ROCK THE TEST

**THE NEWEST SAT SOLUTIONS MANUAL
TO THE COLLEGE BOARD'S OFFICIAL SAT STUDY GUIDE**

www.rockthetest.com

Master Learning
Strategies

Published by Master Learning Strategies Inc.
ISBN 978-1-933918-36-5

Thom Brownworth is the Senior Master at The Stony Brook School, one of the most prestigious college prep schools in the nation. He is in his 40th year at the school and has been the Mathematics department chair for more than two decades. Thom received his undergraduate degree from Houghton College and his Masters degree in Mathematics Education from Hofstra University. Thom has also done extensive graduate study in computer science at Stony Brook University.

Michael Hickey is in his twentieth year at The Stony Brook School. He teaches Physics and Biology and is also the SAT tutor for the school. A recent course he taught at the school exhibited an average increase on the SAT of 240 points per student with a high of 470 points. Michael graduated from the United States Merchant Marine Academy at Kings Point with a degree in engineering. He has also done extensive graduate study in education.

TABLE OF CONTENTS

Practice Test #1 - Verbal

Section 2

1. **Choice D** is correct.   The portion of the sentence set off by dashes " a realistic room...." describes or defines the blank. "Stage scenery" gives us another clue that the blank is clearly the "setting". None of the other choices fits well. A dirt pile is certainly not a "conventional" setting and that's why it challenges typical or "conventional" stage scenery.

2. **Choice B** is correct. "Ironically" is the key word since it sets up a seeming contradiction. The first blank is defined by "much more". Thus Choices C, D and E can be eliminated. "Lavishness" fits the first blank but "adapt" does not fit the context of the second. One would think that an affluent (wealthy) society would not suffer at all but "overabundance" can be just as dangerous as want. "Corpulence" (obesity)

3. **Choice E** is correct. Anyone "suffering from various ailments" would flock to a person, place or medicine which holds even the hope of remedy. "Therapeutic" effects are palliative or healing. Note the difference between "effects" and "affects". Effects are results while affects are influences. "Succulent" (juicy) nor "redolent" (aromatic) nor "cerebral" (brainy, pensive) nor "mandatory" (imperative, obligatory) fit the context.

4. **Choice C** is correct. The first blank is defined by the part of the sentence which comes before the comma. Because Salazar's research **is** "more valuable and comprehensive", the sentence is set up to be positive. Negative words such as "undermined", "debacles", "dissolved" and "misconceptions" would not complement "valuable and comprehensive". Therefore, all the other Choices do not fit. Salazar's research, on the other hand, would "provide" a foundation for future "investigations" if it was valuable.

5. **Choice A** is correct. Once again, the part of the sentence after the comma gives us the key to answering the question. If the launch was delayed by nearly a week, something must have hampered preparations. "Thwarted" means hampered or caused difficulty in accomplishing a task. "Forfeited" (surrendered, sacrificed) nor "Implemented" (carried out) nor "discharged" (carried out, deposited) nor "redoubled" (strengthen, double the effort) fit the context.

6. **Choice B** is correct. The first blank is defined by "offended" and the second blank parallels the first. Thus both words should be negative. "Harangue" means to passionately or vehemently address a person or group, typically in a negative or pejorative fashion. Temperance suggests moderation while this guest was clearly "intemperate". <u>Any positive words</u> in any of the Choices can therefore be eliminated. "Flattering", "praising", "conciliatory" (peaceable), and "accommodating" are all positive and can be eliminated.

7. **Choice A** is correct. "Long and arduous" and "limping slowly" give us the clues we need. "Halting" suggests stunted motion with a lack of fluidity. It may also be used of speech. "Robust" (strong) nor "constant" nor "prompt" nor "facile" (easy) fit the context.

8. **Choice D** is correct. The term "melodramatic" indicates sentimental extravagance or exaggerated emotion. This is precisely what "histrionic" can mean, although histrionics may simply mean studies in theatre. "Imperious"(regal, belittling) nor "inscrutable" (beyond understanding or mysterious) nor "convivial" (good company, fond of feasting) nor "solicitous" (full of concern, apprehensive)

9. **Choice E** is correct. Line 2 indicates that "dolphins are able to understand sign language, solve puzzles, and use objects in their environment as tools." Line 5 goes on to say that "dolphins possess a <u>sophisticated</u> language". These are clearly characteristics typically attributed to humans.

10. **Choice B** is correct. In his last sentence, the author of passage 1 is clearly trying to make a close comparison between dolphin and human intelligence. The author of Passage 2, after informing us that a number of studies on dolphin intelligence are inconclusive, makes this definitive statement, "The fact is, we don't know, and comparisons may not be especially helpful." His final sentence makes his position clear—"Until we know more, all we can say is that dolphin intelligence is different." Choices A and C are <u>incorrect</u> although both may be true!! **BE CAREFUL !!** Just because a statement is true does NOT mean it's correct. It must answer the question asked. The test makers are very good at tempting you with appealing answers, which may be true but don't answer the question. The more questions like this you see, the more adept you'll become at recognizing the "trap" answers.

11. **Choice D** is correct. As was stated in the previous answer, the author of Passage 2 is skeptical of any studies comparing the intelligence of one species with another. Choice A is incorrect because the author of Passage 2 does not believe "dolphin and human intelligence is roughly equal". B is incorrect because Passage 2 does not say that dolphins outperform other animals. C is incorrect because Passage 2 doesn't state that dolphins are less intelligent than other mammals. E is incorrect because Passage 1 does not discuss brain size.

12. **Choice D** is correct. Both passages clearly indicate that dolphins have some intelligence. What kind of intelligence and what it means is what is called into question. The other Choices are not supported by the Passages.

13. **Choice E** is correct. The reason that Pilgrims are mentioned in the first paragraph is to show that things haven't changed much over the past 350 yrs. Many of the same misconceptions are held today and, therefore, the reference to Pilgrims "draws a <u>parallel</u> to the current condition".

14. **Choice D** is correct. Parallel construction is found in lines 11 and 12. "Motivated more" and "charged more" are parallel and, therefore, are synonymous. "Inspired" is, therefore, closest to "charged".

15. **Choice B** is correct. The second paragraph begins, "This idea is certainly not new, Rousseau..". Clearly, Rousseau is introduced to us in the context of time, specifically, a long time. "Longevity" hits the mark.

16. **Choice A** is correct. The first sentence of the third paragraph begins, "It's a great story…" and ends with "but there's a problem". All along the author has been decrying the fact that Native Americans have been <u>misconceived</u> throughout their entire history. The "problem" is that the "ancestor-descendant model" introduced in the second paragraph is <u>wrong</u>. "Fallacy", "deception" and "error" all hit the mark, but these misconceptions are neither "harmless" nor "beneficial". Choices C and D can be eliminated.

17. **Choice A** is correct. The previous answer gives the foundation for this choice.

18. **Choice C** is correct. Following the line of reasoning of the author, Native Americans had to have the practical skills and sense to survive to the present time just as any culture would. In lines 34-37 the author lists these survival characteristics.

19. **Choice A** is correct. Whenever people use the terms "They" or "Them" they immediately exclude themselves in the equation. Frequently these terms are used to put down or demean one group or another. From the context, this is how the Europeans perceived the Native Americans.

20. **Choice B** is correct. Lines 66-70 give us some insight into why these misconceptions have persisted. Western historians are described as "culture-bound by their own approach to knowledge". This indicates that they would be "disadvantaged' and that their approach would be "narrow".

21. **Choice B** is correct. An "educated guess" as to the history and culture of the Native Americans would have to be made because there is no archaeological documentation. This would be necessary because "oral histories and religious rituals" would not be written down.

22. **Choice C** is correct. The "Every modern observer…of the South Pacific or Zaire or New Hampshire or Austria…" was exposed to folklore about the Native Americans. In other words, those from every corner of the globe have been exposed to these misconceptions. These references clearly indicate the "universality of certain notions". Choice A is incorrect because although other cultures have heard of the Native American, they have not been "influenced" to the point of accepting the practices of their culture.

23. **Choice B** is correct. If most students start from a negative perspective (line 82), then it is clear that the misconceptions that they hold must be dispelled. "Disillusionment" often means disappointment or dissatisfaction. It this case, however, it means to leave without illusion or naiveté.

24. **Choice A** is correct. The previous answer lays the foundation for this choice. Choices B through E are not supported by the passage.

Section 5

1. **Choice D** is correct. The key word in this sentence is "instead" because this gives us an important clue about the relationship between the two words. The correct answers must be contrasting. In addition, the phrase "worth exploring" is in a series with the second word which must, then, be positive. As a result, the first blank must be a negative attribute. Therefore, Choices B and C can be eliminated. Although Choice B is contrasting, it doesn't fit the context as well as D.

2. **Choice E** is correct. It is clear by the flow of the sentence that the two answers parallel or explain one another. Although "adulation" works in the first blank, "superiors" certainly does not work in the second. "Sycophants" are yes men who will use "flattery" either to avoid punishment or to get what they want.

3. **Choice D** is correct. "Thin, pliable….. transparent" are all important attributes of "membranes", whereas "callous" (hard) and "inflexible" would be poor characteristics for wings. "Arable" (farmable) doesn't fit.

4. **Choice E** is correct. If its writers want to reflect the "mixture" of dialects in their nation, the missing word should highlight the differences in the languages. "Articulation" (enunciation or precision), "intonation" (pitch), spontaneity (relaxed, natural), and "profundity" (depth) all fail to fit the context. The prefix *homo* means "same" as in homogenous, whereas *hetero* means "other" as in heterozygous. "A variety of dialects" would suggest "heterogeneity".

5. **Choice B** is correct. The phrase "only to discover" suggests a contrast. The word "palliative" means soothing or healing and self-serving excuses will certainly not have this effect; in fact, they often may have the opposite effect. "Reprehensible" (damnable), "depreciatory" (demeaning), "litigious" (arguable) and "compendious" (brief, succinct) don't fit.

6. **Choice D** is correct. Each of the other choices is a common idiom whose meaning is self-evident. In other words, if someone is ecstatic, it is not uncommon that they actually jump up and down. In lines 5-6 the author muses about how certain sayings came into being because they are <u>not</u> self-evident like "the whole nine yards" and neither is "talking through your hat". Have you ever seen someone "talking through their hat"? What does that even mean? That's the author's point.

7. **Choice B** is correct. The answer to this question if found in lines 7-11. The last sentence of the paragraph contradicts the one just prior to it. If Josh Billings never left his home town before 1860, how could the saying "joshing around" have been in use since 1845 and still be attributed to him?

8. **Choice B** is correct. The entire paragraph must be read to answer this question. The topic sentence of any paragraph gives the main idea of the paragraph. The first sentence of the piece gives us just that, as it speaks of the development of major cities from the Middle Ages up through the 20th century. Central marketplaces, often at the crossroads of trade routes, were places where cities sprang up all throughout history. Choice B would set up this paragraph nicely. "Crime rates" and "portraits of famous people" and "building of large cathedrals" have little to do with the reasons why cities are built.

9. **Choice C** is correct. By beginning the paragraph with the phrase "The following study is concerned with…" the author is clearly explaining an approach with an eye toward the reasons behind how and why Western cities were birthed. An important key to many of the critical reading passages is taking note of the verbs that are used. The passage does not "criticize", "justify" or "defend" anything.

10. **Choice C** is correct. Having to "put up with….prospective buyers coming to gape" is certainly intrusive, while people who've "stopped and stared and admired" are clearly appreciative. (A) is incorrect as we don't know whether the first group is "uneducated" or not. (B) is incorrect because the first group never "slights" (offends) the artist. (D) is incorrect because the author never tells us that the first group "rejects the artist's methodology".

11. **Choice A** is correct. The first paragraph answers this question. Since the author is a writer and not an artist, she feels uncomfortable at the thought of a public viewing and evaluation of her work. Therefore, she seems to feel that most artists would feel the same way. She soon finds out that this is not the case. Choices B through E are never discussed in the paragraph.

12. **Choice B** is correct. As indicated in the previous answer, the author expects the artist to be as uncomfortable as she is. The second paragraph begins, "I was wrong". "Reality" differed from "expectation." The author is not "idealistic", "speculative", "disappointed" nor "possessive" throughout the passage, therefore, Choices A, C, D, and E are incorrect.

© 2009 Master Learning Strategies Inc.

13. **Choice C** is correct. The size and of the painting compared to the size and of the author's home were incongruous. The painting "deserved" better and needed to be displayed in a fashion to bring out the best in it. (A) is incorrect because the passage doesn't speak about the artist's unique accomplishments. (B) is incorrect because the author's home does not reach the "widest possible audience". (E) is incorrect because "size" not "elegance" appears to be the attribute that needs to be complemented.

14. **Choice B** is correct. The end of the second paragraph and the beginning of the third answer this question. The word pragmatic means practical. In practical terms, she had made the "right" decision, but clearly she speaks with so much emotion about the painting that she now regrets that decision. "Souvenirs" and "trust" and "ability to appreciate smaller paintings" is not mentioned.

15. **Choice C** is correct. The answer to this question is found in lines 40-42. The metaphor is that of marriage and divorce which in most cases elicits strong emotions in man and wife. "Painful memories and "childhood places" are not mentioned.

16. **Choice E** is correct. Line 60 reads "..recite it like a poem, and so in a sense I can never lose it." One can typically recite something and never lose it only if it is committed to memory and therefore "preserved vividly in the narrator's mind." "Sharing with others", "the narrator's sense of identity" and "the narrator's longing for beautiful objects" are not mentioned.

17. **Choice D** is correct. Phrases like "I went back to the exhibition day after day….and became almost maudlin….torturing myself with wanting it back" indicate clearly that her focus is not the artist, nor the painting itself, but the <u>personal</u> loss she felt. We are never told of any "pressure to divorce it" or "difficulty maintaining it" or "empathy she felt toward the creator".

18. **Choice C** is correct. Although the story is about a painting, the main intent of the author is to convey the deep, emotional torment she felt in this series of events. Once again, take note of the verbs that are used here. The passage does not "defend" or "argue" or "stimulate" anything and, therefore, Choices B, D, and E can be eliminated.

19. **Choice E** is correct. At the end of the second paragraph we learn that after hours and hours of observing various birds, Wilbur Wright is inspired. His imagination, like those of many throughout the centuries, is captured by the thought of flight. The poem in lines 31-36 also uses imaginative language while describing flight and line 41 describes engineers as the new poets of the times. Choice B is incorrect because the passage does not use "contemporary" (present-day) poetry. "Lifestyles" and "principles of flight" are not discussed.

20. **Choice C** is correct. When constructing anything earth-bound, a building or bridge or locomotive, the primary concern is strength which typically translates into mass. However, when constructing anything intended to fly, reducing weight is the primary concern and strength secondary. Lines 3-9 are intended to illustrate the contrast between "earth-bound" engineering and "heaven-bound" engineering. Choice A is clearly the opposite of what we are looking for.

21. **Choice D** is correct. The second paragraph contains the answer to this question. The Wright brothers were not a large engineering firm who happened to become interested in manned flight. They built bicycles. It was from this modest beginning that they became both famous and successful.

22. **Choice E** is correct. The poem in lines 31-36 describes the soul breaking free from the body and soaring upward. The soul is the seat of the deepest longings of a person. (A) is incorrect because the passage does not contrast the "imaginative and practical" sides of engineering.

23. **Choice A** is correct. Lines 40-42 elaborate on the opening sentence of the paragraph which describes the new engineering that allowed people to fly as a "kind of poetry". The end of line 40 indicates directly that artistry can be seen in machinery. "Practicality" and "technical language" are not discussed nor are "artistic pretensions". Therefore, Choices C, D and E can be eliminated.

24. **Choice B** is correct. When someone becomes famous for one thing or another, he or she is apt to be deified --- too lofty to be a mere mortal. Lines 47-48, however, indicate that although Wilbur Wright had lofty ideas, he was just a normal, middle-class, "regular" guy. © is incorrect because this was <u>not</u> the generally accepted view. (E) is incorrect because this line would tend to do the exact opposite of "perpetuating the legacy of a hero".

Section 7

1. **Choice E** is correct. The original sentence is wordy and awkward. Good writing is precise and succinct. E is the best response. B is incorrect because it sounds as though he found out sometime <u>after</u> he walked into the office that his plan was approved. This construction would be okay if one wanted to add emphasis or to finish a series, for example, "*and then*, they told him.." but there is no context to suggest such an emphasis. C is incorrect because "when it was learned by him" is known as the passive voice which generally should be avoided.

2. **Choice E** is correct. The original sentence is grammatically incorrect. As it is written the introductory phrase "Burdened……skis," modifies "Sarah's search" instead of "Sarah". B is incorrect because it has the same construction. C is incorrect because the baggage cart is not "burdened". Choice E not only conveys the information but it does so in a concise, descriptive manner.

3. **Choice C** is correct. As it stands, the original sentence leads to confusion. To whom does the "he" refer, James or Sam? Also, if we assume it is Sam, since he is last in the series, then the original sentence indicates that they all stumbled over a rock which is not the intent of the sentence. Choice C clarifies the intent well. Choices D and E clarify the pronoun reference but the flow of each sentence is more stunted than C.

4. **Choice D** is correct. The phrase "this was a disaster many workers had feared" is an independent clause and could stand alone. Therefore a semi-colon could have been used but that is not one of the choices. As it stands it is a comma splice and incorrect. B is incorrect because the word "because" implies that the council kept the economy from collapsing due to the fear of the workers. Choice E is simply another independent clause replacing one comma splice with another.

5. **Choice C** is correct. The flow of the sentence with the phrase "not only by…." indicates that something additional will follow in the same vein and almost dictates that the phrase "but also by" be used to complement and parallel the construction.

6. **Choice A** is correct. The original sentence is correct. as is. Choices B, C, D and E graphically illustrate the awkwardness of "ing" construction which, unfortunately, is commonly used in writing and speaking; "of allowing", "by allowing", "still having" and "in allowing" are all awkward and inappropriate.

7. **Choice D** is correct. The underlined portion of this sentence refers to fieldwork which is not a person or persons (they), therefore, the original sentence is incorrect as is. Choice D conveys the information cleanly and refers back accurately to the subject which is linguistic research.

8. **Choice A** is correct. All of the other choices are awkward or confusing. B is incorrect because it destroys the parallel construction comparing "sustainable observation" to "intermittent observation". C is incorrect because "providing" is awkward "ing" construction. E, though correct does not flow as well as A.

9. **Choice D** is correct. The original sentence is incorrect because it is not a sentence at all but a <u>sentence fragment</u> because there is no verb. "Referring" is used as an adjective in the original sentence but can only be used as such when preceded by some form of the verb "to be", as in "I am referring". Choice D changes "referring" to "refers" thereby making it a verb which the sentence needs.   Both C and E get the thought across but in an awkward, wordy manner.

10. **Choice E** is correct. In the original sentence, "they will be…..century" is a complete thought or independent clause and can stand alone and is, therefore, a comma splice. A is incorrect. B is still a comma splice and incorrect. C is incorrect because a semi-colon joins two independent clauses. Although the first part of the sentence is independent, the second "being….century" is not. D is incorrect because it doesn't follow the correct comparison form "as _____ as" nor is the tense correct "is" does not complement the last century.

11. **Choice B** is correct. The original sentence is incorrect because the initial phrase "With billions ….mined" modifies the subject "some" and is clearly inappropriate. Some have the misconception that a sentence cannot begin with the word "because". This is not true. The word "because" sets up a consequence or result when it is used at the beginning of a sentence. Choice B conveys the thought nicely.

12. **Choice C** contains the error and should read "and it has been" since it refers to "fable".

13. **Choice C** contains the error and should read "lifestyles were" since it refers to "they" and the word "came" gives us the appropriate tense.

14. **Choice B** contains the error and should read "professional writers" since the subject, Susan and Peter, is plural.

15. **Choice B** contains the error. "Either….or" is the proper construction as "Neither…..nor" is the proper construction. The sentence should read "before either tea <u>or</u> coffee…".

16. **Choice C** contains the error. Since this phrase begins with "<u>one</u> must be…" in order for there to be parallel construction it follows that "<u>one</u> will practice".

17. **Choice B** contains the error. Parallel construction dictates that the sentence should read "<u>has to enter</u> a password" in order to be correct.

18. **Choice D** contains the error and should read "<u>has</u> collaborated on…" to be consistent with what appeared earlier in the sentence.

19. **Choice B** contains the error. Since "writings" is the subject of the sentence and plural, it requires the plural verb "<u>have</u> continued" in order to be correct.

20. **Choice A** contains the error and should read "have repeatedly <u>arisen</u>".

21. **Choice B** contains the error. Assuming that this is written present-day, anything that has occurred in the nineteenth century is past tense. The sentence should then read "<u>has been</u> the change…"

22. **Choice D** contains the error. The subject of that portion of the sentence is plural (children) and, therefore, the sentence should read "becoming creative artists…"

23. **Choice C** contains the error and should read "<u>was</u> calculated" since it refers to "the announcement" which is singular. This is a frequent trick of the test writers, putting a plural noun in the clause just prior to a verb modifying a singular noun. In other words, we're apt to still "hear" the word "days" and think that "<u>were</u> calculated" sounds correct. Be careful of this pitfall.

24. **Choice B** contains the error and should read "cleverly" since it is an adverb modifying designed.

25. **Choice E** is correct. The sentence is grammatically correct as it stands.

26. **Choice C** contains the error. "harmful effects" is the plural subject of this clause and requires the plural verb "have".

27. **Choice E** is correct. The sentence is grammatically correct as it stands.

28. **Choice C** contains the error. If one is preoccupied at all, he is "preoccupied *with*" something not "*in*" something

29. **Choice A** contains the error. The error here is in consistency of tenses. "Contrasting" is the present progressive tense which indicates on-going action in the present. whereas "Contrasted" or "In contrast with" is required by the context which is past tense.

30. **Choice D** is correct. The phrase "that are arising" is confusing because it could be referring to either the "statements" or the "candidates". A, B and E do not address this problem and can, therefore be eliminated. C is grammatically incorrect because "is" is singular, whereas, both "statements" and "candidates" are plural.

31. **Choice D** is correct. The original sentence is poorly written. A goal dictates an infinitive. For example, "His goal is to win….to challenge….to defeat….to be successful etc. "Their goal, after all, is to be elected" would be perfectly fine but this sentence is neither the original one nor an answer choice. Choice D expresses the intent well and correctly.

32. **Choice A** is correct. Because there are three different nouns in the previous sentence and because "It" is used to introduce the sentence, it is helpful to clarify to the reader exactly to what "It" refers. In this case it is clear that the "It" refers to the strategy of "smearing the opponent".

33. **Choice B** is correct. This piece is written from the standpoint to an outside observer—in the third person. Line 6 is a complete change of voice and perspective and should be deleted.

34. **Choice D** is correct. The original sentence is incorrect because it contains a comma splice. Both phrases separated by the comma are independent clauses and could be joined by a semi-colon or a comma and conjunction. Choice D is concise and to the point. B is incorrect because it would leave the reader hanging. C is incorrect because changing "report" to "verify" changes the meaning of the sentence. To report is to communicate data while to verify is to determine if something is accurate. E is awkward.

35. **Choice E** is correct. This sentence flows well with what has preceded it. Choice A is incorrect because the reader would anticipate reading about the "bright side". Choice C is incorrect, because a conclusion should summarize the piece whose focus is negative campaigning not the media.

Section 8

1. **Choice C** is correct. Someone or something which is unable to avoid traps will certainly become "prey". A "peer" is a contemporary, an "ally" is a friend. A "nemesis" is an enemy. None of these fit the context.

2. **Choice C** is correct. As refrigeration retards spoilage, the "distribution" (expansion) and "variety" of food available to the average American family would increase greatly. A and B would be opposite effects of refrigeration and transportation. E is incorrect as dearth means lack.

3. **Choice A** is correct. The word <u>although</u> sets up a contrast. Therefore, despite having different styles, something must be the same. Since they were from the same locale, it would be almost unavoidable ("inevitable") not to "compare" them.

4. **Choice B** is correct. "Demonstrative" is a word used to describe someone who easily displays his or her emotions. Since Gaston is typically <u>not</u> that kind of person, reporters were surprised. Choice E is incorrect as wistful means full of yearning or desire.

5. **Choice E** is correct. If a written piece or a person is described as dense it means that it or they are not easily understood. Conversely, if something is easily understood it can be described as transparent. "Opacity" or opaqueness is usually used with reference to an object's inability to transmit light. Floridity (flowery, ruddy) doesn't fit.

6. **Choice C** is correct. "Negligible" means of little or no consequence (same root as neglect) as one might expect the stance of oil companies to be looking to drill in pristine areas. Irrepressible (can't keep down) nor momentous (significant) nor magnanimous (generous) fits.

7. **Choice B** is correct. Jerry is careful to conceal that fact that he is from a poor section of Boston where the air is foul because that's where the factories are. His fear of rejection or prejudice leads him to lie about being from the wealthier neighborhood of Belmont. The author of Passage 2 was clearly surprised that people of the Hodgkinsons social stature "would bother putting themselves out" for someone like him. Even when he comes to the conclusion that they like him, he is anxious about it. There is no indication in either passage that either one is interested in social advancement (A) or influenced by the lifestyles of their friends (D).

8. **Choice A** is correct. Jerry is satisfied in his present situation because he is in Africa and has no desire to return home. If he does, he may have to face the truth and he has no interest in doing so. The author of Passage 2, on the other hand, feels like a child of the slums and, yet, with a university degree doesn't feel like he fits in there nor the middle class and certainly not with the affluent. B is incorrect because the narrator is able to do this. There is no indication of "philanthropic concerns" or "befriending people of all social classes"

9. **Choice D** is correct. As soon as the narrator says, "but at the time…" we know that the subsequent condition he describes changes in the future. For example if someone says, "I got accepted to Harvard, but at the time I thought I wanted to go to law school…", implies that the speaker has since changed his/her mind. Choice A is incorrect _even though the statement may be true!!!_ **BE CAREFUL !! This is a favorite trick of the makers of the SAT.** They will give you a statement that is true, but will not answer the question that is asked or be supported by the passage. "The truth can sometimes by more damaging than a lie" is true, but it is not supported by the passage in this case and does not answer the question. Choice B is incorrect because the narrator does recognize Jerry's deceitfulness. Choice C is incorrect because we don't know anything about Jerry's background yet or how the narrator feels about it.

10. **Choice E** is correct. If Jerry's lies were "always believed", they couldn't have been too   outlandish and, therefore, had to be moderate (not exaggerated). Choices A, B, C and D are incorrect because none fits the context.

11. **Choice A** is correct. Because Jerry is so far from home and nobody knows who he really is, his lies are minor or "insignificant". If he were home, however, the same lies would have a significant or "major" consequence to him or others.

12. **Choice A** is correct. The last sentence of the Passage gives us the key. "In Africa, no one could dispute what Jerry said he was…" Thus, the "inhabitants could not easily verify his American social status". B is incorrect because he is accepted. C is incorrect because the narrator implies that he is more respected in Africa due to his false impressions. D is incorrect because with privilege comes responsibility wherever one is. E is incorrect because we know nothing of Jerry's friends.

13. **Choice D** is correct. Passage 1 gives us no indication that Jerry has changed. On the other hand, the first sentence of the last paragraph in Passage 2 begins, "The truth was I had changed,…" and goes on the say how. The other Choices are not supported by the Passages.

14. **Choice D** is correct. Up to line 39 the narrator is fearful and insecure about revealing his true status. But in lines 39 and 40 he says, "Yet whatever I said seemed to make no difference in their acceptance." This sentence clearly shows a transition from "apprehension to a desire to reveal himself" because he feels guilty of "trying to pass" as someone that he is not.

15. **Choice E** is correct. The second half of the second paragraph in Passage 2 contains the keys to this question. The narrator indicates that some hosts lead boring, unstimulating lives and would, therefore, be "hungry" to hear and live ("vicariously") every detail of the lives of their guests. The Hodgkinsons are the exact opposite which catches the narrator by surprise.

16. **Choice E** is correct. In line 45 the phrase "in the world" is followed by "leading stimulating lives" and implies that they were "in contact with interesting people and ideas."

17. **Choice C** is correct. Although "anxious" could mean either impatient or frightened, the context best fits the word "uneasy". "Meticulous" (detailed) and eager do not fit at all.

18. **Choice A** is correct. In Passage 1 Jerry has "created" his own identity through a web of lies. The narrator of Passage 2, however, describes several factors, both "external and internal" determine one's identity. The other Choices are not supported by the Passages.

19. **Choice E** is correct. Both Jerry and the narrator are Americans and it is clear from the reading that their stata in American society have considerable influence on how they perceive themselves "Even when living abroad".

Section 10

1. **Choice D** is correct. The original sentence is a sentence fragment because it is missing a verb. "Coming" without some form of the verb "to be" is being used as an adjective. We have also discussed before the awkwardness of "ing" construction. In Choices B and C "they" is redundant and should not be used. E is incorrect because it keeps the sentence as a fragment lacking a verb.

2. **Choice E** is correct. The original sentence is incorrect because as it stands "patients" modifies "medical directors" and that is not the intent of the sentence. B is incorrect because "The belief of" is awkward and wordy. C begins fine but is incorrect because the "medical directors" do not believe "you". D leads to an incomplete sentence because there are two dependent clauses without an independent clause which can stand alone.

3. **Choice E** is correct. The original phrase is incorrect because "Lecturing at the university" modifies "read the poetry" and that makes no sense. It should modify "Professor Clark" which should follow immediately after the initial phrase. Therefore E is the only possible answer.

4. **Choice C** is correct. The original sentence is terribly awkward with the phrase "because of being her…". Although B is grammatically correct, it is not the most concise and fluid way to put it. C is the best response.

5. **Choice A** is correct. The original sentence is correct. as is. All of the others are poorer representations of the first.

6. **Choice B** is correct. The underlined portion of the sentence should parallel the verb construction of that part of the sentence which precedes it. "Could not continue" should be followed by "could rely". B is a better choice than E since it is more succinct.

7. **Choice B** is correct. The original sentence is awkward and wordy. There is no reason to add "it is" and "who" to the sentence. It's a good rule to use the most concise and direct way to say something. Adding words frequently leads to confusion or awkwardness. B gets the point across directly.

8. **Choice E** is correct. The original sentence is very awkward and lacks parallel structure. The phrase "is safer, quicker, and cheaper" should be paralleled by "is greater". Both C and E have this construction but "human misery toll" is a poorer way to express it.

9. **Choice A** is correct. The original sentence is concise and grammatically correct. The part of the sentence which follows the dash modifies and elaborates upon the first part of the sentence, as it should.

10. **Choice C** is correct. Although gourmets may be "prized for their rarity" it is more likely that "wild truffles" are. The original sentence is, therefore, incorrect. "Wild truffles" should, then, immediately follow "Prized for their rarity". C is the only choice that has this construction. D adds "As". E is incorrect because it makes no sense at all.

11. **Choice D** is correct. Agreement in number is the key to this question. "Evidence" is singular and needs the verb "shows". "Friendships" is plural and needs the verb "tend". D is the only choice with both verbs correct.

12. **Choice B** is correct. The original sentence is incorrect because a "duo" is a <u>single</u> pair. Two people cannot become "singing duos". B is correct. E has an awkward "ing" construction.

13. **Choice C** is correct. The original sentence is incorrect because there should be a natural break between the first action (the sister's reading) and the second (the brother's reading) but there is not. B is incorrect because "and" is not a sufficient connection between the sister reading the sports section first and the brother reading the comics first. C is concise, direct and the semi-colon serves to establish this relationship well.

14. **Choice D** is correct. The original sentence is incorrect because there is clearly a contrast introduced to the reader. However, the conjunction "and" is used and is, therefore, incorrect. The transition words "yet", "however", "although" and "but" would all set up the appropriate contrast between "urban" and "rural" scenes.

Practice Test #1 - Math

Section 3

20 questions – first third - easy

1. **Choice B** is correct. Find x in the equation then substitute to find the value

   $2x + 3 = 9$ so $2x = 6$ or $x = 3$ Now substitute. $4x - 3 = 4(3) - 3 = 12 - 3 = 9$

2. **Choice D** is correct. The smallest auditorium would be 1,200 (8*150) so answers A, B and C are wrong.

   The largest would be 1,600 (8*200) so E is wrong.

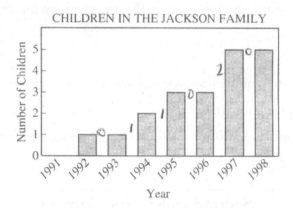

3. **Choice A** is correct. The figure is not drawn to scale so the correct answer may not look correct. All five

   segments start at point X so we have lots of right triangles with one leg of size 8. Find the longest other leg

   and we have the longest hypotenuse. The other leg sizes starting from the left are 5, 2, 0, 3 and 4. 5 is the

   longest.

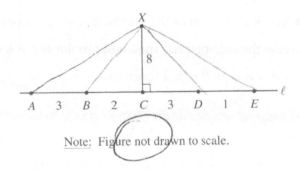

Note: Figure not drawn to scale.

4. **Choice D** is correct. In the year the twins were born the family size would have gone up by two children.

   From the graph we see that in 1997 the number of children is 2 more than in 1996.

© 2009 Master Learning Strategies Inc.

5. **Choice B** is correct. Be careful of averages. If the average of x and y is 5 then the total of x and y is 10. (2*5) If the average if x, y and z is 8 then the total of x, y and z is 24. (3*8) So adding z made the total go up from 10 to 24.

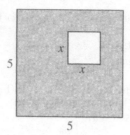

6. **Choice E** is correct. The area of the shaded region is the big square minus the small square hole.

BIG – small is $25 - x^2$

7. **Choice D** is correct. We have two multiplication problems and three of the numbers are the same in both problems. In the first problem we know that the product is 1 so none of the numbers is 0. In the second problem at least one of the numbers has to be 0 to get 0 as the answer. S, t and v are not 0 from the first problem so only u is left to be 0.

Second third - medium

8. **Choice C** is correct. Add up the points in the quarters and see how much is left for the last quarter. One-sixth of 36 is 6, one-fourth is 9 and one-third is 12 which makes 27 points. This leaves $36 - 27 = 9$.

9. **Choice B** is correct. Try 4. 2^8 on your calculator is 256 and 8^3 is 512 so answer C is wrong. Try something smaller to see of they get closer together. Try 3. 2^6 is 64 and 8^2 is 64.

10. **Choice E** is correct. Try 1. 4 less than 3 (3 times the number) is –1. 2 more than 1 is 3. C is wrong. Try 2 since it seems we need to increase the side that has the higher multiplier. 4 less than 6 is 2. 2 more than 2 is 4. Closer but still wrong. Try 3. 4 less than 9 is 5. 2 more than 3 is 5.

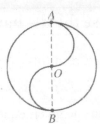

11. **Choice C** is correct. The circumference of the big circle is 36π which makes the radius 18. The radius of

each semicircles is half of the big radius or 9 so the length of the curved path is $2*9\pi$ or 18π. Another

thought! We are taking linear measurements of similar objects. The small circle is half the big circle so half

of 36π is 18π

12. **Choice C** is correct. This problem is near the end of the medium questions so the answer might not seem

correct. Answer E makes it tricky. f is a LINEAR function so the equation is $y = mx + d$ What if we test out

some equation. If we make $m = 24$ then $24(1) + d = 24$ from the chart so $d = 0$. With this equation

$24(0) + 0 = a = 0$ and $24(2) + 0 = b = 48$. This makes $a + b = 0 + 48 = 48$ Since we picked our equation from

our head we know it only finds wrong answers. This means answers A, B and D, which aren't 48, are

wrong. We have two answers. Either it is always 48 or it is sometimes 48 and sometimes something else. Try

another equation. Lets choose a slope of 10. Working this out just like the first one d is 14. a is 14 and b is

34. Did you get these values? 14 + 34 = 48 again! Does this convince you that the answer is 48? The

problem is not worth enough to spend more time. Put down C and move on.

Math Method : Using the chart we have three equations. $m(0) + d = a$, $m(1) + d = 24$ and $m(2) + d = b$. The

problem wants us to find $a + b$ so lets add the first and third equations. We get $2m + 2d = a + b$. But

$2m + 2d = 2(m + d) = 2(24) = 48$.

13. **Choice A** is correct. Lets find a couple more terms. The next (fourth) term is $-5 + 2 = -3$. The fifth term is

$-3(-1) = 3$. The sixth term is $3 + 2 = 5$ and the seventh term is $5(-1) = -5$ and the eighth term is

$-5 + 2 = -3$. The terms we have so far are 3, 5, -5, -3, 3, 5, -5, -3 Looks like they are repeating. The fourth

and eighth terms are both -3 so every multiple of 4 terms we get -3. How close to 55 terms can we get? 52

is that close so term number 52 is -3. We have to go 3 more terms to get to 55 so the value is -5.

14. **Choice A** is correct. A reflection is like a mirror. In this case the mirror is the x-axis. Points above the x-axis will be paired with a point directly below it. Lets find two points on the line and their images. (0, 5) and (1, 7) are both on the line (put the x values in the given equation to find the y value.) Directly below (0, 5) and the same distance from the x-axis is (0, –5) and below (1, 7) is (1, –7) Put our reflection points into their answers and see which one works. $y = -2x - 5$ works for both points.

15. **Choice C** is correct. From the graph at age 6 Elina was 45 inches tall. At age 12 she is 60 inches tall. This means she grew 15 inches. We want to know her percentage increase which means we need to divide her increase by something. The words in the problem tell us what that should be. "…than her height at age 6?" lets us know we need to divide by her height at age 6. This makes the problem 15/45 or .3333 on the calculator. But we want a percentage which means we need to multiply the number by 100 making it 33.33.

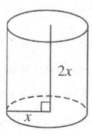

16. **Choice E** is correct. Lets put in our own value of x and find some wrong answers. Let x be 2 so the cylinder has radius 2 and height 4. The volume is area of the Base * height and the base is a circle so the formula is $\pi r^2 h = 3 \times 2^2 \times 4 = 48$ Which of the answers is 48?

A) cylinder with r = 4 and h = 2 $3 * 4^2 2 = 96$ Wrong

B) cylinder with r=4π and h = 2 $3 * (4*3)^2 2 = 864$ Wrong

C) cube with edge 4 $4^3 = 64$ Wrong

D) cube with edge 4π $(4*3)^3 = 1728$ Wrong

E0 solid 2 by 4 by 2π $2 * 4 * 2 * 3 = 48$ Possible

The answer is E

17. **Choice B is correct.** Put in my own numbers. $a = 2$, $x + 1 = 5$ so $2 + 2(5) = r = 12$. We should look for 5.

A) $\frac{12}{4} = 3$ B) $\frac{12-2}{2} = 5$ C) $\frac{12+2}{2} = 7$

D) $\frac{12}{2} - 2 = 4$ E) $\frac{12}{2} + 2 = 8$

Only B remains

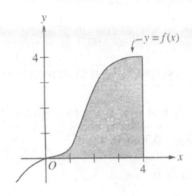

18. **Choice D is correct.** $a \le 4$ says the x value is less than 4 which is true. Cross off any answer without I. B is wrong.

$b \le a$ says the y value is less than the x value. Draw the line from $(0, 0)$ to $(4, 4)$ which is the line $y = x$. Are any shaded pint above this line? Yes so II is false. Cross off any answers that have II. C and E are wrong which leaves only A or D.

$b \le f(a)$ says that the y value of the point is below the y value on the curve. This is true. Cross off A. Only D remains.

19. **Choice C is correct.** Put in my own numbers. $n = 12$ This bottle will be accepted.

A) $|12 - 12| = |0| = 0 = \frac{1}{8}$ WRONG

B) $|12 + 12| = |24| = 24 = \frac{1}{8}$ WRONG

C) $|12 - 12| = |0| = 0 < \frac{1}{8}$ Possible

D) $|12 + 12| = |24| = 24 < \frac{1}{8}$ WRONG

E) $|12 - 12| = |0| = 0 > \frac{1}{8}$ WRONG

Only C remains

20. **Choice E** is correct. The first few numbers are –25, –24, –23 and when I add these we get a big negative number. To get a positive answer we need to include positive numbers to balance the negative ones and then more. Just to get 0 as the sum we need positive numbers from 1 to 25 to match the negative ones from –1 to –25. This is 25 positive numbers and 25 negative numbers which is 50 numbers. But don't forget 0. It is a number in our list so we have a total of 51 numbers to get a sum of 0. The next number in the list is 26 so our sum is 0 + 26 or 26. Just what we want., 52 numbers.

Section 6

8 questions – first third - easy

1. **Choice E** is correct. What **can** it equal. Just put in their numbers. Try easy ones first.

   C) $1 + \frac{2}{1} = 5 + \frac{2}{5}$ or $3 = 5$ plus something. WRONG

   E) $5 + \frac{2}{5} = 5 + \frac{2}{5}$ The same! The answer is E

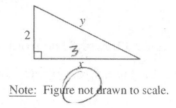

Note: Figure not drawn to scale.

2. **Choice A** is correct.. Pythagorean Theorem. $2^2 + x^2 = 2^2 + 3^2 = 4 + 9 = 13$

3. **Choice D** is correct. To show something is not true we need to make sure the conclusion is false. In this case we need to find a number that is NOT divisible by 4. In their answer list only 18 is NOT divisible by 4.

Second third - medium

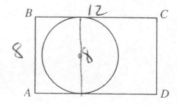

4. **Choice A** is correct. The diameter of the circle is the shorter of the two lengths for the rectangle since it needs to fit inside. So the diameter is 8 and the radius is 4. $\pi 4^2 = 16\pi$

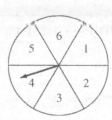

5. **Choice A** is correct. To get a fraction greater than 1 the numerator must be larger than the denominator. The answer will be successful ways / possible ways. There are 36 ways to pick the two numbers which is why all the denominators are 36. How many successful ways are there? If we get a 6 for the denominator then there are no numbers larger than 6 to get. If we get a 5 there is only one success, the number 6. Continue the logic to 4 (2 ways), 3 (3 ways), 2 (4 ways) and 1 (5 ways) which adds up to 15 successful ways.

6. **Choice D** is correct. The language w is directly proportional to x translates directly into the equation $w = kx$ where k, for that problem, is always the same. We need to see if we can make a nice multiplication problem for the number pairs in the tables.

   A) Multiply 1 by 3 to get 3. The multiplier is 3. 2 times 3 is 4? No so A is wrong.

   D) 7 times 3 is 21 so its multiplier is 3. 8 times 3 is 24? Yes. 9 times 3 is 27 Yes. This one works.

Last third - hard

7. **Choice D** is correct. Put in my own number for k. Since we have to divide k by 3 lets use 300. So Dwayne collects $300 each day and pays out $300/3 or $100 each day. This means he saves $200. At this rate he needs to save for 5 days. We need to find an answer that gives us 5.

   A) $\frac{300}{1500} = 5$ WRONG   B) $\frac{300}{1000} = 5$ WRONG

   C) $\frac{1000}{300} = 5$ WRONG   D) $\frac{1500}{300} = 5$ Possible

   E) $1500(300) = 5$ WRONG   Only D remains.

8. **Choice B** is correct. Guesstimation should work here. P times Q. P looks like −0.5 and Q looks like 1.7. −0.5*1.7 = −0.85. Which is to the left of P but not all the way past −2. Best value looks like B and the question asks **could represent**.

© 2009 Master Learning Strategies Inc.

10 questions – first third - easy

9. **Choice 3** is correct. Use a direct solution on this easy problem. Since $x = y + 1$

$$5y + 2x = 5y + 2(y+1) = 5y + 2y + 2 = 7y + 2 = 23 \text{ so } 7y = 21 \text{ and } y = 3$$

10. **Choice 450** is correct. A 50% increase would mean and increase of 150. $300 + 150 = 450$

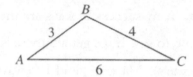

11. **Choice 52, 78 OR 104** is correct. If the angles are all the same in the second triangle, then the two triangles are similar (AA similarity theorem) and all linear measurements are proportional. We need to find the constant of the proportion. If the side of 3 goes with the side of 24 then the constant is 8. So the big perimeter is 8 times the small perimeter. The small perimeter is 3+4+6=13 and 8*13=104. We could stop here and answer 104 and be correct. But there are two other acceptable answers. If the small side of 4 goes with the 24 then the constant is 6 and 6*13=78, If the small side of 6 goes with the 24 then the constant is 4 and 4*13=52.

Second third - medium

12. **Choice 202** is correct. A sum of 1,000 for 5 consecutive numbers means they are all close to $\frac{1000}{5} = 200$. A 201 gets balanced by a 199 and this makes 3 numbers. A 202 gets balanced by a 198 giving us 5 numbers.

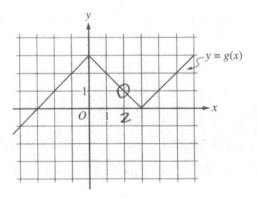

13. **Choice 3** is correct. $h(1)$ means the value of x is 1. 2x = 2. Thus $h(1) = g(2) + 2$ From the graph $g(2) = 1$ so $g(2) + 2 = 1 + 2 = 3$

14. **Choice 24** is correct. When we choose an actor for the first part we can choose any one of the four actors. Now when we choose for the second part there are only 3 parts left. So for each of the four first choices we have 3 choices, making 4*3 or 12 choices for the first two parts. With each of those 12 choices we have two actors left for the third part giving us 24 choices. We have only one actor left for the last role so the answer is 24

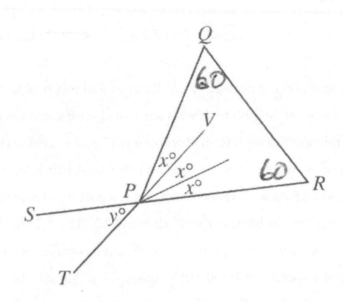

15. **Choice 40** is correct. We know that $\triangle PQR$ is equilateral which means the angles are 60° each. So in angle P

$3x = 60$ or $x = 20$ But we want y. $< SPT \cong < RPV$ because vertical angles are congruent which gives us $y = 2x = 2(20) = 40$

Last third - hard

---

16. **Choice 1.2 OR 6/5** is correct. Do this problem like Simon Says. Just do what is says.

Left side $4 \Delta (5y) = 4 + 3(5y) = 4 + 15y$

Right side

are equal $4 + 15y = 5y + 16$ which solves to y=1.2

© 2009 Master Learning Strategies Inc.

17. **Choice 1** is correct. What are the values of p and t? Plug in the x values and find out. Using $(0, p)$ $0 = p^2 - 4$ gives two answers. 2 and –2. So one of the points on the line is either $(0, 2)$ or $(0, -2)$. Using $(5, t)$ $5 = t^2 - 4$ also gives two answers. 3 and –3. So one of the points on the line is either $(5, 3)$ or $(5, -3)$. To get the largest possible value of the slope we want to pick the lowest left side and the highest right side. So we want the slope of the line from $(0, -2)$ to $(5, 3)$ slope= rise/run = 5/5 = 1.

18. **Choice 18** is correct. Averages do not average nicely! Be careful of this problem. Don't use averages. Lets get an approximation. If she went 30 mph both ways she would have spent the same amount of time going and coming, which is 30 minutes. 30 mph for half an hour is 15 miles. That is the shortest possible distance. If she went 45 mph both ways she would go 22.5 miles in that same half hour. So the correct answer is somewhere between 15 and 22.5 miles. Experience should teach us that Ester would spend more time at the slower speed. So the distance should be nearer to 15 than to 22.5. Rate * Time = Distance! Lets make a couple of guesses. At the slow rate of 30 mph times say 35 minutes makes 30*35/60=17.5 miles. That gives us 25 minutes left for the fast speed. 45*25/60=18.75 miles. Close but not the same! Try 36 minutes at the slow speed. 30*36/60=18 miles. At the fast speed we have 24 minutes or 45*24/60=18. Bingo. 18 miles.

    Math Method: Fast $45 * t = d$ where t is the part of the hour going fast. The part of the hour going slow would be $1 - t$ Slow $30 * (1 - t) = d$ which is the same distance! $30 * (1 - t) = 45t \Rightarrow 30 - 30t = 45t \Rightarrow 30 = 75t$ or $t = \frac{30}{75}$ But we want d not t. $d = 45t = 45\left(\frac{30}{75}\right) = 18$

Section 9

16 questions – first third - easy

.1 **Choice B** is correct. $5t = 45 \Rightarrow t = 9$ So $tk = 9k = 1$

2. **Choice B** is correct. 4 turns is 2 inches. 8 turns would be 4 inches which is a little too much. The only answer that is a little less than 8 is 7.

3. Choice C is correct. Put in my own numbers. An x of 2 and a y of 3 makes the first equation true. 3x is 3*2 or 6 and 2y is 2*3 or 6. That makes — – .

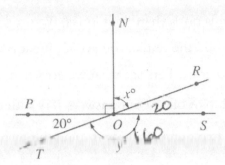

4. **Choice C** is correct. We can easily find out what the values of x and y must be. y and 20 make up a straight angle so $y + 20 = 180$ or $y = 160$. _____ is 20° since vertical angles are the same size so $x + 20 = 90$ or $x = 70$. This means $y - x = 160 - 70 = 90$

5. **Choice D** is correct. There are to be 4 sessions, 2 breaks and one lunch. So the total time is 4(1.5) + 2(0.25) + 1 = 7.5. From Noon to 4:30 is 4.5 hours which means we need 3 more hours. 3 hours before noon is 9 am.

Second third - medium

6. Choice A is correct. This question asks which number **could** be so we only have to try their numbers. The two facts we need to make sure happen is that the three expressions make integers and that $x + 1$ is the median or middle number. Since their number answers are all integers and there is not division in the expressions all the results will be integers. Lets try A. here x is 5. That makes $2x - 5 = 5$, $x + 1 = 6$ and $3x - 8 = 7$. 6 is the median. It works. Look at another one. Let x = 7. $2x - 5 = 9$, $x + 1 = 8$ and $3x - 8 = 13$. But 8 is not the median of these three which is why B is wrong. The answer is A

7. **Choice E** is correct. We are given an expression for profit and asked which value of n will make the profit be $100. We only need to put in their numbers and find out which one works. We usually start with answer C. $P(150) = 0.75(150) - 50$. Either you use your calculator for the answer or looking notice that the result will be too small. We need more wreaths sold. This also means that anything smaller than 150 is also too small. The correct answer is either 175 or 200. 200 is easier to try. $P(200) = 0.75(200) - 50 = 150 - 50 - 100$.

8. **Choice D** is correct. This problem is not as hard as it looks. We need to find two numbers that multiply to 24 and when you square them and add the results you get 73. What two numbers multiply to 24. 4 times 6, 3 times 8, 2 times 12 come to mind quickly. Lets see what we get when we square them and add the results. $4^2 = 16$ and $6^2 = 36$. $16 + 36 = 52$. Not one of our answers. Try with the next pair. $3^2 = 9$, $8^2 = 64$ and $9 + 64 = 73$. BINGO! We have our two numbers. Now to find the answer. $(x + y)^2 = (3 + 8)^2 = 121$

Math Method : Do FOIL and multiply out the binomial. $(x + y)^2 = x^2 + 2xy + y^2 = 73 + 2(24)$, which is the same 121.

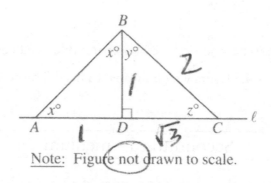

Note: Figure not drawn to scale.

9. **Choice D** is correct. First note that the figure is NOT drawn to scale. The SAT people have tried to disguise the answer by making the diagram a little off. Make sure you write the known sizes on the diagram. Write 1 and $\sqrt{3}$ where they belong. Now lets examine anything else we know. In the triangle on the left both small angles are the same size. This makes it an isosceles triangle. That makes BD the same length as AD. Write in 1 for BD. $\triangle BDC$ is a right triangle and we know the lengths of the two legs. $1 + 3 = 4$ so the hypotenuse is $\sqrt{4} = 2$. And here we have another one of the SAT people's favorite right triangles. The hypotenuse is exactly double the small leg so the triangle is a 30°, 60° right triangle. Looking at the answers we don't even have to figure out which one to use.

10. **Choice B** is correct. When you see 30 percent of something it means we will be multiplying the numbers in the order listed. The problem also seems to be missing a number for us to do the problem. But the answers are all numbers so that "missing" number can be anything we like. Since we are using percents we like to use 100 for the missing number. So 30% or 40% of something would look like $0.30 * 0.40 * 100 = 12$. Now the other part. 20% of w% of something is $0.20 * \frac{w}{100} * 100 = 0.2w$ which are both supposed to be equal. Thus $12 = 0.2w$. 0.2 times which of their answers would be 12? The answer is B

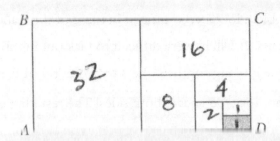

11. **Choice B** is correct. Since we are not told what the area of the shaded rectangle is, we should make it up. It is small so make it 1. The rectangle on top of the shaded one is the same size so that is also 1. The square just to their left is twice the shaded area so that would be 2. Write it in the diagram. Now the rectangle just on top of the three regions we know is twice the square so it is 4. Likewise the other areas are each doubling making them 8, 16 and 32. The problem asks for the area of the shaded region over the area of the rectangle ABCD. The shaded region is 1 and the whole rectangle has area 64. (Add up all 7 regions we found.)

Last third - hard

12. **Choice B** is correct. Just put in your own numbers and see which answers work. Both x and y are negative so lets choose –2 for y and –3 for x. That makes –6 < –2 < 0. Now put the same values in the answers.

   A) –2(–3) = 6

   B) –(2(–3) + –2) = 8

   C) 2(–3) = –6

   D) 0

   E) –(–2) = 2

   The largest of these is 8.

13. **Choice C** is correct. Again we put in our own number for n. Carlos delivered 5 packages on Monday. 4 * 5 = 20 so he delivered 20 on Tuesday. 5 + 3 = 8 so he delivered 8 on Wednesday. Carlos delivered 5 + 20 + 8 = 33 packages, which makes the average for each of the three days 11. Put in 5 for n in each answer and see which one gives us 11.

   A) 2(5) – 3 = 7   B) 2(5) – 1 = 9

   C) 2(5) + 1 = 11   D) 2(5) + 3 = 13

   E) 6(5) + 1 = 31

© 2009 Master Learning Strategies Inc.

14. **Choice E** is correct. This problem looks very difficult because of the fraction in the exponent and the negative in one of the exponents. It will be very difficult to pick out numbers to make the sentence true so we would spend too much time looking for them. Lets try to get rid of the problems first. Remember that an exponent of $\frac{1}{2}$ means square root. So square both sides! The resulting equation is $a+b=(a-b)^{-1}$ Oh that -1 exponent! What does it mean? Reciprocal! So the equation is now $a+b=\dfrac{1}{(a-b)}$ or $\dfrac{a+b}{1}=\dfrac{1}{(a-b)}$

Now cross multiply and you get $(a+b)(a-b)=1$ The answer is E

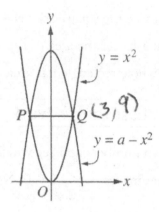

15. **Choice E** is correct. Looking at the graph we know the graph is symmetric on the left and right of the y-axis. Since PQ = 6 then it has to be 3 on each side of the y-axis. That makes the coordinates of Q (3, something) Put 3 into the first equation to find the y value. $3^2=9$ so the coordinates of Q (3, 9). But $y=a-x^2$ crosses at that point so its equation gives the same value of 9. So $9=a-3^2=a-9$ or $9=a-9$ or $a=18$. The answer is E

16. **Choice D** is correct. We need to make up our own sets here and see what happens. Make X be the set with members {a, b ,c } so $x=3$. Make Y have a member in common with X. Let Y be {c, d, e, f} so $y=4$. Now Z has all the members of X or Y but NOT any common members. This means Z does not have member c! So Z is {a, b, d, e, f} which makes $z=5$ and $k=1$ since there is one common member. Now we look for an answer that produces 5!

A) 3 + 4 + 1 = 8

B) 3 + 4 − 1 = 6

C) 3 + 4 + 2 = 9

D) 3 + 4 − 2 = 5

E) 6 + 8 − 2 = 12

The answer is D

Practice Test #2 - Verbal

Section 2

1. **Choice D** is correct. The blank is defined by what follows the comma. If Sondheim "strives for an element of surprise", then he would avoid being "predictable". "Erratic" (inconsistent) and "idiosyncratic" (quirky, eccentric) don't fit the context.

2. **Choice C** is correct. Once again, the phrase preceding the blank gives us important clues. If "the pandas had already been weakened by disease and drought", any other negative event would have a magnified effect. A "harsh winter" would thus be "catastrophic". "Regressive" (backward) nor "moderate" (insignificant, negligible) don't fit.

3. **Choice A** is correct. If we look at the first blank only, we see that it is modified by the word "practical". Marriage is certainly not practical "entertainment" nor "attitude" nor "bargain" nor "misfortune". That leaves only A. "Devoid" (empty) fits the second blank because although there may be love, the overriding concern is "economic advantage."

4. **Choice B** is correct. Looking at the second blank in this question is the easiest strategy. If "Maggie is a procrastinator", she will tend to extend or "prolong" discussions because she would rather postpone her duties. The other second choices do not fit the second blank and can be quickly eliminated. "Temporize" means to draw out in discussion.

5. **Choice C** is correct. Look at the first blank only. The first part of the sentence sets up a parallel between glass and the atmosphere. Since glass is transparent it "admits" light yet traps heat inside a car or room. In like manner, we are all well familiar with the greenhouse effect where the atmosphere does the exact same thing on a global scale. The other first blank choices do not fit and can be eliminated.

6. **Choice C** is correct. The key word here is "yet" which sets up a contrast. The speaker had a positive trait and a negative one. "Praised for style" but "ridiculed for vacuity (emptiness)

7. **Choice D** is correct. The blank is defined by what follows the colon. "Quickly became irritated…" describes a "petulant" (peevish, insolent) person. "Fastidious" (excessively neat, proper) nor sedulous (dedicated, persistent) nor "vindictive" (vengeful) nor "mercenary" (one who works for money) fit.

© 2009 Master Learning Strategies Inc.

8. **Choice A** is correct. The construction of the sentence, particularly "although most of them are not so sentimental", clearly implies that the appropriate answer would mean sentimental. Treacle is a blend of molasses and corn syrup. "Treacly" would be the adjective form meaning excessively sweet. "Cursory" (superficial) nor "prosaic" (common, dull) nor "meticulous" (precise) nor "consecrated" (holy) fit.

9. **Choice C** is correct. In the first eight lines of the Passage, there are two examples of irony—situations in his writing which were completely different than was found in his actual life. A is incorrect because female readers were drawn to him. B is incorrect because the Passage does not give an example of his financial matters. D and E are also not supported by the text.

10. **Choice B** is correct. Lines 8 and 9 indicate that the source of Balzac's creativity is "not sensitivity but *imagination*" and immediately following this line is the experience of being locked in the closet. The Passage goes on to say that his "fiction originally sprang from the intuition he first discovered" in that closet.

11. **Choice E** is correct. Anyone who has a close relative who has some degree of fame has had to weather the storm of expectation because he or she will "inevitably be compared" to them. Sadly, the same would be true if the relative is infamous.

12. **Choice C** is correct. The Passage is short enough to show that the only possible answer has to do with the "perception of her father as a role model."

13. **Choice A** is correct. Line 18 begins "But unlike a man, whose self-worth rose through his economic exertions…" immediately tells the reader that the situation was the exact opposite for women at that time in history. "Mutually exclusive" means that the two cannot co-exist. In other words, it would bring shame upon a woman at the time if she were to exert herself in pursuit of economic gain.

14. **Choice C** is correct. The author of the Passage has made it clear that a man's identity and self-worth are found in his work or "occupation" which is one's "vocation". An <u>avocation</u>, on the other hand is a hobby or something one does purely for the love of it (hence the word amateur) and not to be paid for it (as a professional would be).

15. **Choice E** is correct. The fifth class was introduced in the nineteenth century (1851, line 26). The trade tokens referred to in lines 37-38 lend contrary evidence to the idea of a fifth class of non-working women because the initials of both the husband and the wife were found on these tokens in the late seventeenth century. These, however, disappeared sometime during the eighteenth century.

16. **Choice D** is correct. The influence of the queen is not mentioned at all in Passage 1, whereas, all of the other Choices are.

17. **Choice D** is correct. Lines 42-46 describe the beginning of the end of the role of women in business. The man described here as having been born in 1790, remembers his mother "confidently joining the family auctioneering business". This clearly happened in the early 1800's. But in little more than fifty years the fifth class was introduced. It would, naturally, take some time for most women to surrender the roles in business to their spouses and for another generation to follow suit. The early 1900's would, consequently, see the death of the "practice of married couples jointly running businesses".

18. **Choice D** is correct. The word "hail" can be defined by any of the Choices given. The context, therefore, always gives us the best clue. What is being "hailed"? *A temporary emancipation* is the answer. "Emancipation" (freedom) would not be "called out to" nor "gestured to" nor "come from" nor "summoned" but it certainly would be "**welcomed**".

19. **Choice E** is correct. Lines 85-90 describe Mary Kingsley's "distaste for the 'new women' agitating for freedom,.." and incorrectly being identified as one of them. Therefore, there was a clear "contradiction between her personal motives and the way her actions were interpreted". Choices A-D are not supported by the text.

20. **Choice C** is correct. Lines 65-67 give us the primary reasons that Victorian women traveled and these are: "scientific research…missionary work…and to escape domestic confinement." It is clear that both "educational pursuits and humanitarian concerns" fit these objectives but there is no mention of "entrepreneurial" (business) interests.

21. **Choice A** is correct. A specific example of a Victorian traveler would be one who traveled to Greece to "examine ancient ruins". These would obviously be an educational pursuit even if it was solely for the individual. Choices B-E do not fit the descriptions of the reasons women traveled during the Victorian era as described in lines 65-67.

22. **Choice B** is correct. The fifth class, again, were the confined Victorian women who could not work for fear of public ridicule. "Caged birds" would be a very apt description of them. "Dorothy Middleton and Mary Kingsley" had clearly escaped such a fate, as would the "new women".

23. **Choice B** is correct. An important key to remember when answering a general question such as this one in a critical reading section is to realize that an "extreme" answer is almost always wrong. The tone of these Passages is neither overtly positive nor harshly negative. It seems evident that the Passages were written by those who did not experience the things about which they were writing, in other words, in the third person. Almost anyone who experiences injustice of any sort and personally writes about it would tend to be much more expressive than these authors are. Therefore, neither "affection, regret, indignation (anger) nor hostility (really angry!) are in evidence. Rather, "analytical detachment" is the best description of the Passages here.

24. **Choice A** is correct. Lines 14-20 in Passage 1 make it clear that women were "discouraged from pursuing careers in their native country" which supports the assumptions in Passage 2. Choices B-E are not supported by the text.

Section 5

1. **Choice B** is correct. The word "predictably" gives us our first clue and tells us that the blank will not contradict the rest of the information in the sentence. A "detail-oriented" person would be someone who is good at "keeping track of a myriad (thousands) of particulars…" To be "adept" (apt) is to be skillful at something. "Remiss" (careless) and "humorous" and "hesitant" and "contemptuous" (scornful) miss the mark.

2. **Choice E** is correct. A "controversial tax" in any country, at any time, will certainly fuel a <u>negative</u> response from the populace. This choice must go in the first blank. Any of Choices A, C or E would work. "…that could <u>not</u> be…" precedes the second blank which intimates a word or phrase meaning suppressed or held down. The best choice here would be "quelled" which means exactly that.

3. **Choice E** is correct. "Inbreeding" is the process of mating closely related organisms in order to produce the most desired traits. Since all organisms inherently have a handful of mutations, which are typically both <u>harmful</u> and recessive, mating closely related ones increases the chances of these <u>harmful</u> traits being expressed. (Hence the historical genetic consequences of royal families intermarrying.) What follows the comma in the sentence defines the answer. "Deleterious" means harmful and fits well. "Ineffable" (indescribable, unspeakable) nor "articulated" (well-spoken) nor consummate (ultimate) nor "presumptive" (assuming) work.

4. **Choice A** is correct. The flow of the sentence gives us the clue. The word "that" gives us an indication that there is a cause and effect here. The words "therefore", "consequently", "hence" and "thus" would also do the same. We are, therefore, looking for a pair of words which parallel one another since there are no contradictions in this sentence. One who "vacillates" (wavers, waffles) is one who shows "inconsistency" or is erratic. No other pair works.

5. **Choice E** is correct. "A judicious biography" is one which is wise or balanced. By the context, it is clear that this example is one in which the "balanced" definition is exhibited. The first blank is defined by the phrase "both strengths and weaknesses" and a word meaning balanced would fit. "Equitable" (equal or even-handed) fits well. The second blank is defined by "two extremes" and must be a positive word since "indictment" is a negative one. The word eulogy is usually used of a message given at a funeral by a friend of the deceased. It literally means "good word" from the Greek "eu" (good) and "logos" (word, study or purpose).

6. **Choice B** is correct. This question is very straight-forward and discusses the hardships on farm families that the majority of the population never sees. The first sentence of the piece, as with any good writing, introduces the main topic of the paragraph with the phrase "…brutal work schedule that few could tolerate." My thanks and my prayers are with our faithful farmers and their families whose hardships bring the blessings we take for granted every day.

7. **Choice D** is correct. Once again, Passage 1 is very clear about the strenuous nature of the work that needs to be done every day on a working farm. Passage 2 speaks of the "nostalgia" (wistful, excessively sentimental) view that non-farmers have of life on the farm. One week at "farm" camp would cure most of us of that nostalgia in a New York minute.

8. **Choice B** is correct. Unlike a century ago, the "majority" of the population of the United States is not agrarian (non-farmer). The author of Passage 1 would then be exposing the realities of the hardships of farm life to them. Although the may be "bored by the routine chores performed on a farm" or even "admire the efficiency of the average family farm", there is no indication of this in the written passage. **BE CAREFUL!!** The test makers are apt to tempt you into making a conclusion that is not supported by the written passage.

9. **Choice E** is correct. This is the only accurate description. The authority quoted is not the New York Times. It is politician Darrell McKigney, an ex-farmer.

10. **Choice A** is correct.   Since Waverly goes out of her way to be condescending (look down upon) and make fun of the ad June created, and laughs along with the other <u>at</u> June, rather than <u>with</u> June, the answer must be negative. "Unsophisticated and heavy-handed" hit the mark.

11. **Choice A** is correct. Line 10 begins " I was surprised at myself…" and ends with "…how humiliated I felt." She wasn't so much surprised that June could say such a thing, as we'll see in a moment, but more by the way she allowed it to affect her. Thus she was "unaware of her emotional vulnerability".

12. **Choice D** is correct. "I had been outsmarted by Waverly once again.." obviously indicates that this had taken place before.

13. **Choice C** is correct. The last sentence of any paragraph or passage usually sums up the action in that paragraph or passage. The final phrase in the last sentence of the first portion of the reading says, "…and now betrayed by my own mother". The writer is writing this passage months after the incident and still feels the deep hurt of her mother's comment, particularly in front of friends and family.

14. **Choice B** is correct. Clues to the answer are found in the phrases " ' I guess my mother's telling me…." and "I knew by the wonder in his voice…" that the author is "not the only one who ponders the meaning of a jade pendant."

15. **Choice A** is correct. Lines 37-38 says, "I always notice other people wearing these same pendants…". This gives us the indication that the gift that June received from her mother was certainly not an isolated incident or some coincidence, but rather, "a widely observed tradition" in the Chinese community.

16. **Choice E** is correct. The main idea of a passage can frequently be discovered by reading the first and last sentences of each paragraph. The last sentence of the first paragraph states, "The long-standing fear that many people have about bats tells us less about bats than about human fear." The first sentence of the third paragraph states, "Bats have always figured as frightening or supernatural creatures in the mythology, religion, and superstition of peoples everywhere." Both of these sentences strongly suggest that "our perception of bats has its basis in human psychology."

17. **Choice D** is correct. The word "classic" could mean any of Choices B, C or D. The context, however, dictates that Choice D, "well-known" is correct.

18. **Choice A** is correct. The first part of the first paragraph indicates how innocuous (harmless) bats are. The second part of the paragraph states that the anticoagulant (doesn't allow blood to clot) essential to a bat feeding on a steady flow of blood, is not toxic to humans and may, therefore, have a beneficial use in the future with respect to people who have clotting problems.

19. **Choice C** is correct. "Normal" is clearly a relative term. What is "normal" to one person or country or species may not be "normal" to another. In like manner, if we consider daylight "normal" time because it is the time that we are most productive, we may erroneously consider that to be true of all species and, consequently, subconsciously consider nocturnal animals to be "abnormal". Our perception has "limitations of a point of view".

20. **Choice E** is correct. The question asks us which Choice detracts LEAST from the author's argument in the second paragraph. Therefore, we are either looking for something that supports his point of view in the second paragraph or has nothing to do with his argument at all. Here the author uses a number of examples of how our view of night and darkness is bad or evil. "…we associate night dwellers with people up to no good…" or "in the night we become vulnerable…" That "some dream imagery has its source in the dreamer's personal life" has nothing to do with the author's argument and is, therefore, the best response.

21. **Choice A** is correct. The examples in paragraph three come from the studies of ancient cultures throughout the world. "Anthropology" literally "man study" is the clear choice.

22. **Choice C** is correct. The third paragraph of the Passage is a classic way to write a paragraph. A thesis statement is given—"Bats have always figured as frightening or supernatural creatures in the mythology, religion, and superstition of peoples everywhere."—and is followed by a number of specific and excellent examples which illustrate the thesis well. "Different sides of an issue" are not discussed nor are "details given that culminate (conclude with) in truth"

23. **Choice B** is correct. Lines 48-49 indicate that the "Ancient Egyptians prized bat parts as medicine for a variety of diseases". This clearly answers the question of the "usefulness" of bats.

24. **Choice B** is correct. Stoker is the author of *Dracula* and the author mentions him to illustrate the point that the enduring legacy of a small, furry mammal turned monster proves that "our fear of bats reveals more about us than about bats."

Section 7

1. **Choice E** is correct. The error in the original sentence lies with faulty parallelism. "…museums <u>in</u> Great Britain…" must be compared to "museums <u>in</u> Canada".

2. **Choice B** is correct. As the original sentence stands it is incorrect because it is a comma splice, that is, it contains two independent clauses separated only by a comma. There are a number of ways to approach this. One could separate the sentences altogether with a period after "Education". Or one could use a semicolon there followed by "it manufactures". But the simplest and smoothest way is Choice B.

3. **Choice B** is correct. Once again, we have a faulty parallelism in the original sentence. One cannot compare a "campus newspaper" to a "hometown" as the original does. Newspapers must be compared with newspapers and hometowns with hometowns. Hence B is correct. Both D and E are incorrect because the phrase "as much <u>as</u>" needs to remain intact, though not together.

4. **Choice E** is correct. A good grammar rule to adopt is to say things as concisely as possible. Extra words more often confuses the issue rather than clarifies it. The original sentence is simply too wordy and awkward. The pronouns "they" and "it" are excessive and unnecessary. B illustrates another good rule. The conjunction "and" makes this sentence a compound sentence. It is better to use a complex sentence rather than a compound sentence where possible. Choice E is an excellent example of a complex sentence.

5. **Choice D** is correct. The original sentence is incorrect because the first part of the sentence, "Having thought….care" modifies "the committee" instead of the appropriate subject which is "the chairperson". In other words, the modifier is misplaced. The correct subject must immediately follow the modifier or confusion and misunderstanding will result.

6. **Choice C** is correct. The plural subject "reasons" needs a plural verb "are" rather than "is" in order to be correct.

7. **Choice A** is correct. The original sentence is grammatically correct and succinct.

8. **Choice E** is correct. As in question 5, the original sentence contains a modifier error. After seeing this and other examples over and over again, hopefully you will see and "hear" an incorrect sentence when you come across it, even if you don't know what it's called. "Margo" is the subject of the sentence and is "Returning to Dayville" **not** "the small town" as the original sentence indicates. Choice E makes things clear and grammatically correct.

© 2009 Master Learning Strategies Inc.

9. **Choice E** is correct. The phrase "as well as" can be used to link two things together but not three. A series of things should be joined by commas and a conjunction. Choice E does not only this, but also disposes of the awkward "ing" word "Having".

10. **Choice C** is correct. The original sentence contains a faulty parallelism as well as being too wordy. If the subject is "moving <u>from</u> the South <u>to</u> the North" then he should also move "<u>from</u> the United States <u>to</u> France".

11. **Choice C** is correct. The original sentence is very confusing. To what does the word "it" in the last line of the sentence refer? The "government", "universities", "research center" or "talent" are all possibilities. A space research center would clearly be dependent upon the government for business and information and would also be dependent upon universities for graduates or "talent". C sets the meaning of this compound sentence straight with a minimum of fuss and a lack of confusion.

12. **Choice C** contains the error and should read "disintegrated" in order to be consistent with the past tense "launched".

13. **Choice E** is correct. The original sentence is correct. as is.

14. **Choice B** contains the error. The construction "either....or" is necessary here not "either...and".

15. **Choice D** contains the error. The plural subject "pottery shards" requires the plural verb "they are" rather than "it is".

16. **Choice D** contains the error. It is not uncommon in daily English to hear the phrase, "the only one of <u>its</u> kind". Clearly then " a kind" is incorrect.

17. **Choice E** is correct. The original sentence is correct. as is.

18. **Choice A** contains the error. Consistency in tense is required here. "Because he <u>was</u> absent when his rivals <u>voted</u>…" Selby "<u>is</u>" worried in the present because he "<u>was</u>" absent in the past.

19. **Choice E** is correct. The original sentence is correct. as is.

20. **Choice D** contains the error. It should read "not only present but <u>necessary</u>".

21. **Choice B** contains the error. It should read "prepared jointly by <u>him</u>" not "by <u>he</u>".

22. **Choice B** contains the error. The original sentence contains a faulty parallelism. The infinitive "to ride" requires the infinitive "to explain" to be correct.

23. **Choice E** is correct. There is no error in the original sentence.

24. **Choice A** contains the error. "Since….then" is a pair of words used to delineate a cause and effect. In grammatical language, "since" makes the first part of the sentence a subordinate or dependent clause. By simply dropping the word "Since", the remainder of the sentence is correct. and gets the point across.

25. **Choice A** contains the error. One has preoccupation "with" something or someone not "on" something or someone.

26. **Choice B** contains the error. The compound subject "Carlos and I" should read "Carlos and me". The way to determine whether to use I or me is to eliminate the other person. In other words, "…the foundation awarded me a grant…" not "…I a grant…".

27. **Choice B** contains the error. The compound subject "…clinics and proposed center…" requires the plural verb "are" not "is".

28. **Choice C** contains the error. Consistency in number is the solution here. The plural subject "multivitamin tablets" requires the pronoun "their" not "its".

29. **Choice B** contains the error. Adjectives are used to modify nouns while adverbs are used to modify verbs. "Constant" cannot modify "changing", therefore, and should read "constantly".

30. **Choice D** is correct. A topic sentence should introduce the main idea or thesis of the entire passage. The entire passage deals with the relationship between employers and employees. Misunderstandings can arise between any two groups when communication is not clear. Therefore, Choice D is an excellent introduction.

31. **Choice** B is correct. The "he or she" in these lines clearly refers to the workers. In order to accomplish a task between two parties smoothly and efficiently, the concerns ("demands") of the workers need to be taken into account by management. The balance, of course, is that the employees need to know their responsibilities and perform them in order to uphold their end of the table, so to speak. B expresses this well.

32. **Choice E** is correct. In order to understand how sentence 7 (which is grammatically correct as is) needs to be revised, it must be read in the context of sentence 6. When they are read together, it appears that "This results from…" is referring to the satisfaction of customers which is confusing. "Unreasonable demands" of employers are the result of "..an employer's lack of consideration". The phrase "Such treatment demonstrates…" puts the emphasis where it belongs.

33. **Choice E** is correct. A grammatical pause is necessary between "employees" and "this". This can be accomplished by a period and a new sentence or a semicolon since they are two independent clauses. However, neither of these are choices. Choice E is the best.

34. **Choice C** is correct. This paragraph speaks about the problems that employers have with employees and Choice C would introduce this paragraph well.

35. **Choice E** is correct. The final sentence of any essay should summarize the body of the essay. This is a great point to emphasize in the essay portion of the SAT. Choice E does the perfect job.

Section 8

1. **Choice D** is correct. The second part of the sentence, after the comma, gives the clue to the answer. "Though" like "Despite" indicates a contradiction. If he "eagerly sought" something but "chose not to heed that advice", then the answer must be akin to "advice". "Counsel" is a synonym for advice as opposed to council which is a group of individuals.

2. **Choice A** is correct. The second blank is easier to answer than the first. "…making that excitement…" "inaudible" (unable to be heard) nor "futile" (hopeless) nor "impersonal" make any sense at all. Hence, B, D and E can be eliminated immediately. Choice C is incorrect because "contempt" means disdain or lack of respect for something.

3. **Choice E** is correct. The first blank is defined by the phrase "that disaster" just after the comma. "Catastrophic" immediately jumps out from the list of first choices. The word "nevertheless" indicates that the answers will be opposites and certainly "constructive" is the opposite of "catastrophic".

4. **Choice D** is correct. Once again we see a pattern. That portion of the sentence following the colon defines something in the first part of the sentence. In this case it is not the blank but the word "cloaked". To cloak, like the garment, is to cover something up. A "shroud", like the Shroud of Turin, which supposedly was the burial cloth of Christ, also covers things up.

5. **Choice A** is correct. The blank follows the semicolon and must clarify some action which takes place in the first part of the sentence, namely, "just as demand was reaching its peak" Clearly, this was the perfect time to introduce her products and was a great opportunity or "opportune" time. "Intermittent" (off and on) nor "dubious" (doubtful) nor "extravagant" (showy, ostentatious) hit the mark.

6. **Choice D** is correct. The first blank is the easiest to find. It is described by the phrase "not automatically reject folkways that might at first seem silly". Choices A, C and E can be immediately eliminated. "Arrogance" and "smugness" both fit but "pursue" does not fit the second blank. "Legitimate" can either be used as an adjective to modify a noun or as a verb meaning to give legal status or authority to or justification for something.

7. **Choice B** is correct. The second paragraph begins with the idea of manipulation and brings to mind a puppeteer. "Wire-pullers" would be an apt description of those behind the scenes who are "molders of public opinion"

8. **Choice B** is correct. "Consumption" typically means eating or drinking but, of course, one does not do that to a television. It must, therefore, be used as an a metaphor for watching or "viewing" television.

9. **Choice D** is correct. Lines 21-24 describe the invalid fears of moralists in the eighteenth century who trumpeted the dangers of reading novels. As a blanket prohibition this would be as invalid as prohibiting the viewing of all television because of the deleterious effect of some programming.

10. **Choice D** is correct. See the previous answer.

11. **Choice C** is correct. There is a parallelism here. *Reality* is to *fiction* as *primary* is to *secondary*. Clearly from the context the word primary refers to "everyday" life and secondary to the "fictional" world of television.

12. **Choice A** is correct. If a person cannot distinguish the difference between a fight among family members of a soap opera and his own family, one would consider him unstable. Advocates of the simulation theory would say that people who don't understand their concerns would be "applying it too literally" or simplistically.

13. **Choice B** is correct. Clearly the author has a positive view of television and is trying to dispel the myths that "evaluators" or critics of television purport. His attitude toward them would therefore be "scornful". "Intrigued" (interested) nor "equivocal" (undecided) nor "indulgent" (permissive) nor "nonchalant" (unconcerned or indifferent) fit.

14. **Choice E** is correct. The entire gist of the piece implies that each of these theories is flawed and that "no reasonable person could take them seriously".

15. **Choice B** is correct. The critics of television seem to think they are the only ones who can think. Are the critics of television not viewers themselves? Seems to be an internal contradiction. That "viewers never engage their analytical faculties" is the only choice supported by the passage. The others are not.

16. **Choice E** is correct. The author is very "descriptive" of the various theories of television critics but also uses "irony" as indicated in the previous answer. How can a critic of television be a critic without viewing it or how can a critic be unaffected by it if it is so dangerous?

17. **Choice D** is correct. The word "sovereign" is typically used of a king or queen or even of God and is synonymous with omnipotent or all-powerful. "Absolute" would be the word that would best describe these attributes. "Opulent" means wealthy.

18. **Choice B** is correct. The "fatal loophole" described in line 62 is that the theories themselves are "symptoms of universal stupefaction." One can't have it both ways. Either the theories are universally dangerous or they are not. If one can be outside the box looking in, then clearly they cannot be universally dangerous. The only other option is that "theorists are themselves victims of television."

19. **Choice A** is correct. The author's attitude toward politicians is "humorous contempt" because although they may spout the evils of television and its effect on the populace, they are the ones who are manipulated by all-consuming power of their own images on television and its affect on voters.

Section 10

1. **Choice B** is correct. The original sentence is incorrect as it stands because the use of the present participle "exploring" dictates that something else should follow "bloodstream". The only way this sentence can be corrected among the choices is the use of the infinitive "to explore" which is Choice B.

2. **Choice B** is correct. It is often helpful to lift out clauses set off by commas in order to get to the core of a sentence. Doing this immediately leads us to the answer. "H. Ford Douglas...eventually recruited" makes the most sense.

3. **Choice A** is correct. The original sentence is correct. as is. Although B is grammatically correct as well, it is not as concise as A.

4. **Choice B** is correct. A faulty parallelism is the problem with the original sentence. "Journalists <u>should</u> present…. and …. <u>should</u> also stir…"

5. **Choice D** is correct. The question of how the "Spartans tested the endurance of potential warriors" is answered by the prepositional phrase "by devising" various ordeals. "Devised" can be used as an adjective but clearly a verb is necessary here to describe what the Spartans did.

6. **Choice E** is correct. The original sentence is incorrect because the phrase "asserted as" is improper. One "asserts that" something is true or not true. This eliminates both A and B. Both C and D, however, are wordy and awkward.

7. **Choice E** is correct. Faulty parallelism is the problem with the original. The correct construction here would be "not only as…but as". E is the best response.

8. **Choice A** is correct. The original sentence perfectly expresses the idea intended.

9. **Choice D** is correct. The original sentence describes a cause and effect. The distance and the methane cloud blocks the radiant energy of the Sun. The problem with the original sentence is that the word "this" is confusing. Does it refer to "Uranus" or the "cloud"? It's a good rule not to use too many pronouns because it could lead to confusion.

10. **Choice B** is correct. As the sentence stands, the introductory phrase modifies "my mistakes" because this immediately follows the comma. This is obviously incorrect. "I" must therefore follow the comma which eliminates A, C and E. "I made numerous mistakes" is appropriately modified by the first part of the sentence.

11. **Choice C** is correct. The original phrase is incorrect because one usually uses the construction "so absorbed that" . C and D are then the only possible choices. Clearly D is more awkward than C.

12. **Choice D** is correct. As it stands the original is incorrect because the phrase "By simply entering…number" cannot modify "a catalog", it must modify a person. This immediately eliminates A, B and E as possible answers. "They" is incorrect. Although D is the best of the choices, it too could use some correction. "One can" is a better response. Even the test makers can make a mistake!!

13. **Choice C** is correct. Parallelism demands the construction "not only *a verb* but also *a verb*". That is why the original sentence is incorrect. The tense of the verb should also be the same. Choice C is the only one which fits the requirements.

14. **Choice D** is correct. Once again, if we lift out the clause set off by commas, the main idea of the sentence is apparent. "The city is populated by many people who…" "…speak languages at home that range from Armenian to Zapotec.". By lifting out the clause the answer becomes quite evident. "…who speak.." is the only choice that makes any sense.

Practice Test #2 - Math

1. **Choice E** is correct. In this problem asks us to find the one answer that **doesn't** work. We could simplify the inequality given and test their answers or we could just test their answers. Looking at the problem we see a variable on the small side and no variable on the large side. It would be smart of us to put in big values first. The largest value given is 3 so put in 3. We get $3b + 1 = 3(3) + 1 = 9 + 1 = 10$ which is not smaller than 10.

2. **Choice A** is correct. In this problem we only need to put in their answers to see which one works. Start with 4 (C). 2^{16} is very much bigger than 16. So C is wrong as is any answer bigger than 4. So the correct answer is either 1 or 2. Try 1, the easier value to calculate. 2^4 is 16. We have our answer.

3. **Choice E** is correct. Even though the problem has a variable, the answers are all numbers. This means that whatever answer we get for a special case works all the time. Let's put in our own number for the variable. Use 5. This makes the problem "How much greater than 3 is 10?" $10 - 3 = 7$. We have our answer but let's try 2 for r as it is the smallest value for r where the results of both expressions aren't negative. Using 2, the sentence becomes "How much greater than 0 is 7?" Same answer!

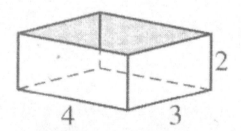

4. **Choice E** is correct. Cutting the vertical edges of the box and flattening them gives us a shape that looks like a plus sign. That makes choices A and B wrong so cross them off. The bottom of the box has lengths 4 and 3. This is the middle of the plus sign. We need to find the shape with the middle that is 4 by 3. In choice C the middle is 2 high and 3 wide. Cross it off. Choice D is 2 high and 4 wide. Cross it off as well. Now only choice E is left so it better be correct. It is 3 high and 4 wide. Super. That must be our answer. Put it down and go on to the next problem.

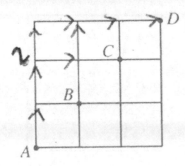

5. **Choice B** is correct. In this problem we are forced to always go up ↑ or right → and also make sure we don't hit points B or C. Let's count the ways we can go. From A we can go either way. For now we will count the paths starting from A and going up. Go up one square. Where can we go from here? Only up since if we go right we hit B. Continue up one more square. At this point we could go up or right. Remember this point. We will come back to it. Choose to go up. Now we have arrived at the top of the large square and may only go right from this point. The path we have followed is three ups and then 3 rights. (↑↑↑→→→) Now we go back to where we had a choice after two ups. Let's go right from here. At this point we can go up but not right. Going right hits point C. So we go up and get to the top of the large square. Now we can only go right to get to point D. This path is ↑↑→↑→→. Once we moved up from point A there was only one point where we were not forced in a single direction. So there are only two paths if we first choose to go up. This means that answer A is wrong since we have found 2 paths and still have other places to look. Now we consider the starting from A by going to the right. This bottom section of the large square is just a mirror image of the top part. This means there will be a path that is the mirror image of each path we found in the top half. So there were two path in the top and there are two paths in the bottom. For the record those paths are →→→↑↑↑ and →→↑→↑↑.

6. **Choice A** is correct. $\frac{3}{7}$ of a number is 42. We are asked what is $\frac{5}{7}$ of the same number. This answer must be bigger than 42! That makes C, D and E wrong. Cross them out! So the answer is either 45 or 70. Since $\frac{5}{7}$ is almost double $\frac{3}{7}$ then the correct answer should be near double 42. 70 fits that bill much better than 45. Put down A and move on.

   Math Method: Solve for n and find the answer. $\frac{3}{7}$ of a number is 42 gives the equation $\frac{3}{7}n = 42$ (The key words here are *of* which means multiply and *is* which means equals.) Multiplying both sides by 7 gives $3n = 294$ so $n = 98$. Now find out what the problem expects. $\frac{5}{7}n = \frac{5}{7}(98) = 70$

7. Choice E is correct. In this problem the marble falls randomly which makes the probability of landing in F the same as the ratio of the area of F to the area of the whole box. So lets look at the areas. There are three squares and three double squares or 9 squares. F is a double square. The ratio (division) of the areas is 2 squares to 9 squares or $\frac{2}{9}$

Second third - medium

8. **Choice E** is correct. Putting in our own numbers for their variables will make this problem look easier. Let's pick 3 for *a* and 5 for *b*. So the problem becomes

I. (4)5 = 20 is odd Wrong!

II. (4) + 5 = 9 is odd. Possible.

III. (4) − 5 = −1 is odd. Possible.

Cross out choices A and D as they both say I is correct. We could try a few more examples and each time II and III come out as possibilities. Looking at II we see the expression $(a+1)+b$ or (ODD + 1) + ODD. ODD + 1 is even so we have EVEN + ODD which is always ODD. II is correct. Looking at III we get (ODD + 1) − ODD = EVEN − ODD which is always ODD so III is correct.

9. **Choice D** is correct. Look at the pattern mentioned. The first 1 is followed by 1 zero. The second is followed by 2 zeros and the third by 3. What would follow the fourth 1? Yes, 4 zeros. So the 98th one would be followed by 98 zeros, the 99th by 99 zeros and the 100th by 100 zeros. That makes $98 + 99 + 100 = 297$ zeros.

10. **Choice D** is correct. This problem is basically asking if you know what $f(2)$ is asking for you to do. It means put in 2 where you see *x*. Put 2 in and find out the value! $f(2) = \dfrac{3 - 2(2^2)}{2} = \dfrac{3 - 2(4)}{2} = \dfrac{3 - 8}{2} = \dfrac{-5}{2}$

Note: Figure not drawn to scale.

11. **Choice A** is correct. "Figure not drawn to scale" means that the diagram is meant to be confusing. $l \perp n$ means perpendicular or right angles. That means all the angles where l and n meet are 90° angles. $x > 90$ would make line m tilt down on the right side. Let's put in 100 for x and see which answers are wrong. Remember that $x + y$ has to be 180° since they form a line. This makes $y = 80$.

A) $80 < 90$ possible

B) $80 > 90$ WRONG

C) $80 = 90$ WRONG

D) $n \perp m$ or $y = 90$ WRONG

E) $l \parallel m$ or angles all 90° WRONG

So A is the only possible answer.

12. **Choice D** is correct. Draw a quick sketch of $y = 5x - 10$. The line hits the y-axis at -10 and slopes up 5. This means it hits the x-axis to the right of 0. This makes answers A, B and C wrong. Cross them out. We are looking for the x value where it hits but what is the y value there? It is 0. Put in 2 or 5, the remaining answers, to see which one gives us 0. Two works since $5(2) - 10 = 10 - 10 = 0$ If you realized from the start that the y coordinate had to be 0 then you could have started that way and gotten the correct answer quickly. But if you are as visual as most people the quick sketch will weed out wrong answers very quickly. It has to be emphasized that it is to be a quick sketch as shown.

13. **Choice E** is correct. The question here is what does the word median mean in a math context. It is the number in the middle when the list is **in order**. Put the list in order and see what we have.

    27°, 33°, 40°, 44°, 50°, 68°

There are 7 numbers so that means the middle number must have 3 to its right and 3 to its left. 40° is given as the median and there are already 3 numbers to its right. We can't put any more on that side. 42° would have to be put on the right so it is the EXCEPTION.

Last third - hard

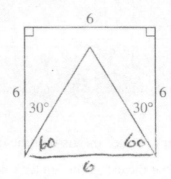

14. **Choice D** is correct. Finding the perimeter means we have to add up the lengths of the 5 sides. We know the length of three of them but need to find the lengths of the missing two. The diagram is drawn to scale so we can measure to get a good approximation. Use the edge of your test booklet to compare how long the missing side is compared with one of the sides of length 6. It looks almost exactly the same. So it looks like we have five sides of length 6 or a perimeter of 30. To have been 28 as the answer the missing sides would both have had to be 5. Is your measurement that much off?

    Math Method: Complete the bottom of the box. The figure has to be a square so the bottom is 6 also. The triangle you created is isosceles with the base angles 60° each. That makes the vertex angle also 60° and it is an equilateral triangle. Since one of the sides is 6 then they all are 6, which gives us the missing sides for the perimeter.

15. **Choice C** is correct. What is a prime number? It is a number which can't be broken up into a multiplication problem of smaller positive integers. Examples are 2, 3, 5, 7, and 11. 9 is not prime since 3*3 = 9. Now what is the *greatest* prime factor of 38? 38 = 2*19. 2 is prime and if you work at it you will see that 19 is also. In this problem we have to add up the two prime numbers we get. One of them is 19 so the answer to the problem is bigger than 19. This makes A and B wrong. What about the other answers?

    C) 24 means the other prime is 5. Does 5 divide 100? Yes

    D) 29 means the other prime is 10. 10 is not prime. OUT

    E) 44 means the other prime is 25. 25 is not prime. OUT

    5 must be the largest prime factor of 100 and it is.

© 2009 Master Learning Strategies Inc.

16. **Choice C** is correct. Draw a quick sketch of l. Remember it has to go through $(0, 0)$ and have a positive slope. Now what **must** be true of any line we draw the is perpendicular to l?

    A) passes through $(0, 0)$ No, we could put it elsewhere.

    B) positive slope. No, our line k goes down

    C) negative slope. Possible. k does slope down

    D) positive x-intercept. No. Slide k down a lot!

    E) negative y-intercept. No. Slide k up.

    Only C is possible!

    Math Method: Perpendicular lines have negative reciprocal slopes so one must be positive and one must be negative. Since l has positive slope then k must have negative slope.

17. **Choice A** is correct. This is a "Follow the Rule" problem. $1 \Uparrow 2 = \dfrac{1+2}{1-2} = \dfrac{3}{-1} = -3$ We need to find a value

    of x that makes the right side -3. Put in their numbers.

    C) $2 \Uparrow 2 = \dfrac{2+2}{2-2} = \dfrac{4}{0}$ which is wrong. Now we see we have to get a negative answer. The only way to do this

    is to make the number we choose bigger so that the bottom of the fraction is negative. This makes D and E

    also wrong so we need to try either 4 or 3.

    A) $2 \Uparrow 4 = \dfrac{2+4}{2-4} = \dfrac{6}{-2} = -3$ Right

    Math Method: $2 \Uparrow x = \dfrac{2+x}{2-x} = -3$. Cross multiply. $2+x = -3(2-x) = -6+3x$ or $2+x = -6+3x$ or

    $8 - 2x$ giving $x = 4$

© 2009 Master Learning Strategies Inc.

18. **Choice A** is correct. Let's put in our own numbers. Suppose the first shirt costs \$12. ($x = 12$) , the discount is \$2 ($z = 2$) and we buy 7 shirts ($n = 7$). This means we buy 1 shirt for \$12 and 6 for \$10 which makes the amount we spent $12 + 60 = \$72$. Now which expression gives us \$72?

A) $12 + (7 - 1)(12 - 2) = 72$ possible

B) $12 + 7(12 - 2) = 82$ WRONG

C) $7(10) = 70$ WRONG

D) $\dfrac{12 + (12 - 2)}{7} = 3.14$ WRONG

E) $(12 - 2) + \dfrac{(12 - 2)}{7} = 11.43$ WRONG

Only A remains as a possibility.

19. **Choice A** is correct. Here we must remember that there are three ratios (fractions) that are equal.

The measure of the central angle to 360°

The length of the arc to the circumference

The area of the sector to the area of the circle.

In each case it is the small piece to the whole circle. The first ratio we can find. $\frac{30}{360} = \frac{1}{12}$. To find the area of the sector we need to find the area of the circle and to find that we need to know the radius of the circle.

We can find the radius because we know the length of the arc so we set both ratios equal. $\frac{1}{12} = \frac{6\pi}{2\pi r}$ and cross multiply gives $2\pi r = 72\pi$ which makes the radius 36. That makes the area of the circle $\pi(36^2) = 1296\pi$.

Now to find the area of the sector we again set two ratios equal. $\frac{1}{12} = \frac{area}{1296\pi}$. Multiply by 1296π and get 108π.

20. **Choice E** is correct. We should use our own numbers. If there are 25 men then there are 100 women and a total of 125 students. These makes it a very small college but the numbers should work out. The problem asks "what percent of those enrolled are men?" to find the percent we divide the number of men by the number of students and then multiply by 100. So we get $\frac{25}{125} \cdot 100 = 20\%$. Now plug in to the answers.

A) $\frac{25}{25+75} = \frac{25}{100} = 0.25 \neq 20$ WRONG

B) $\frac{25}{2*25+75} = \frac{25}{125} = 0.2 \neq 20$ WRONG

C) $\frac{25}{100(2*25+75)} = \frac{25}{12500} = 0.002 \neq 20$ WRONG

D) $\frac{100*25}{25+75} = \frac{2500}{100} = 25 \neq 20$ WRONG

E) $\frac{100*25}{2*25+75} = \frac{2500}{125} = 20$ possible

Only E remains a possibility.

Section 6
8 questions – first third - easy

1. **Choice D** is correct. We can put in their numbers to see which one works. Putting in 9 makes the top 3 + 9 or 12. Divide that by 2 and we et 6. This is too small. We need to use a larger number. Only two of their numbers are bigger. Try 12. 3 + 12 = 15. Divide that by 2 and we get 7.5 which is what we want.

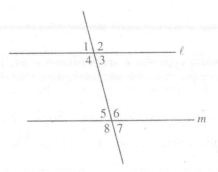

2. **Choice D** is correct. In problems where there are two **parallel** lines cut by a third line, the four big angles are the same size and all four small angles are the same size. In addition any big angle plus a small angle is always 180°. We have to add the measures of angles 2 and 4 which are both big angles. So we must find in their answers a pair of big angles. In this diagram all the big angles are even numbers. So find an answer with two even numbered angles.

© 2009 Master Learning Strategies Inc.

3. **Choice A** is correct. To find the unemployed women we have to start filling in the other boxes in the table. Since we know the total women we might as well start finding the employed women first. That number is 21,000 since that is what we have to add to 27,000 to get 48,000. Write that in the box. Now what do we add to 21,000 employed women to get 21,500 total women? 500 is right.

Second third - medium

4. **Choice E** is correct. The hardest part of this problem is identifying what number to put into the function. k is the number of cars washed and you know this group washed 15 cars. So put 15 into the function wherever you see a k. $4(15) - 30 = 60 - 30 = 30$. They made $30.

5. **Choice D** is correct. Let's put in our own numbers here. In the first equation let $x = 3$ and $r = 5$ so $v = 15$. Now we need to choose only k in the second equation since we have already picked numbers for v and r. $15 = k(5)$ so $k = 3$. Is $5(15) \neq 0$ true? Yes. The question asks which answer is equal to k which we set as 3. Now to test the answers.

A) $1 = 3$ WRONG

B) $\frac{1}{3} = 3$ WRONG

C) $3 - 1 = 3$ WRONG

D) $3 = 3$ possible

E) $3 + 1 = 3$ WRONG

Only D remains

6. **Choice B** is correct. For every 2 white eggs there are 3 brown eggs. This means that the smallest number of eggs in the basket is 5. If you took the number of eggs in the basket you could always put them in groups of 5 where 2 of the eggs are white and the other 3 are brown. So the number of eggs in the basket must be divisible by 5. Only 12, of the numbers given, is not divisible by 5 so that is the correct answer.

Last third - hard

7. **Choice C** is correct. Since $r > t$ we need to simplify the given expression. Does 4 divide 18? No. Does 9 divide 18? Yes $18\sqrt{18} = 18\sqrt{9 * 2} = 18\sqrt{9}\sqrt{2} = 18(3)\sqrt{2} = 54\sqrt{2}$ So the values of r and t are 54 and 2 and their product is 108.

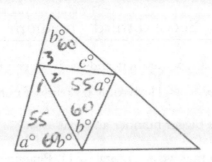

8. **Choice E** is correct. Let's put in our own numbers. $a = 55°$ and $b = 60°$. Once we have written them in we see that we can find the third angle in two little triangles. In our diagram they are marked as angles 1 and 2. They are both 65°. Now we can find angle 3 since it forms a line with angles 1 and 2. That measure is 50°. The little triangle on top now has two known measures, 50° and 60°. That means c = 70°. Now to test their answers.

A) $55 + 3 * 60 - 180 = 55 \neq 70$ WRONG

B) $2 * 55 + 2 * 60 - 180 = 50 \neq 70$ WRONG

C) $180 - 55 - 60 = 65 \neq 70$ WRONG

D) $360 - 55 - 60 = 245 \neq 70$ WRONG

E) $360 - 2 * 55 - 3 * 60 = 70 = 70$ possible

Only E remains possible.

---

10 questions – first third - easy

---

9. **Choice 1404** is correct. The problem can be restated as "If something is 351 then what is 4 somethings?" 4*351 = 1404.

10. **Choice 57.5** is correct. From 53 to 62 is 9 units. To get halfway we would need to add half of 9 to the smaller value. 53 + 4.5 is 57.5. Another way to look at this would be to note that halfway between two things is the average of those two things. Add the 53 and 62 and then divide the result by 2 gives the same 57.5.

11. **Choice 110** is correct. Since two of the angles have the same measure then two of the sides have the same length. So the third side is either 50 or 30. Which one should we choose to make the perimeter the <u>least</u> possible value? 30 of course. 50 + 30 + 30 = 110.

© 2009 Master Learning Strategies Inc.

Second third - medium

12. **Choice 9** is correct. We could test a few numbers and see if we can find the answer. Let's be smart about the way we put in numbers. since $x + y = 11$ we only try pairs of numbers that add to 11. In addition since $x^2 - y^2 = 77$ we know that x is the bigger number and that $x^2 > 77$. Now 6, 7, and 8 are all too small for x. Let's try 9 for x. That says y is 2 so that we get a total of 11. Plugging in we get $9^2 - 2^2 = 81 - 4 = 77$ and it works. We have found the answer.

Math Method: Factor the known expression and get $x^2 - y^2 = (x - y)(x + y)$ plug in 11 for (x + y) $(x - y)(11) = 77$ or $(x - y) = 7$ and solve the two equations. $(x - y) = 7$ and $(x + y) = 11$ by adding them both and get $2x = 18$ or $x = 9$

13. **Choice 13, 14, 15, 16 or 17** is correct. Notice that this problem doesn't say that each slice is the same size. Neither does it say that the number of degrees has to be a nice number. But it doesn't say that they aren't either. We know the total of all the degrees in the tip angles will be 360°. The tip size can't be 20° but it could be 21°. How many slices would that make? $360 \div 21 = 17.14$ slices. Nasty. Try 22°. $360 \div 22 = 16.36$ slices. Nasty. Try 23° $360 \div 23 = 15.65$ slices. Nasty. Try 24° $360 \div 24 = 15$ slices. NICE! Put down 15.

Getting them ALL: If each slice were 20° we would get 18 slices. But the slices must be slightly larger meaning the number of slices has to be less than 18. On the other hand we might make large 30° slices. We would get 12 slices here. But this is too many since the slice must be smaller than 30°. So any number of slices that is larger than 12 and smaller than 18 is a possible answer and will be marked correct.

14. **Choice 5** is correct. There are only 5 terms and this kind of multiplication sequence (geometric) goes up very fast. We should be able to find it quite fast.

$a = 1$, Sequence $1 + 3 + 9 + 27 + 81 = 605$? No.

$a = 2$, Sequence $2 + 6 + 18 + 54 + 162 = 605$? No.

$a = 3$, Sequence $3 + 9 + 27 + 81 + 243 = 605$? No.

$a = 4$, Sequence $4 + 12 + 36 + 108 + 324 = 605$? No.

$a = 5$, Sequence $5 + 15 + 45 + 135 + 405 = 605$? Yes.

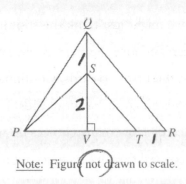

Note: Figure not drawn to scale.

15. **Choice 1/2 or 0.5 is correct.** Let's put in our own values for the sides. For a first try lets use the values of the fractions that they give us. That is $QS = 1$, $QV = 3$, $PT = 3$ and $PR = 4$. We need to find the area of the two triangles. The formula is $\frac{1}{2}bh$. $\triangle PST$ has base $PT = 3$ but the height SV which is unknown. But we can find it because $QS + SV = QV$ or $1 + SV = 3$ or $SV = 2$. That makes the area of $\triangle PST = \frac{1}{2}(3)(2) = 3$ and the area of $\triangle PQR = \frac{1}{2}(4)(3) = 6$. That makes the ratio we want as 3 over 6 or 0.5

Last third - hard

16. **Choice 2 or 7 is correct.** We need to put $2m$ into the function and see what we get.

$h(2m) = 14 + \dfrac{(2m)^2}{4} = 14 + m^2$ which the problem says is $9m$. which makes the equation $14 + m^2 = 9m$. We could guess and check with some numbers or we could solve the equation.

Guess and check would look like this.

$m = 1$, does $14 + 1 = 9$?No.

$m = 2$, does $14 + 4 = 18$? Yes. 2 is an answer!

Solving: $14 + m^2 = 9m$

$m^2 - 9m + 14 = 0$

$(m - 2)(m - 7) = 0$ 2 and 7 are both solutions.

17. **Choice 149 is correct.** We need to find out how many chimes happen at each time. The first time the clocks chime is at 7:30. Here type A clocks and Type C clocks will strike once each. Since there are 13 of these clocks we get 13 chimes.

At 8 o'clock all the clocks chime. Type A and B each chime 8 times making 8 * 15 or 120 chimes. Type C clocks only chime once each making 3 more chimes for a total of 123 chimes.

8:30 is the last chiming in the time period given and it is a repeat of the 7:30 chiming which is 13 chimes.

The total chiming is 13 + 123 + 13 = 149.

18. **Choice 72** is correct. At first glance we might just think this a simple problem. How many ways do we have to choose the first card? 4 since we can't choose the shaded card. Now for the second slot. We still have 4 choices making 4*4 or 16 ways to put the first two cards. Continuing this way would yield 4*4*3*2*1 or 96 ways. But remember this is the last problem in the section. Most people get this one wrong. What happens when we try to put down the fourth card? How many choices do we have? Well that depends on the two cards we have left. If we have a shaded card then we have to put it down because it is not permitted in the last slot. But if we don't have that card we really do have 2 choices for slot 4. This makes it a very much more difficult conditional probability if we continue to think along these lines. The good news is that if we look at the problem differently it will solve easily. Here are two other ways to look at the problem.

Solution 1: What if we calculated the total number of ways there are to arrange the cards in any manner then took off the number of ways the shaded card could be in the first position and then also took off the number of ways the shaded card would be at the end. Lets try. Total ways is 5*4*3*2*1 = 120

Shaded card first is 1*4*3*2*1 = 24

Shaded card last is 4*3*2*1*1 = 24

Answer is 120 – 24 – 24 = 72

Solution 2: This time we will change the order of the slots that we put down the cards.

1st slot: 4 choices since the shaded card can't go here.

5th slot: 3 choices since the shaded card can't go here.

Now we have no more restrictions to consider.

2nd slot: 3 choices since all cards can go here.

3rd slot: 2 choices since all cards can go here

4th slot: 1 choice since that is all the cards we have left.

Answer is 4*3*3*2*1 = 72

Section 9
16 questions – first third - easy

.1 **Choice C** is correct. This is a very simple "plug in their number" problem. Start with 8 girls on the bus which is choice C. Since the number of boys equals the number of girls at the start, there are also 8 boys. After the four boys got off there are four left. We now have to check if the number of girls is twice the number of boys. 8 is twice 4. Yes, so that is the answer.

2. **Choice D** is correct. We need to find a graph with negative slope which means that the line will slope down from left to right. Graphs A and B are positive slope. Cross them off. The second condition is a positive y-intercept. The line must cross above the origin. C hits below and E hits at the origin. Cross them off. Only D is left.

3. **Choice B** is correct. We need to find the cost per donut. The unit of measure says take the cost and divide it by the number of donuts. The cost for a box of 6 donuts is $1.89. Dividing by 6 shows 0.315 on my calculator. That is closer to $0.30 than $0.40. Put down B and move on to the next problem.

4. **Choice B** is correct. This also deals with the same price list at the top of the column. There are many ways to purchase 21 donuts. There are fewer ways to purchase exactly 21 donuts. For example you could purchase all 21 as single donuts and pay $0.40 each. So 21 times $0.40 is $8.40. But if we purchase some of the 21 in boxes we save money so $8.40 is too much. If we get 2 boxes of 12 we get 24 donuts which is too many. We can only get one box of 12 and the remaining 9 donuts can be gotten as 1 box of 6 and then three single donuts. That makes our cost $3.59 for the box of 12 plus $1.89 for the box of 6 and $1.20 for the three single donuts. $3.59 + $1.89 + $1.20 = $6.68.

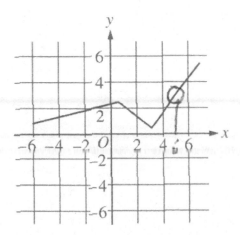

5. **Choice C** is correct. $h(5)$ is asking for the y-value on the graph when the x-value is 5. There is no line at the x-value of 5 so we should draw one in ourselves. Keep going up until we hit the graph. Then draw it over to see where it hits the y-axis. We can see that it hits somewhere between 2 and 4. In fact it looks very close to halfway between. That would make it about 3. Write down answer C and move on to the next problem.

Second third - medium

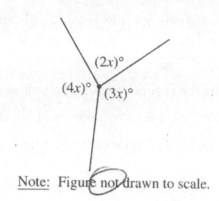

Note: Figure not drawn to scale.

6. **Choice C** is correct. "Figure not drawn to scale." Be careful because the correct answer might not look correct for this diagram. Looking at the three angles shown we see that they go all the way around the vertex point. This makes the sum of the three angles how many degrees? Right, 360° is the total. There is a trap set for those who think of the three angles of a triangle being 180° so don't fall into that one.

$$2x + 4x + 3x = 360$$
$$9x = 360$$
$$x = 40$$

© 2009 Master Learning Strategies Inc.

7. **Choice D** is correct. We are only dealing with positive integers for their variables. $x^{-\frac{1}{2}} = \frac{1}{3}$ is a nasty

looking problem. Let's look at the other one. $y^z = 16$ looks a little easier. What could the values of y and z

be? Well, $16^1 = 16$ works but we are also told that $z > y$ which means that the exponent needs to be larger

that the base. $4^2 = 16$ has the same problem but $2^4 = 16$ does work. Now we know that $y = 2$ and $z = 4$.

The question asks what is $x + z$? But we know $z = 4$ so we are really being asked what is $x + 4$? Now we

have to go back to that nasty equation. Let's use their answers to make the work a little simpler. Start with

11. That makes $x = 7$ since $7 + 4 = 11$. What is $7^{-\frac{1}{2}}$? Putting $7^{\wedge}(-1/2)$ into our calculator we get 0.05399

which is nowhere near 0.333. Cross off C and try again. Do we need to go higher or lower? Hard to tell.

Lets go lower and use 7. That makes $x = 3$ since $3 + 4 = 7$. Putting $3^{\wedge}(-1/2)$ into the calculator gives

0.1924. Wrong but closer. Cross off B. Use 5 next. This makes $x = 1$. $1^{\wedge}(-1/2) = 1$. Cross off A. Now try

13. This makes $x = 9$. $9^{\wedge}(-1/2) = 0.333$ which is the correct answer.

Math Method: Finding x can be followed in the math equations below.

$$x^{-\frac{1}{2}} = \frac{1}{3}$$

$$\left(x^{-\frac{1}{2}}\right)^{-2} = \left(\frac{1}{3}\right)^{-2}$$

$$x = 9$$

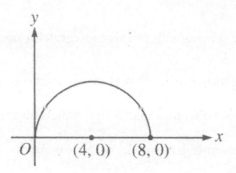

8. **Choice C** is correct. This question asks "Where are the *y*-coordinates equal?" We can do this by drawing on the diagram. An *x*-coordinate of 1 means we should draw a line straight up from 1 hit the graph. This will give us our *y*-coordinate. But how to locate 1. We should be able to approximate accurately enough to find their answer. Mark the halfway point between 0 and 4 as accurately as we can and we have 2. Now get the halfway point between 0 and 2 and we have 1. If you have a need to be super accurate you can use the edge of your test booklet and make a mark on the edge both at 4 and at 0. Fold the two marks together and we have 2. Fold again and we have 1. But this is much too accurate for this problem. Now from 1 draw a line straight up until it hits the semi-circle. Now draw straight over to the right until it hits the graph again. Now draw straight down until it hit the *x*-axis. Is this 6 on the graph? No, it seems to be about half way from 6 to 8 which we ought to call 7. Are one of the answers "1 and 7"? No! We cross off A and B since they have both been shown to be off. Now try the same pattern with 2. We go up, over and down and seem to hit around 6. "2 and 6" is an answer so let's put that down and go on to the next problem.

9. **Choice B** is correct. What is *p*? It *could* be only <u>one</u> of their answers but it might be lots of other numbers. Don't waste time finding all the answers. Plug in their numbers and find the one that works. We need to evaluate "3 is the remainder when $2p + 7$ is divided by 5." Start in the middle with 4. $2(4) + 7 = 15$ and $15 \div 5$ has a remainder of 0 which is not the 3 we wanted. Cross off C. Which way to go? Hard to tell. Try going up to get a larger remainder. Use 5 so $2(5) + 7 = 17$ and $17 \div 5$ has a remainder of 2. D is wrong so cross it off. Try 6. $2(6) + 7 = 19$ and $19 \div 5$ has a remainder of 4. Wrong again so cross off E. Try 3. $2(3) + 7 = 13$ and $13 \div 5$ has a remainder of 3. That's it! Put down B and move to the next problem.

10. **Choice B** is correct. Imagine Stacy's class lined up in height order. All the students who are taller are on Stacy's right and the shorter ones are on her left. How many students are on her right. Since she is the 12th tallest there are 11 on her right. Since she is the 12th shortest there are also 11 on her left. So the 11 on her right plus the 11 on her left plus Stacy gives $11 + 11 + 1 = 23$ which is answer B.

11. **Choice A** is correct. We know from the equation that the shape of the graph is a parabola. All the answers show parabola graphs so we are on the right track. We are given the fact that "*a* and *c* are negative constants." What does *a* being negative mean? *a* determines which way the graph points. If *a* is negative the graph points down. Cross off D and E since these graphs point up. What does *c* being negative tell us? It is the *y*-intercept. Which of the three graphs that remain have a negative *y*-intercept? A does. B has 0 as the *y*-intercept so cross it off. C also has 0 so cross it off. Only A remains.

Last third - hard

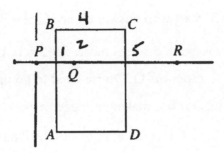

Note: **Figure not drawn to scale.**

12. **Choice B** is correct. "Figure not drawn to scale." Be careful! The answers are all numbers so there must be something in the problem that adjusts the spacing to always make the distance PR the same value. So let's make up our own coordinates that will make the problem simple to calculate. Suppose we let P be right on the origin and the line from P through Q and R be the *x*-axis. Now we only have to find where on the *x*-axis R is to find the value for PR. We need to pick a value for where AB might hit the *x*-axis. Lets be easy on ourselves, and make it hit at 1. The problem says that P and Q are symmetric about line AB. This means that Q is as far to the right as P is to the left. So we need to go 1 more over from 1 to get to Q. That makes Q be at 2. Good so far. Now where does CD hit the *x*-axis? BC = 4 so C is 4 to the right of B. But B was at 1 so C must be at 5. This makes going from Q to the line CD the same as going from 2 to 5. That makes it 3. So R is 3 to the right of line CD. 5 + 3 = 8 and there we have answer B. Put it down and go on to the next "hard" problem.

13. **Choice C** is correct. Let's use our own numbers. What shall the initial price of the telephone be? $100 is a good number to use since we want to find the percentage that the final price is to the initial price and 100 is an easy number to divide by. Follow the problem. We increase 10%. So 10% of 100 is 10. Now the new price is $110. Next we decrease by 25%. 25% of $110 is $0.25 * 110 = 27.5$. This makes the final price $110 – $27.50 = $82.50. Calculating final price divided by initial price gives us $82.50 \div 100 = 0.825$ which is 82.5% or answer C

14. **Choice E** is correct. Use their answers and follow their directions. There is a trap in this problem. Their answers are not the value of w. It is $3w$. How do we convert their answers to the value of w? Right. We have to make it smaller so we divide by 3. Start with answer choice C. $\frac{4}{3} \div 3$ is 0.44444. What a nasty number to use. Let's use some easier numbers to start. 3 seems nicer. $3 \div 3 = 1$. Use $w = 1$ in their sentence. $1 * 4$ is the same as $4 + 1$. 4 does not equal 5 so cross off D. Do we need to go up or down? $1 * 4$ is smaller than $4 + 1$ so we need to make the first one bigger. But making w bigger makes both values bigger. Which one gets bigger faster. $4w$ gets bigger faster than $4 + w$. So let's try 4 as $3w$. That makes $w = \frac{4}{3}$ and we follow their sentence again. $\frac{4}{3} * 4$ is the same as $4 + \frac{4}{3}$. Using the calculator we get 5.333 for both answers. Mark it down and move on to the next problem

15. **Choice C** is correct. Right triangles. The SAT people love certain right triangle triples. The integer ones they love are {3, 4, 5}, {5, 12, 13} and {7, 24, 25} and multiples of them. They ask to have the triangle be *consecutive even* integers. None of our triples are even but if we double them they are. {3, 4, 5} becomes {6, 8, 10} which is the answer to the value for x. Since x is the shortest side then $x = 6$. Substitute this value into their answers to see which one works.

A) $6 + 6 + 1 = 6 + 2$ OR 13=8 WRONG

B) $6^2 + (6+1)^2 = (6+2)^2$ OR $36 + 49 = 64$ WRONG

C) $6^2 + (6+2)^2 = (6+4)^2$ OR $36 + 64 = 100$ possible

D) $6 + 6 + 2 = 6 + 4$ OR 14 = 10 WRONG

E) $6^2 = (6+2)(6+4)$ OR 36 = 80 WRONG

Only C is possible.

Another Method: Did you remember that right triangles make the Pythagorian Formula true? Remember that is $a^2 + b^2 = c^2$ where c is the hypotenuse or longest side. So the equation they want will probably match that form. A and D don't have squares so they don't match. E doesn't have two squares added on one side and a square on the other. Probably not the answer we want. Both B and C match the pattern. But which is the correct answer. We need to remember that the sides of the triangle are *consecutive even* integers. {2, 3, 4} are consecutive but not even. {2, 4, 6} are even and they are consecutive since there are no even numbers that come between any of these. By how much do they go up? Each on is two more than the last one. Look at answer choice B. These three numbers go up by 1 so it is not the right answer. Look at answer choice C. Each of the three numbers go up by 2 so it does fit the requirements.

16. **Choice D** is correct. We need to use Process of Elimination on this problem. "x is and integer greater than 1" lets us know we don't have to consider negatives or fractions for x. Nice!

I. $y \neq x$ Can this be false? If it were then $y = x$ or they have the same value. We know that $y = x + \frac{1}{x}$.

How much is $\frac{1}{x}$? Since x is more than one the bottom of the fraction is bigger than the top. This makes it a number somewhere between 0 and 1 and the bigger x is the smaller the fraction is. Good. So y is a little more than x. That means they are not equal and statement I. is always correct. Cross out any answer to the problem that doesn't include I. Cross out B.

II. y is an integer. How can this be? X is an integer and y is x plus a little fraction. That makes it some kind of fraction. So II. Is false! Cross out any answer that includes II. Cross out C and E. This leaves A and D. So we need to find out if III is always true.

III. $xy > x^2$ OR $xy > xx$. What do we know about y? It is always a little bit bigger than x. This we found out in part I. above. So we are multiplying x on the left side with a little bit bigger number than we are multiplying it on the right. That means the left answer will be a little bit bigger than the right answer. So III. Is always true. Cross off A and write down answer choice D, the only one left.

Practice Test #3 - Verbal

Section 3

1. **Choice D** is correct. The phrase "now, however," gives us the clue that what follows must contradict what came before it, namely, that "taking massive doses of vitamins was relatively <u>harmless</u>". The answer must then be synonymous with <u>harmful</u>. "Toxic" (poisonous) is the obvious response. "Inane" means foolish and doesn't fit.

2. **Choice D** is correct. What follows the comma is what defines the blank. To "critically examine" something is to "scrutinize" it.

3. **Choice C** is correct. Here we have an effect followed by its cause. A country would only have its name changed as a result of political unrest. Therefore, the answer must mean <u>because of</u> "political turbulence". To "testify to" something is to lend credence to it or support it. No other answer fits.

4. **Choice C** is correct. The second blank should be easier to find. Neither "subtracted" nor "extrapolated" fits the context, thus, A and E can be eliminated. From the context it would seem as though the first blank would mean "diverse". The word "multifarious" means just that.

5. **Choice A** is correct. The second blank is, again, the easiest to answer. If these computer games are so "intricately contrived" then it would take a player of considerable skill to "master them". Choices C, D and E can immediately be eliminated. Since the conjunction "and" is used in a series with "elaborately contrived", then "_____ strategies" must parallel that description. "Byzantine" (intricately involved, labyrinthine) fits the bill. "Nefarious" (illegal) nor "devious" (deceitful) nor "onerous" (burdensome) fit.

6. **Choice B** is correct. The passage here describes Edmund Wilson as a writer who would write "on the fly" so to speak. Many writers may send letters only after many revisions or deep thought. Wilson is not described in such a way but as "spontaneous". The clues are that he was not "a self-conscious letter writer" or "one who tried to sustain studied mannerisms".

7. **Choice E** is correct. The "young, middle-aged and old Wilson" precedes the descriptors "speaks directly" and "informal" which are consistent with those found in the first sentence. This would seem to indicate that Wilson never changed his style throughout his lifetime.

8. **Choice C** is correct. Lines 3-4 indicate that "our heroes have to be perfect to be useful." The fear was that if any of their flaws were exposed it would be harmful to the Black community. "Perfect" is synonymous with "above reproach".

9. **Choice B** is correct. From the context it is clear that "paintings" is used as a metaphor for "historical biographies" of past Black leaders.

10. **Choice B** is correct. *Australopithecus* was supposedly one of the ancestors of present-day human beings. Just the mention of this term would bring to mind images of cavemen and dinosaurs to most people. This was quite a different world from the one in which we live today. This image would "dramatize" the difference.

11. **Choice A** is correct. If the light from Andromeda was generated 2 million yrs ago, then we are "looking into history" so to speak. The author in lines 6-7 clearly would love to be able to do the opposite, that is, "observe events that occurred on Earth in the distant past."

12. **Choice E** is correct. The area to peruse is the second paragraph. Lines 11-12 precede the references in the question (lines 13, 15) and says, "The possibilities are staggering" indicating that if time travel were possible, tremendous things could be accomplished. This is precisely why "time travel is such a fascinating topic".

13. **Choice B** is correct. Certainly anyone who speaking on a topic within his own field would lend a degree of authority to his presentation. In other words, this is not just any person on the street "talking through his hat."

14. **Choice C** is correct. Lines 16-35 give all of the author's concerns about "causality violations". If you peruse these lines you will see that A, B, D and E are all mentioned. Not C.

15. **Choice B** is correct. The gist of lines 37-42 is that people were oblivious to the fact that time flows in discrete intervals before mechanical clocks were invented. "When… mechanical clocks were invented, making off time in crisp, regular intervals, it must have surprised people…" Choice B states the complete opposite of this statement and would thus undermine it.

16. **Choice D** is correct. In the context of telling the reader that the body has its own internal clocks (plural), he gives us the examples of the brain and "…another clock is the heart" implying that, although they are both clocks, they are not in synchrony or marking time the same way.

17. **Choice E** is correct. The term "ruthless" usually means "merciless" but in the context it is describing how "Time marches on". It is "relentless", persistent, persevering, inexorable; nothing will stop it.

18. **Choice C** is correct. All the while the author is wistful about time travel. Here he uses the metaphor of our lives or time as a chronologically typed manuscript. If it is so, "…skipping upward on the page" is like "traveling back in time in his imagination" as he smokes his great-grandfather's pipe.

19. **Choice C** is correct. The entire passage is an analysis of exactly why most people feel the sentiments they feel in response to a certain work of art. Thus, the "essence" or the "nature" of the feelings of pleasure are focused upon.

20. **Choice C** is correct. The term "figures" could mean a variety of things but the context indicates "representations" of men or women is the best response. Choice E is incorrect because there is no indication from the passage that they necessarily have to be famous.

21. **Choice B** is correct. The gist of this paragraph is that to the majority of people aesthetic pleasure means "a state of mind that is essentially indistinguishable from their ordinary behavior" or "all their other mental activities are directed is the same as daily life". Hence, "the story of John and Susie" represents "a typical interpersonal relationship" --- John and Susie are, of course, very typical, impersonal names as in "John Doe".

22. **Choice D** is correct. If interpersonal relationships or experiences are what typically resonate with most people and most of modern art doesn't deal with that, then most would find "little of human interest to engage them.

23. **Choice E** is correct. It is only clear at the end of the piece that the author appreciates modern art and, although he looks down on ("condescends") those who do not; he understands and "tolerates" their lack of appreciation.

24. **Choice A** is correct. Appreciation of a work of art does not "invite sentimental intervention" but rather the "content of the work" itself, that is, the "artistic elements" alone are appreciated by those who are knowledgeable of modern art.

Section 6

1. **Choice C** is correct. The original sentence is awkward and incorrect. "They" is extraneous because we already know who "they" are. The subordinate clause "Having come this far" appropriately modifies the subject, "delegates". D is incorrect because the comma is unnecessary. E is incorrect because the phrase "so that" is unnecessary.

2. **Choice D** is correct. Consistency of tense is the key here. The original sentence is incorrect because it is not in the past tense as the first part of the sentence is. Choice D is the only choice with the appropriate tense.

3. **Choice C** is correct. Since "effects" is a plural noun, it requires the plural verb "are" to complement it. C and D are the only possible choices but D is awkward.

4. **Choice E** is correct. The original sentence in order to be correct must continue because the subject "The issue" has no verb. Since the sentence gives two options or possibilities, "either…or" or "whether…or" construction is dictated. Choice E is the correct choice.

5. **Choice D** is correct. The original sentence would be correct, though awkward, if "doing" was replaced by "did". D is a better revision because it clarifies what she did by using the phrase "accomplishing this feat" instead of using the general pronoun "it".

6. **Choice D** is correct. The original sentence is incorrect because the comma joins two phrases which can stand alone. "…having been…" is also awkward "ing" construction which should be avoided. D is the best response.

7. **Choice A** is correct. The original sentence is correct. as is.

8. **Choice C** is correct. The original sentence is horribly awkward. "Being as", again, is awkward "ing" construction. C is direct, straightforward and grammatically correct. "Although" in Choice D indicates a contrast which is not described in the remainder of the sentence and is, therefore, incorrect.

9. **Choice E** is correct. The word "Although" at the beginning of the sentence sets up a contrast which is not defined in the remainder of the sentence and, thus, makes the original sentence incorrect. "…never having painted…" is also awkward and roundabout. Choice E is direct and logical.

10. **Choice D** is correct. The original sentence would be fine if the word duration was removed. D is the only response which is smooth and grammatically correct. B is incorrect because "it made it" is awkward. C is incorrect because of similar construction. "…to make it to seem…" is awkward and roundabout.

11. **Choice B** is correct. The original sentence is incorrect because there is disagreement in number. The subject "first novels" must be complemented by "they" in the underlined portion of the sentence. Although B-E all have either "these" or "them" in their construction, B is the best of them.

12. **Choice A** contains the error. The musical "tells" how not "telling" how.

13. **Choice B** contains the error. Whether *a noun* or *a noun* parallel construction is dictated here. "Whether…a curse or a blessing.."

14. **Choice A** contains the error. The term "which" should not be used to refer to people but "who" in this case or "whom" in others.

15. **Choice D** contains the error. The sentence should read "were" slaveholders since that was their condition at the time of the speech and nothing likely changed.

16. **Choice A** contains the error. "One challenge…was *to preserve* her ethnic identity…" is the way this sentence should be written. The infinitive is dictated here.

17. **Choice D** contains the error. "When" sounds awkward here. A better choice would be "because", "since" or "for".

18. **Choice D** contains the error. "More clear" not "more clearer" is grammatically correct.

19. **Choice B** contains the error. The plural subject "reforms" requires the plural verb "have not" not "has not".

20. **Choice C** contains the error. Crabs, the plural subject, requires the plural pronoun/verb combination "they feed" not "it feeds".

21. **Choice B** contains the error. "In the catching of " is an awkward way to express an idea when the simple infinitive "to catch" will suffice.

22. **Choice B** contains the error. The sentence should read "sensitive to criticism" not "sensitive to be criticized". The original is too awkward.

© 2009 Master Learning Strategies Inc.

23. **Choice E** is correct. The original sentence is grammatically correct.

24. **Choice D** contains the error. Parallel construction is dictated here. "The tiger is *the fiercer* and the lion is *the stronger*."

25. **Choice C** contains the error. "Two causes" are introduced in the first part of the sentence and must be identified in the second. "...and a decrease in jobs" identifies the second cause after "less funding".

26. **Choice B** contains the error. The singular subject "number" requires a singular verb "accentuates."

27. **Choice D** contains the error. The problem with this sentence is that an object ("novel') cannot be compared to a person ("Charlotte Bronte") as is being done here. Novels to novels or people to people are fine. The lack of parallelism can be solved by substituting "than Charlotte Bronte's novel *XYZ*".

28. **Choice A** contains the error. The plural subject "trucks" needs the plural pronoun "they".

29. **Choice E** is correct. There is no error in this sentence.

30. **Choice A** is correct. The second sentence is an aside, a diversion from the main idea, in anticipation of the reader's response.

31. **Choice A** is correct. If the author found a book containing the letters, it would be logical to insert a sentence saying where he was (library) when he did so.

32. **Choice D** is correct. As written, the second sentence is a sentence fragment lacking a verb. Choice D clarifies the relationship between the two sentences smoothly and correctly.

33. **Choice E** is correct. As it stands, the sentence indicates that "An earl rebelled because a messenger rode..." This certainly is not what is meant to be communicated. E clarifies the action. As a result of the rebellion, the messenger rode.

34. **Choice B** is correct. As it stands the original sentence is incorrect because "their" modifies "letters" which certainly do not have "anxieties". "The Pastons are the ones with the anxieties and, thus, B is the best response.

35. **Choice C** is correct. There are no questions, rhetorical or otherwise, posed to the reader in this passage. Every other device is used.

Section 7

1. **Choice E** is correct. What follows the comma defines the blank. "Exchanging goods for goods" as opposed to money for goods, as we do so far more often today, was common for centuries and is called "bartering".

2. **Choice E** is correct. The phrase "no longer" indicates a contrasting relationship and contrasts with "agree" in the second part of the sentence. "Dispute" would be a contrast.

3. **Choice C** is correct. The phrase within the commas defines the blank. To perceive "unconsciously" is to be "intuitive". "Autonomy" (self-governance) nor "incoherence" (lacking rationale) nor "sophistry" (appears right but is wrong) nor "receptivity" (openness) fit.

4. **Choice A** is correct. The second blank is easier to find. Since lab exercises and classroom teaching are distinct from one another, if they are to be "coordinated" they must be "integrated" (joined or unified). Computer labs can certainly "supplement" (add to) classroom instruction.

5. **Choice A** is correct. If someone or group "detests" (hates) something, they certainly will not be "advocates" or "proponents" (those who are behind or for something) but rather "critics" or "belittlers". The "epitome" of something is a prime example of it, thus, Choice A is the best response.

6. **Choice C** is correct. The phrase "keen judgment" defines the blank. "Acumen" is keen judgment or savvy.

7. **Choice B** is correct. The construction of the sentence clearly indicates that both blanks complement one another and mean "obscure" or "baffling". The words "arcane" and "abstruse" both mean difficult to understand or mysterious. "Lucid" (clear) nor "didactic" (instructive) fit.

8. **Choice C** is correct. The key clue here is the phrase "difficult to reconcile" which indicates a contrasting relationship between the two blanks. The first blank must be synonymous with "openhanded" and the second the opposite. The best choice for the opposite of "openhanded" for the second blank would be "pettiness". "Magnanimous" fits because it means generous of spirit. "Insolence" (rebellion) nor "solicitous" (eagerness, apprehension) fit.

9. **Choice D** is correct. Both passages indicate that the buyers are influenced by the marketers "connotations" and "subtleties" of the names of the SUV's.

10. **Choice A** is correct. Passage 1 begins with the phrase "advance of the giant sports utility vehicle.." Passage 2, on the other hand, doesn't address the size of the vehicle.

11. **Choice D** is correct. As indicated in answer 9, "connotations" and "subtleties" exemplify one another.

12. **Choice C** is correct. No one wants to be weak and out of control, but, in fact, the opposite. Marketers play on this desire. "Conquering rugged terrain" and "taming the wilderness" are clues to this answer.

13. **Choice C** is correct. There is no indication in Passage 1 about how war affects women, but the main idea in Passage 2 is exactly that.

14. **Choice A** is correct. A "fissure" is a crack or rift in a rock or between people. The rift between civilians and soldiers had everything to do with the ignorance of the civilians toward the soldiers' plight.

15. **Choice C** is correct. Northcliffe's report of "airy confidence" regarding the battle of the Somme completely distorted the truth. The footnote dramatically "emphasizes the inaccuracy" of the reports.

16. **Choice E** is correct. Civilians were kept in the dark not only by the soldiers' unwillingness to express the danger to their loved ones but the "censored reports by the press".

17. **Choice B** is correct. Substituting the word believe in this sentence would best fit the context. "No wonder communication failed between the troops and those who could *believe* prose like that.."

18. **Choice A** is correct. The thesis statement of the author of Passage 2 is immediately followed by the example of Vera Brittain. Thus she serves to support his argument.

19. **Choice E** is correct. The phrase "wives and mothers" is preceded by "munitions workers, bus drivers, soldiers in the 'land army'" which clearly indicates that these positions were all together new to women and these were certainly positions of authority compared to their previous domestic experiences.

20. **Choice B** is correct. This paragraph follows what was described in the previous answer. The "…political and economic *revolution*" which "temporarily dispossessed male citizens of their primacy" clearly indicates that women had filled roles and "pursued rights previously unavailable to them".

21. **Choice E** is correct. Because women were politically, socially and economically elevated by the circumstances of the war, there was a natural tension between wanting their men safe at home and enjoying their new-found social and economic freedom. This may have seemed like "gloating" to some.

22. **Choice B** is correct. The words "menial" and "fatal" denote subservience and death and are used to describe the lengths that women would go to just to "break out" of their traditional roles. They were most definitely "stifled".

23. **Choice E is correct.** For different reasons, neither of these publications dwelt on the realities of war because they were too harsh to contemplate.

24. **Choice C** is correct. The separation or isolation from civilian society, both physically and emotionally, is clearly pointed out in both Passages.

Section 9

1. **Choice B** is correct. If sea urchins are becoming more scarce, divers must "descend" to more dangerous depths, thus "increasing" the potential for injuries.

2. **Choice B** is correct. "Boasting" clearly defines the blank. "Egotism" is synonymous with boasting.

3. **Choice D** is correct. Parallel construction dictates that the first blank means "steadfast" and the second means "tactful". "Steadfast" (steady, persevering) is synonymous with "resolute" and "tactful" (wise, discerning) with "diplomatic".

4. **Choice C** is correct. By the context of the sentence, the blank must mean the opposite of "little control". "Autonomy" (self-governance) indicates total control. "Consecration" is holiness and "effacement" is humiliation.

5. **Choice C** is correct. The second blank is easiest to answer. If someone is "forcibly detained" they must be "bad guys". This eliminates A, B and D. Choice E is incorrect because "supportive" acts would not be punished. That leaves us with the answer. "Sedition" is rebellion and "insurrectionists" are rebels.

6. **Choice A** is correct. Clearly Leguizamo's characters extended the scope or range of roles for Latino actors. This was a necessary "corrective" measure to the inequality shown them before. "Corollary" (consequence) nor "precursor" (something which comes before) fit.

7. **Choice D** is correct. This is the story of one person's perception of another. None of the other choices fits.

8. **Choice C** is correct. Both of these phrases are descriptive and lend evidence to he "attentiveness" Virginia had toward Clayton.

9. **Choice A** is correct. This almost poetic use of language by the author especially the phrase, "an uncanny complexion, as if the shades swirled just under the surface", metaphorically describes Clayton's "complicated nature".

10. **Choice A** is correct. Lines 14-15 serve to abruptly change this poetic mood to something more practical before moving on to the next paragraph.

11. **Choice D** is correct. Lines 22-25 describe the cellos like "novitiates" or those who have entered a religious order. The term "sanctity"(holiness) is, therefore, the best fit.

12. **Choice B** is correct. The "crush" referred to in line 42 is the "crowd" of people going to the rehearsal because they are later referred to as the "mob" in that same sentence.

13. **Choice E** is correct. The phrase "sailing above the mob" indicates that he is unaffected by the crowd and "immersed in his private world."

14. **Choice C** is correct. Not only does Clayton always seem to be humming something but immediately following rehearsal he wants to practice some more. He is "consumed" by his interest in music.

15. **Choice C** is correct. The phrase "agonizing bliss" would at first seem to be oxymoronic or paradoxical since they are opposites. However, knowing that Virginia is fascinated, if not infatuated, by Clayton, we realize that she is willing to allow the "wind to whip her blue" or feel physical discomfort just to be with him.

16. **Choice A** is correct. Lines 59-61 are referenced below "A jug of wine, a loaf of bread, and thou," indicating that like Fitzgerald's character, being with Clayton is the only thing that matters and the lack of food is a distant second.

17. **Choice D** is correct. These lines describe the physical similarities between Clayton and his cello in the eyes of Virginia. D is the correct response.

18. **Choice D** is correct. This allusion to the bumblebee, an insect that flies in contradiction to the laws of aerodynamics, by Clayton is in reference to the challenges he has faced as a cellist being a very tall man. His perseverance and "resolute determination" have prevailed.

19. **Choice E** is correct. When someone does something over and over again, it becomes "natural". A musician, in like manner, will be "natural" or "at home" with his instrument. Despite Clayton's physical size, he is "graceful" or "natural" behind the cello. However, when he is not playing, he is fairly clumsy.

Section 10

1. **Choice B** is correct. The original sentence is incorrect because it implies the Allies knew the end from the beginning that the treaty would inevitably fail. When they signed the treaty they believed it "would ensure" peace.

2. **Choice C** is correct. The original sentence would be correct if "consisting" was replaced with "consists". This is not an answer choice, however. Choice C does the job of revision nicely.

3. **Choice E** is correct. The original sentence is redundant. "Permanently" and "keep it off" mean the same things. E would be the correct way to state this idea.

4. **Choice E** is correct. The proper English phrase is "no sooner had _____ *than* _____". This eliminates A, B and D. Choice E is a much better choice than the awkwardness of C.

5. **Choice E** is correct. The essence of this sentence is "One reason *was*...." Choice E is the only possible response.

6. **Choice C** is correct. A parallel comparison dictates that "Chaplin will *not be remembered*" any more than "Wayne *will be remembered*".

7. **Choice E** is correct. The original is incorrect because two extraneous pronouns, "you" and "it", are used. Choice E gets the idea across smoothly and concisely.

8. **Choice A** is correct. The sentence is correct. as is.

9. **Choice D** is correct. The word "was" is unnecessary and "publishing" should be replaced by "published". Choice D does this nicely. C simply turns the entire second half of the sentence into a clause without a verb. E is simply too stunted.

10. **Choice D** is correct. "Until being.." is awkward "ing" construction and, therefore, makes this sentence incorrect. The pronoun "its" is also incorrect since it modifies "walruses" which is plural. D is the best answer.

11. **Choice A** is correct. The original sentence is correct. as is.

12. **Choice B** is correct. This sentence is incorrect as it stands because "the effect" is modified by "Persuading…" "Richard Coniff" is the one who persuades and should immediately follow the introductory clause. This eliminates A, B and E. Choice B is a smoother response than D.

13. **Choice A** is correct. The original sentence is correct. as is.

14. **Choice E** is correct. "Mickey was made to talk." is too roundabout and the simple preterit tense "made Mickey talk" is applicable here.

Practice Test #3 - Math

Section 2
20 questions – first third - easy

1. **Choice D** is correct. Solving directly is simple but let's practice using their answers. Use answer C which is 3. Does $3(3) + 9 = 5(3) +1$? That is does $18 = 16$? No, so choice C is wrong. We need to make the right bigger. Since $5x$ increases faster that $3x$ we should use a bigger x value. Try 4. Does $3(4) + 9 = 5(4) + 1$? That is does $21 = 21$? Yes. We have found the answer.

2. **Choice B** is correct. Use their numbers again. Start in the middle with 3 and the value of m. The problem says we multiply by m and add p. So we multiply by 3 and add what? $7(3)$ is 21. $21 + (-6)$ is 15. So $p = -6$. See if it works for the next term. Multiply 15 by 3 and add -6 and we get $45 - 6 = 39$. But we wanted 31. 3 is the wrong answer. Our answer for the third term turned out too large. Perhaps we should try a smaller multiplier like 2. $7(2)$ is 14. Add 1 to 14 and you get 15. So if 2 is the multiplier then 1 is what we add. Try with the next term. $15(2) + 1 = 31$. Correct. Try it on the forth term. $31(2) + 1 = 63$. Right again. The answer is 2.

3. **Choice B** is correct. With each color there are four sizes. Since there are three colors there are 3 fours. $(3)(4) = 12$.

4. **Choice D** is correct. This problem is asking for us to put -3 and 3 into the function and see which one produces a larger value for -3. Test each answer.

   A) $f(-3) = 4(-3)^2 = 36$ and $f(3) = 4(3)^2 = 36$ $f(-3) = f(3)$

   B) $f(-3) = 4$ and $f(3) = 4$ $f(-3) = f(3)$.

   C) $f(-3) = \frac{4}{-3} = -1.333$ and $f(3) = \frac{4}{3} = 1.333$ $f(-3) < f(3)$

   D) $f(-3) = 4 - (-3)^3 = 31$ and $f(3) - 4 - (3)^3 = -23$ $f(-3) > f(3)$ which is the correct answer. We can write it down and go o but here is the way to do E for completeness.

   E) $f(-3) = (-3)^4 + 4 = 85$ and $f(3) = (3)^4 + 4 = 85$ so $f(-3) = f(3)$

5. **Choice E** is correct. Problems that say something *is proportional to* are problems giving you a simple formula. We simply replace that phrase with *equals k time* and write the equation. Here is the same problem with the extra words left out. Force (*f*) is proportional to (= *k**) stretch. (*s*) $f = ks$. In these problems *k* is called the *constant of proportionality* because once you find its value in one part of the problem is remains the same for the whole rest of the problem. How to find that value? Plug in their numbers. We know a force of 15 gives a stretch of 8 so $15 = 8k$. Dividing by 8 gives us $k = \frac{15}{8}$ which is almost 2. Now put in the 20 for stretch in the new situation. $f = \frac{15}{8} * 20 = 37.5$

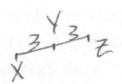

6. **Choice E** is correct. Make a little diagram. Sketch a short line and mark the ends as X and Z Y is the midpoint so make a point in the middle and label it Y. We should have a diagram that has the letters X, Y and Z equally spaced. Pick a value for the length of one of the short pieces. Say 3. Now the other segment is also 3 because we have a midpoint. That makes the total segment XZ = 6. Let's look at their choices.

I. $YZ = \frac{1}{2}XZ$ or $3 = \frac{1}{2}*6$ True. Always? Yes because we are saying the small piece is half of the whole thing. Mark off any answer not having I as an answer. A, D and E remain.

II. $\frac{1}{2}XZ = 2XY$ or $\frac{1}{2}*6 = 2*3$ or $3 = 6$ WRONG. Cross out any answer that contains II. A and E remain.

III $2XZ = XZ$ or $2*3 = 6$ True. Always? Yes because we are saying that double the small piece is the whole length. Midpoints cut <u>exactly</u> in half! Cross out A and only E remains.

7. **Choice C** is correct. We pick our own numbers for *s* and *t* making sure that $5s = 6t$. If $t = 5$ and $s = 6$ then we have the expression that $30 = 30$. Good. Now for the value of *r*. $2r = 5s = 5*6 = 30$ so $r = 15$. Now we try there answers looking for 15.

A) $\frac{12}{25}(5) = 2.4$ WRONG

B) $\frac{6}{5}(5) = 6$ WRONG

C) $3(5) = 15$ possible

D) $15(5) = 75$ WRONG

E) $30(5) = 150$ WRONG

Only C remains

Second third - medium

8. **Choice A** is correct. Again we pick our own numbers (CAREFULLY) and see which answer matches. 5 busses seating 20 passengers means there is room for 100 people. But three seats are empty so there must have been 97 people. We have just picked $n = 5$, $x = 20$ and $k = 97$. Now we look at their answers.

A) $5(20) - 3 = 97$ possible

B) $5(20) + 3 = 97$ WRONG

C) $5 + 20 + 3 = 97$ WRONG

D) $5(97) = 20 + 3$ WRONG

E) $5(97) = 20 - 3$ WRONG

Only A remains.

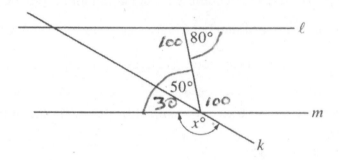

9. **Choice A** is correct. Remember when you have two parallel lines cut by a third line then all four big angles are the same size, all four small angles are the same size and a big and little angle add to 180°. So 50° + the unknown angle size is equal to 80°. That makes that little piece next to the 50° equal to 30°. Also the 30° angle and the $x°$ angle make a straight line. That means the two of them add to 180° so $x = 150$.

10. **Choice B** is correct. Which answer produces a FALSE answer? Plug them in and see. Just be careful to put the parentheses in the same place in your calculator.

A) $3*(-3)^2 = 27$, $(3*(-3))^2 = 81$ $27 < 81$ True

B) $3*(0)^2 = 0$, $(3*(0))^2 = 0$ $0 < 0$ FALSE

C) $3*(\frac{1}{3})^2 = \frac{1}{3}$, $(3*(\frac{1}{3}))^2 = 1$ $\frac{1}{3} < 1$ True

D) $3*(1)^2 = 3$, $(3*(1))^2 = 9$ $3 < 9$ True

E) we did find a value.

© 2009 Master Learning Strategies Inc.

11. **Choice C** is correct. It looks like we are missing the actual dimensions of the wheels. But all their answers are numbers so it doesn't matter what value we pick for the diameter. Let's pick simple numbers to use. We just have to make sure we pick numbers where the back wheel has **twice** the diameter of the front wheel. Pick 2 feet for the back wheel and 1 foot for the front wheel diameters. How far does the bicycle go when the back wheel turns once? It goes whatever the circumference of the back wheel is. $C = \pi d = 2\pi \approx 6$ feet. The answers they give represent how many times the front wheel turns to have the bicycle go this same 6 feet. Each turn will move the bicycle what ever the circumference of that wheel is. $C = 1\pi \approx 3$ Their answer times 3 has to equal 6. Oh, that is simple! It is 2.

   Math Method: Both the wheels are circles and all circles are similar figures. When you have similar figures, all linear measurements are proportional. Since we cut the diameter in half then we have also cut the circumference in half. So we need to of them to go the same distance.

12. **Choice C** is correct. The probability that a number picked at random is positive is the number of positive numbers divided by the total number of numbers. Since that probability is $\frac{3}{5}$ why don't we use 3 as the number of positive numbers (p) and 5 as the total. This leaves 2 numbers that must be negative. (n) So $\frac{n}{p} = \frac{2}{3}$

13. **Choice B** is correct. Let's make the problem look simpler by putting in the numbers we know.

   $$c(20) = \frac{600(20) - 200}{20} + k = 590 + k = 640$$

   Now what number do we add to 590 to get 640?

Last third - hard

---

14. **Choice A** is correct. We have to use only positive numbers and no fractions or decimals. We start with $x = 1$. That gives us $2 + 3y < 6$. If $y = 1$ then the statement is true. This means that (1, 1) is a point. Can we find any others? Try $y = 2$. $8 < 6$ is false so 2 is not allowed. In fact if we make y any larger the statement is always false. So now we need to try another value of x. $x = 2$ gives is $4 + 3y < 6$. If we try the lowest possible value of y we get $7 < 6$ which is false. In fact no value of y will work. And the larger we make x the worse the inequality becomes. So only (1, 1) works.

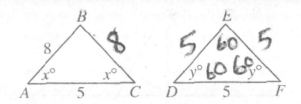

Note: Figures not drawn to scale.

15. **Choice C is correct.** "Figure not drawn to scale." Be Careful.! To find perimeter we need to add up the sides. In △ABC we know that two angles are congruent. So the two sides across from them have the same size. Put in 8 as the missing side and find the perimeter. $8 + 5 + 8 = 21$. Now for the perimeter of △DEF. If the two angles shown are both 60°, what is the third angle size? Right 60°. So in this triangle all three sides are the same length, namely 5. The perimeter is 15. We need to add 6 to 15 to get 21. 6 is our answer but it doesn't look right because △ABC was not drawn correctly.

16. **Choice E is correct.** Two positive consecutive odd integers are 3 and 5; 7 and 9, 93 and 95 and many others. Let's take one pair and test their answers. Let $x = 7$ and $y = 9$. That means $y^2 - x^2 = 9^2 - 7^2 = 32$. Now we test the answers.

A) $2(7) = 14 \neq 32$ WRONG

B) $4(7) = 28 \neq 32$ WRONG

C) $2(7) + 2 = 16 \neq 32$ WRONG

D) $2(7) + 4 = 18 \neq 32$ WRONG

E) $4(7) + 4 = 32$ True

Only E remains.

Math Method: We know $y = x + 2$ since consecutive odd integers are always separated by 2. Thus

$$y^2 - x^2 = (x + 2)^2 - x^2 = (x^2 + 4x + 4) - x^2 = 4x + 4$$

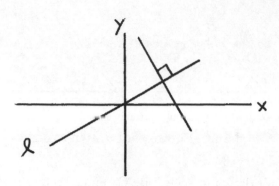

17. **Choice A** is correct. We must remember that perpendicular lines have related slopes. Always when you multiply the two slops you must get –1. So what are the slopes of the lines? We can't tell yet about line l but the other line has slope –4. To get this we need to move the $4x$ over to the other side. What number times –4 will give –1. 0.25 is the number and that is the slope of line l. And the equation is $y = 0.25x$. (Line l goes through the origin so the y-intercept is 0) The point $(t, t+1)$ is on that line. Let's see if any of the values they give us are on line l.

A) $-\frac{4}{3} + 1 = -\frac{1}{3}$ so $-\frac{1}{3} = 0.25(-\frac{4}{3})$ possible

B) $-\frac{5}{4} + 1 = -\frac{1}{4}$ so $-\frac{1}{4} = 0.25(-\frac{5}{4}) = -0.3125$ WRONG

C) $\frac{3}{4} + 1 = 1.75$ so $1.75 = 0.25(\frac{3}{4}) = 0.1875$ WRONG

D) $\frac{5}{4} + 1 = 2.25$ so $2.25 = 0.25(\frac{5}{4}) = 0.3125$ WRONG

E) $\frac{4}{3} + 1 = 2.333$ so $2.333 = 0.25(\frac{4}{3}) = 0.333$ WRONG

Only A remains.

18. **Choice A** is correct. Lets put in our own numbers. The average of 3 and 5 is 4 so $x = 3, y = 5$ and $k = 4$. The average of 3, 5 and 10 is 18/3 = 6. This makes $z = 10$ and the average we want is 6. Try their answers.

A) $\frac{2(4) + 10}{3} = 6$ possible

B) $\frac{2(4) + 10}{2} = 9$ WRONG

C) $\frac{4 + 10}{3} = 4.666$ WRONG

D) $\frac{4 + 10}{2} = 7$ WRONG

E) $\frac{2(4 + 10)}{3} = 9.333$ WRONG

Only A remains.

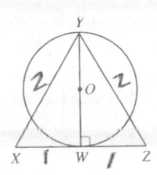

19. **Choice C** is correct. Here again we see that the SAT writers love to use those few special right triangle sizes. The one they use here is 1, $\sqrt{3}$, 2. If we didn't remember it, then we could use the Pythagorean Theorem to get it. That makes the diameter of the circle $\sqrt{3} \approx 1.7$, which makes the radius 0.85. So the area of the circle is $\pi(0.85)^2 = 2.268$. Which of their answers is about 2.268?

A) $\frac{\sqrt{3}\pi}{4} \approx \frac{3.1}{4} \approx 0.77$ Too far off.

B) $\frac{2\pi}{3} \approx \frac{6}{3} = 2$ Closer.

C) $\frac{3\pi}{4} \approx \frac{9}{4} = 2.25$ Very close

D) $\pi \approx 3.1$ Too big.

E) $\frac{3\pi}{2} \approx \frac{9}{2} = 4.5$ Much too big

2.25 is the closest.

20. **Choice C** is correct. When you divide a number the remainder is less than the divider. That makes k bigger than 3. If we divide by a number larger than 15 then the remainder will be 15. This makes k somewhere from 4 to 14. We can almost do this in our head. $15/4 = 3R3$, $15/5 = 3R0$, $15/6 = 2R3$, $15/7 = 2R1$, $15/8 = 1R7$, $15/9 = 1R6$, $15/10 = 1R5$, $15/11 = 1R4$, $15/12 = 1R3$, $15/13 = 1R2$, $15/14 = 1R1$. So 4, 6 and 12 give a Remainder of 3.

Section 4

8 questions – first third - easy

1. **Choice A** is correct. $(s + t) - 6 = 3 - 6 = -3$ Easy.

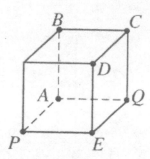

2. **Choice C** is correct. We need to check the distance from the point they give to P and also to Q. If we look at A or E they are each one side away from P and also from Q. If we look at B or D they are each one side diagonal away from P and also from Q. Point C is one side away from Q but it is the distance through the cube away from P. That is much further than a side length.

3. **Choice D** is correct. 78% is just a little more than $\frac{3}{4}$ so the shaded part must be a little more than $\frac{3}{4}$ of the circle. A and B are both less than $\frac{3}{4}$. E is much more than $\frac{3}{4}$. That makes only C or D as possible correct answers. Now we have to consider the other parts. The black is 2% and so is the striped. So both the black and the striped will have to be the same size and very small. In C the black is there but the striped is not. Looks like that is not the correct answer. Only D remains.

Second third - medium

4. **Choice D** is correct. The numerator (top) is 5 less (smaller) than the denominator (bottom). They give us possible bottoms and we need to get 0.75. Let's test their answers.

A) $\frac{3}{8} = 0.375$ WRONG   B) $\frac{7}{12} = 0.583$ WRONG

C) $\frac{11}{16} = 0.687$ WRONG   D) $\frac{15}{20} = 0.75$ possible

E) $\frac{19}{24} = 0.133$ WRONG   Only D remains

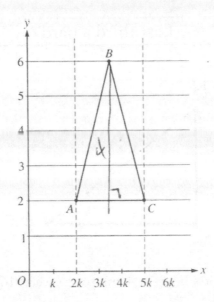

5. **Choice E** is correct. The area of a triangle is $\frac{1}{2}bh$. We can read the height from the graph as from 6 to 2 or

4. Since the area is 18 we have $18 = \frac{1}{2}b4 = 2b$. We can see that the base is 9. We can read from the graph that

the base is from $5k - 2k = 3k$. So the base is both 9 and $3k$ or $k = 3$

6. **Choice D** is correct. Let's put in our own number for the value of k and see what m has to be. Then we will

test their answers. 10 seems a nice number to put in for k since it is easy to use with all the other 10s.

Putting in 10 for k we get $10m^2 10^{-1} = m^2 = 100m$. Dividing both sides by m we get $m = 100$. What do they want

to find? $m^{-1} = 100^{-1} = 0.01$

A) $\frac{10}{10} = 1 \neq 0.01$ WRONG

B) $\frac{10}{90} = 0.111 \neq 0.01$ WRONG

C) $\frac{\sqrt{10}}{10} = 0.316 \neq 0.01$ WRONG

D) $\frac{1}{10*10} = 0.01$ possible

E) $\frac{1}{90*10} = 0.00111 \neq 0.01$ WRONG

Only D remains.

Last third - hard

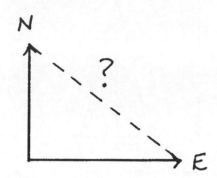

7. **Choice E** is correct. Edna walks for 4 hours at 4 kph so she walks 16 km. Nancy walks the same four hours but only walks at 3 kph so she walks 12 km. They walk at right angles to each other so we have a right triangle. We have the two legs so we square them and add the results to get the square of the long side. $16^2 + 12^2 = 400$. Square each answer they give us and we will find that $20^2 = 400$.

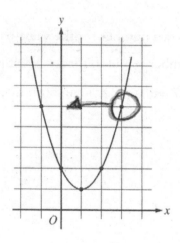

8. **Choice C** is correct. $f(b)$ means the b is an x value. $f(b) = f(3)$ means the two y values are the same for the two different x values. Locate on the graph where $f(3)$ is and look over on the graph to where the parabola it at the same height. What is the x value there? It is -1.

10 questions – first third - easy

9. **Choice 7** is correct. Each person needs 4 bottles of water for the trip. The family has 5 members so that makes 20 bottles of water needed. Water comes in packages of three so 6 packages gives 18 bottles of water, which is too few. 7 packages makes 21 bottles of water, which is too many. But we can't buy less and have enough water.

10. **Choice 13** is correct. Absolute value equations usually give two answers. Let's look at the first problem. $|10 - k| = 3$ means what is inside of the absolute value symbols might have been 3 or it might have been –3. If $k = 7$ then the equation is true. Let's check that answer in the other equation. $|7 - 5| = 8$. This is false so the value of k is NOT 7. This is the place many people get stumped. How can we find the other value? Remember that $10 - k$ could have been three but it also could have been –3. What value of k would make $10 - k = -3$? 13 is the answer. Let's try that in the second equation. $|13 - 5| = 8$ which is true so we have found the value of k.

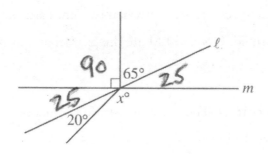

11. **Choice 135** is correct. Find the values of the other angle sizes. We know the angle marked with a square is 90°. The angles across the top of line m total 180° so we find that the missing amount needs to be 25°. Again the angles across the top of line l total 180° and again the missing angle size is 25°. Adding up all 5 know angles sizes gives us 225°. Adding in whatever $x°$ is gives us 360°. Subtraction finds the correct answer.

Second third - medium

12. **Choice 46** is correct. Imagine all 9 numbers written in a line. We will start to write them. The middle one (median) is 42. Write that down. Now the rest of the numbers are some above and some below. We could start writing them. 43 above and 41 below. Then write the next two, 44 above and 40 below. Now we have 5 numbers in the list so we continue writing. 45 above and 39 below for 7 numbers and finally 46 above and 38 below. The problem asks for the largest which is 46.

Another Thought: If we have 9 numbers in an ordered list then we have the middle number and 8 others. Of these 8 numbers, 4 are higher and 4 are below. Since these are consecutive integers going up 4 numbers is simply adding 4 to the middle number.

13. **Choice 28** is correct. $2f(p) - 20$ reduces to $f(p) - 10$. Using the first equation we have $f(p) - 10 = p + 1$ so $p = 9$. We are asked for $f(3p) = f(27) = 27 + 1 = 28$

© 2009 Master Learning Strategies Inc.

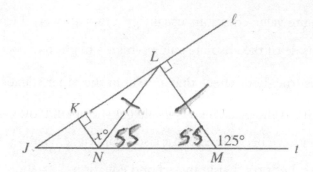

14. **Choice 70** is correct. We have two sides of a triangle congruent so the angles opposite them are the same size. One of these angles and the 125° angle make a line so they total to 180°. This makes each of these two angles 55°. Once again we need to remember that when two lines are parallel and cut by a third line there are lots of congruent angles formed. KN and LM are the parallel lines. t is the third line. So $x°$ and 55° add together to 125°. That makes $x = 70$

15. **Choice 7/15, .466 OR .467** is correct. The question asks for a fraction. The top will be orange juice and the bottom will be the total mixture. But we know the total mixture. It is 1 cup. This makes the fraction orange juice over 1. Dividing by 1 is easy. Our answer will be however much orange juice we have. Doing the problem in decimals may make it a little easier on the calculator. We start off with $\frac{1}{5} = 0.2$ cups of orange juice. Then we add enough mixture to give us 1 cup. How much mixture do we add? $1 - 0.2 = 0.8$. How much of the mixture is orange juice? One-third of the mixture. The word "of" in this context means multiply so we get $1 / 3 * 0.8 = 0.266666666667$. Adding on the original 0.2 gives us 0.466666666667. When we grid in this answer we need to be as accurate as possible so we should start on the left. But there is no 0 to start so we start with the decimal point. Should we put down .467 or .466? Both answers are correct but .467 requires us to round. Correctly rounding is a source of error and the SAT people don't require us to round. We should put down the digits on the calculator until we run out of space. .466 is the answer we use.

Last third - hard

16. **Choice** 3 is correct. We can use our own numbers here since the answer is a ratio of the variables. $a + 2b$ and 125% of $4b$ are equal. What values shall we pick? 125% of $4b$ would be easy to find if $4b = 100$ or $b = 25$. That makes $a + 2(25) = 125$. So $a = 75$ and $\frac{a}{b} = \frac{75}{25} = 3$

Math Method: $a + 2b = \frac{125}{100} 4b = 5b$ or $a + 2b = 5b$

so $a = 3b$ and dividing both sides by b gives $\frac{a}{b} = 3$

© 2009 Master Learning Strategies Inc.

17. **Choice 4/9 OR .444** is correct. $\sqrt{x}$ is pointing to the sixth mark so the value is six-ninths.

$\sqrt{x} = \frac{6}{9} = 0.666666666666$. To find out what x is we need to take off the square root sign. So we square both

sides and get $x = 0.444444444444$

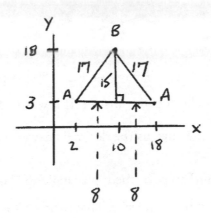

18. **Choice 2 OR 18** is correct. A quick sketch puts the value of x out beyond 10. (There is another sketch we
could have drawn where A is to the left of B but the problem asks for a possible value so ours is good
enough.) We can make a right triangle by starting at B and going right until we are over A and then going
down to point A. How far over did we go? From 10 to x is the amount. How far did we go down? From 18
to 3 or 15 units. So we have a right triangle that has sides $x - 10$, 15 17. Do you remember that special
triple? 8, 15, 17 is that one. Don't worry too much if you didn't remember it. We can use the Pythagorean
Theorem to get it. Either way we now know that $x - 10 = 8$ or $x = 18$. The other answer would come if our
diagram had point A to the left of point B. Everything would be the same except the missing side would
have been $10 - x$. Here $10 - 8 = 2$.

Section 8
16 questions – first third - easy

.1 **Choice B** is correct. The correct answer has to be in all three sets. Let's eliminate wrong answers.

Set E: The number has to be EVEN. Cross out C.

Set P: The number is positive. Cross out D and E.

Set F: The number < 5. Cross out A.

Only B remains.

2. **Choice B** is correct. Test their answers. Start with C. $8 + \sqrt{529} = 8 + 23 = 31 \neq 15$ Cross out C and we need to

get smaller. Try B. $8 + \sqrt{49} = 8 + 7 = 15$ Got it!

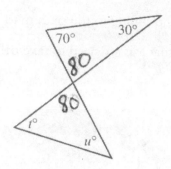

3. **Choice A** is correct. How many were polled? 35 + 14 + 1 = 50 people. There were 35 in favor so the fraction requested is $\frac{35}{50} = 0.7$. Looks like A is the answer. If it wasn't such an obvious answer we could have divided each fraction so see which one gave us the decimal answer we got.

4. **Choice C** is correct. What is the third angle in the top triangle? 80° is the one that makes the three add to 180°. The vertical angle below is also the same size. That makes $t + u + 80 = 180$ or $t + u = 100$

5. **Choice D** is correct. We need to find the change in each year mentioned see which one is greatest.
   A) From 3.75 to 3.50 or a change of 0.25
   B) From 3.50 to 4.25 or a change of 0.75.
   C) From 4.25 to 4.75 or a change of 0.50.
   D) From 4.75 to 3.75 or a change of 1.00.
   E) From 3.75 to 4.50 or a change of 0.75.
   D has the largest change.

Second third - medium

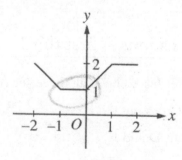

6. **Choice B** is correct. This question asks for k, an x value that gives a y value of 1. $g(k) = 1$ Looking at the graph we see that the y values are 1 from −1 to 0 on the x-axis. So the correct answer will have to be in that range. −1.5 is too far left and answers C, D and E are positive.

7. **Choice A** is correct. $2^a \cdot 2^b \cdot 2^c = 2^{a+b+c} = 64 = 2^6$. This is only true when $a+b+c=6$. What are the requirements on these three variables. They are all positive. They are also all different. Suppose $a=1$. B has to be different so let $b=2$. This forces $c=3$ so the sum would equal 6. Does this work in our problem? Let's see. $2^1 \cdot 2^2 \cdot 2^3 = 2 \cdot 4 \cdot 8 = 64$. Good. We didn't make careless mistakes. Now we find $2^1 + 2^2 + 2^3 = 2+4+8 = 14$ which is answer A. We don't have to go further. The question implies that there is only one answer by giving five different number answers. Only one of them is considered correct. Actually it is possible to find other values of a that will work. But the conditions will force us into choosing the same three values, just different letters on the numbers. The final sum will always be 14. But this is more than you need to know to answer the problem correctly.

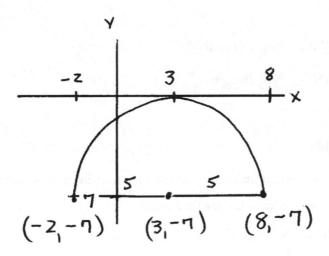

8. **Choice E** is correct. Making a quick sketch we draw a circle and locate the center. The point on the circle has the same y value so it is the same height. The x value is smaller than the y value so this points the point on the left of the center. Actually it is 5 units left. The other end of the diameter would be 5 units to the right of the center. $3+5=8$. Cross off A, B and C since they don't have an x value of 8. What would the y value be? Our diameter is horizontal so all the y values are the same. They are all –7. (8, –7) is the answer.

© 2009 Master Learning Strategies Inc.

9. **Choice D** is correct. Let's pick a height and see if any of the inequalities work. A 40 inch child can ride so the inequality should be true.

A) $|40 - 10| = 30 < 50$ possible

B) $|40 - 20| = 20 < 40$ possible

C) $|40 - 30| = 10 < 20$ possible

D) $|40 - 40| = 0 < 10$ possible

E) $|40 - 45| = 5 < 5$ WRONG

We now need to pick another height and test it on the four remaining possibilities. A 50 inch child is right on the borderline. Since all the answers are "less than" this child can't ride but the answer should be an "equals."

A) $|50 - 10| = 40 < 50$ WRONG – Not an equals

B) $|50 - 20| = 30 < 40$ WRONG – Not an equals

C) $|50 - 30| = 20 < 20$ possible

D) $|50 - 40| = 10 < 10$ possible

We now need to pick another height and test it on the two remaining possibilities. A 30 inch child should also be able on the border. So we look for another equal.

C) $|30 - 30| = 0 < 20$ WRONG – Not equals

D) $|30 - 40| = 10 < 10$ possible

Only D remains

10. **Choice B** is correct. The area of a cylinder is area of the base times the height. The base is a circle making the first volume $v = \pi r^2 h = \pi(25)4 = 100\pi$. The second volume is $\pi(25)8$ or 200π. 200π is twice 100π.

11. **Choice A** is correct. This SAT "function" problem is "true" only when $n < k < r$. We are asked what could make $-2 \blacklozenge (n,0)$ "true." The n has to be the smallest of the numbers given so it must be smaller than -2. Let's look at their choices.

I. -3 is smaller than -2. It is a possible value.

II. -1 is not smaller than -2. Throw this one out.

III. 3 is not smaller than -2. Toss this one too.

Only I is possible so that is our answer.

Last third - hard

12. **Choice B** is correct. Pick our own numbers here. "20% of x" means we have to multiply. If $x = 100$ then 20% or 100 is 20. Now 80% or y has to be that same 20. This means that y has to be a little bit more than 20. Use our calculator to see if we can find something that works. $0.8 * 24 = 19.2$. Too small. $0.8 * 25 = 20$. Success. $y = 25$. Now test their answers.

A) $25 - 0.16 * 100 - 16$ WRONG

B) $25 = 0.25 * 100 = 25$ possible

C) $25 = 0.60 * 100 = 60$ WRONG

D) $25 = 1.00 * 100 = 100$ WRONG

E) $25 = 4.00 * 100 = 400$ WRONG

Only B remains.

Math Method: The original statement yields the equation $0.2x = 0.8y$. All the equations are in the "$y =$" form so put the equation in that form. $y = \frac{0.2}{0.8}x = 0.25x$ which matches choice B.

13. **Choice C** is correct. The questions asks us which *must* be true. We could try to find WRONG answers. Take the simple answers and try to show they are wrong.

A) Pick 2 for x. $x + y$ is even so pick 4 for y. $(2+4)^2 + 2 + z = 38 + z$ is odd so pick 1 for z. This works so x doesn't have to be odd. Cross off A.

B) Pick 1 for x. $x + y$ is even so pick 3 for y. $(1+3)^2 + 1 + z = 17 + z$ is odd so pick 2 for z. This works so x doesn't have to be even. Cross off B.

E) Pick 1 and 3 again so xy is not even. If we pick 2 for z again we see that our statements are true so xy doesn't have to be even. Cross off E.

If time is a problem then guess either C or D. Otherwise continue finding counter examples.

C) z is even so let $z = 2$. Can we find some values so x turns out to be even? $x + y$ is even so if x is even then y has to be even. Pick $x = 4$ and $y = 6$. Then $(4+6)^2 + 4 + 2 = 106$ which is not odd. This is a possible correct answer. Leave it in and try D.

D) z is again even. Let $z = 2$. We need to find a way to make xy odd. Pick $x = 1$ and $y = 3$. Is 1 + 3 even? Yes. Is $(1+3)^2 + 1 + 2 = 19$ odd? Yes. All conditions are met so D is WRONG. Cross off D.

Only C remains.

© 2009 Master Learning Strategies Inc.

14. **Choice E** is correct. Let's test their choices.

I. Normally when we raise to a power the number gets larger. But not for decimal numbers in the 0 to 1 range. Multiplying a decimal by a decimal in this range makes the answer get smaller. So x^3 will be smaller than x^2 just as it says. This is why this problem is a "hard" problem. I is true. Cross off B since it doesn't have I in the list.

II. What happens when we cut a number in half. It gets closer to 0. For numbers in the 0 to 1 range this means they are getting smaller. So II is also true. Cross off A and D since they don't include II. Only C and E are left.

III. This one is like I. In the 0 to 1 range, raising to a power makes the number smaller. So this one is also true making E the correct answer.

15. **Choice A** is correct. First we need to understand the graph. There are 12 dots on the graph. Each dot represents a single hamster. The dot at (1, 40) represents a hamster that had 1 practice then did the run in 40 seconds. So there were 3 hamsters who were timed at 40 seconds. One had 1 practice, one had 3 practices, and one had 5 practices. Let's look at their answers.

A) $t(p) = 44$ means that no matter what the number of practices, the number of seconds is 44. All our timings are from a low of 40 to a high of about 48. This is a very crude measure but it might be OK. Leave it in until we find something better.

B) $t(3) = 3$. Was the time for a hamster with 3 practices 3 seconds? No. Way off. Cross off B.

C) $t(3) = 44*3$ Was the time for a hamster with 3 practices 132 seconds? No. Way off. Cross off C.

D) $t(3) = \frac{3}{44}$ Was the time for a hamster with 3 practices almost 0 seconds? No. Way off. Cross off D.

E) $t(3) = 3 + 44$ Was the time for a hamster with 3 practices almost 47 seconds? Close. Also a possibility. Now we must choose between A and E. A is a horizontal line at 44. E is a line with slope 1 going from $(1,45)$ to $(5,49)$. Looking at the graph we see that hamsters with 1 practice and hamsters with 3 practices have the same results. Look at 5 practices. 2 of the 3 hamsters are the same timings as the 1 and 3 practice hamsters. The number of practices doesn't seem to help much I this experiment. Choice A is a little better than choice E.

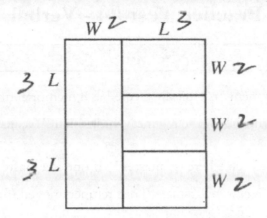

16. **Choice E** is correct. Let's put in our own numbers here. What shall we use for L and W? Looking along the sides we see that on the left that 2L is the same length as 3W on the right. So we need to pick numbers where $2L = 3W$. Making $L = 3$ and $W = 2$ does the job. There are lots of others also but these seem pretty simple to use. How big is the rectangle to be used? $3*2 = 6$. How big is the total to be covered? $12L *10L = 36 *30 = 1080$. How many 6's are needed to make 1080? Do the division to get 180.

© 2009 Master Learning Strategies Inc.

Practice Test #4 - Verbal

Section 3

1. **Choice D** is correct. "A monument" is typically erected as a memorial or remembrance of something or someone. The "statue" is "a symbol" of the regime. "Indictment" (accusation) nor "mockery" (ridicule) fit.

2. **Choice A** is correct. The context clue here is "master". If one is a master at any skill he is "adept" (apt) at it. "Congenial" (friendly) nor "reclusive" (isolated) nor temperamental (fussy, moody) work.

3. **Choice B** is correct. The second blank is easiest to answer. If we cover up the answers and guess what word would fit here we might say "snatch". Choices A, C and D definitely do not fit and can be eliminated. "Pilfer" (steal) and "raid" both work but B is the answer because "penchant" (strong inclination) fits the first blank while "remedy" does not.

4. **Choice A** is correct. Once again, the second blank is easier to determine. The context clue here is "winning the support of church authorities". The term "legitimacy" is really the only choice which fits. It is also logical that if her theology is "inseparable from" her science that she would have the support of the church authorities.

5. **Choice A** is correct. "Pre-revolutionary French nobility" implies privilege for the rich and noble and disdain for the commoners. "Elitist" would certainly describe the separation of the one from the other, and "perquisites" are privileges gained. "Irreproachable" (blameless) nor "reprehensible" (worthy of censure) work.

6. **Choice C** is correct. Although both of the authors show appreciation for Linnaeus' work, clearly the author of Passage 1 is much more appreciative because he has nothing negative to say about him or his work. The majority of what Passage 2 has to say is about the negative aspects of classification and Linnaeus' role in it.

7. **Choice D** is correct. The author of Passage 1 distances himself from his subject, never using the first person. The author of Passage 2 does so immediately in the first sentence and makes it personal – "I am a heretic about Linnaeus."

8. **Choice A** is correct. "The extent to which classification contributed to natural science" is touched upon by both pieces. No other answer fits.

© 2009 Master Learning Strategies Inc.

9. **Choice D** is correct. The author of Passage 1 indicates that even Linnaeus "would probably admit that classification is only a tool and not the ultimate purpose" as some of his immediate successors thought. Choice D embodies this idea.

10. **Choice B** is correct. If one needs to "grow accustomed" to something, it's because it is constant or "persistent".

11. **Choice C** is correct. Line 16 is preceded by the description of the actor dying in one film and magically being "resurrected" in another. The people felt duped because they thought that what they were watching was real.

12. **Choice A** is correct. No one can dispute that seeing a live musical performance is better than hearing one, even if they are the best technological reproductions. In fact, some would say the lack of "perfection" is what makes the live performance authentic and, therefore, better. The inhabitants of Macondo felt the same way. The phonographs lacked the "heart and soul" of the musicians.

13. **Choice D** is correct. After the movies and the phonograph and now the telephone the passage indicates "It was as if God had decided to put to the test every capacity" and "…no one knew where the limits of _reality_ lay." Clearly they couldn't make the "usual assumptions about their world".

14. **Choice C** is correct. The description of the emotion of the people alternating "between excitement and disappointment, doubt and revelation" indicates that these devices promised one thing but delivered another. They "were not all they seemed to be."

15. **Choice D** is correct. Obviously the entire passage describes the effects or the "people's responses" to the introduction or "influx" of these inventions to their culture.

16. **Choice A** is correct. "I am not an adept aesthetician (evaluator of beauty)" is an "assertion", a clear and definitive statement about someone or something. "…I could not presume to analyze" is a disclaimer because Martha Graham is the acknowledged expert.

17. **Choice B** is correct. Lines 5-6 are preceded by the context clues "…the instincts of a mathematician or physicist…". She could not or would not use such language unless she frequently "used mathematical forms."

18. **Choice E** is correct. These lines are surrounded by these words, "…visual, kinesthetic, and emotional effects" and "…evokes many ideas and emotions…". Both of these phrases "evoke a vast number of associations."

19. **Choice D** is correct. This answer is supported in the text by the example of the Renaissance painters using emotional symbols that mean exactly the same thing today or Jung's discovery that "all people share a 'collective unconsciousness'", that is, "…people from disparate traditions nonetheless dream in the same terms"and "some of these patterns are universal.

20. **Choice D** is correct. The author equates the "meeting of the eyes" with "..any amount of electrical shock or charge" and the lack of visual contact with "cutting one dead." These, indeed, are powerful images.

21. **Choice D** is correct. See answer 19.

22. **Choice A** is correct. "Emphases" is really the only choice that fits the context.

23. **Choice E** is correct. If one is speaking of grasping "emotional responses" or "life experiences" in the context of "conscious analysis", it is clear that this is a mental exercise and "understood" is the best response.

24. **Choice B** is correct. The common phrase "center of attention" can be literal or figurative. If someone sits in the physical center of a restaurant, he or she would typically feel "exposed" to some degree and, therefore, lack a certain "relative privacy."

Section 6

1. **Choice D** is correct. The sentence is incorrect as it stands because the subject "One" requires the singular verb "was" not "were". In like manner, in the second part of the sentence "something", being singular, requires "was" as well.

2. **Choice C** is correct. In order to be consistent with the construction in the first part of the sentence with the use of the present participles "toppling" and "uprooting", we must use "snapping power lines".

3. **Choice B** is correct. Once again, consistency of tense is the key here. "As I entered.." is the preterit (past) tense, thus, the verb "turned" is necessary to complement it.

4. **Choice B** is correct. The sentence is poor as is because "more sorrier" is grammatically incorrect; "more sorry" would be the correct way to express that. In addition, when does one use I or me? Eliminating the other half of the compound subject is one way to know, or, in the case of comparisons, by extending the comparison. For example, "No one is sorrier than *I* am sorry" makes sense. "…*me* am sorry does not."

5. **Choice C** is correct. One does not "determine *about*" something or someone but "determines *whether or if*" one thing or another. Choice C makes more sense than B.

6. **Choice D** is correct. Although not technically incorrect, the original sentence is somewhat roundabout. Choice D is much more direct and succinct.

7. **Choice D** is correct. The original sentence would be perfectly fine if the "or did not" was eliminated. Without that as a choice, D communicates the idea correctly and well.

8. **Choice E** is correct. There are two grammatical errors in the original sentence. First, since Baldwin High School is a singular noun, it requires the singular pronoun "it" not "they". Second, the first comma in the sentence separates two independent clauses and is insufficient punctuation to do so. This is called a comma splice. Choice D provides the proper punctuation but is incorrect because there is a contrasting relationship between the first part of the sentence and the second. "As a result" indicates a cause and effect relationship which is not indicated. We need a word which illustrates the contrast like: however, yet, though, but etc. Choice E fits the bill.

9. **Choice A** is correct. There are no grammatical errors in this sentence.

10. **Choice D** is correct. The original sentence is incorrect because as it stands "most people" is modified by "criticized" but clearly that is not the intent of the sentence. Amelia Earhart was the one criticized and should, therefore, immediately follow the comma. This eliminates A, B and C. Choice E is awkward and lacks a verb.

11. **Choice A** is correct. This sentence is correct. as is.

12. **Choice D** contains the error. "As expensive *as*" not "as expensive *than*" is grammatically correct.

13. **Choice E** is correct. There is no error in this sentence.

14. **Choice D** contains the error. As it stands the sentence is incorrect because it compares "artists" with "times". In order to be correct it would have to say "American artists differed from artists of earlier times."

15. **Choice C** contains the error. The subject "issues" is modified better by the plural noun "those" rather than the ambiguous "that".

16. **Choice E** is correct. There is no error in the original sentence.

17. **Choice C** contains the error. The common English phrase is not "necessary *in* the enjoyment of…" but "necessary *for* the enjoyment of."

18. **Choice B** contains the error. To maintain consistency with "*Driving less* frequently" the sentence should read "*turning off* all appliances."

19. **Choice A** contains the error. The phrase "was celebrated" indicates that the action is in the past and since the word "had" precedes the verb to swim, it requires the past participle "swum".

20. **Choice B** contains the error. The singular subject "agency" requires the singular pronoun "it" not "they".

21. **Choice C** contains the error. The proper idiom is "still a threat *to* travelers" not "a threat *of* travelers".

22. **Choice B** contains the error. A verb requires an adverb modifier. "Correct" is modifying "reading" in the original sentence and should be "correctly" in order to make grammatical sense.

23. **Choice E** contains the error. There is no error in the sentence.

24. **Choice A** is correct. If you lift out the phrase set off by commas, it is easier to see that the singular subject of the sentence is "record" and requires the singular verb "provides".

25. **Choice C** contains the error. The preposition "as" here is incorrect because it means "during" the action. A "result" happens *after* a certain circumstance not *during* the circumstance. The word "as" should be replaced with "when".

26. **Choice C** contains the error. The singular word "tourist" requires the singular verb "expects" for agreement.

27. **Choice A** contains the error. The sentence should begin "For *us*…" not "For *we*…"

28. **Choice D** contains the error. Proper usage dictates an "either….or" relationship or a "neither….nor" relationship. The "or" should be changed to "nor".

29. **Choice A** contains the error. The subject is a compound one including "directory and centers" and, therefore, "is" should be replaced by "are" in order to be correct.

30. **Choice B** is correct. The sentence is incorrect as it stands because it lacks a subject. Although "I" is the implied subject it is not present and Choice B is the only choice that has it.

31. **Choice E** is correct. The pronoun "it" being used twice in such close succession brings confusion. If "the creature" replaces the first pronoun, the meaning will be immediately cleared up.

32. **Choice D** is correct. It is very clear that this piece is relating a personal experience. Hopefully all the questions on the SAT will be that easy!!!

33. **Choice B** is correct. Separating the two sentences as is done in the original only serves to stunt the expression of both. Combining them both smoothly is the idea. There is an implied "however" here. Just because one may know certain facts about skunks does not mean he is any more "immune" to the defense mechanism they possess than one who knows nothing. Therefore, a contrasting conjunction would be helpful. Choice B does it best.

34. **Choice B** is correct. This sentence is redundant because what it expresses is painfully obvious. Deleting it is the best thing to do.

35. **Choice A** is correct. Clearly the last sentence is meant to be a joke. No family would ever leave a house just because a skunk had taken up residence there. The humor of the last sentence is in the same tone as the previous "Welcome to Aromaville!"

Section 7

1. **Choice D** is correct. The context clue is "exaggerated fear" which is synonymous with "phobia". The term "quixotic" comes from the literary character Don Quixote who imagined grand things from simple, daily ones. It, therefore, means "unrealistic".

2. **Choice E** is correct. The second blank is easier to find. If "an outbreak of disease" occurs at a school, one would expect that, in order to protect the healthy students, the school would "ensure" (make sure) that all school children are immunized. No other second choice fits. "The challenge" is for schools to "anticipate" the outbreak before it actually occurs.

3. **Choice B** is correct. The context clue her is "general merriment" which is synonymous with "gaiety". The other words are self-explanatory.

4. **Choice C** is correct. "Demagogues" are those who incite rebellion. If the "hysteria" is not to be blamed on them, it is because, although they used it to their advantage, "they didn't actually _create_ it."

5. **Choice E** is correct. The portion of the sentence which follows the colon defines the blank. If most of their activities occur up in trees, the word which describes this is "arboreal". "Indigenous" (native) nor "transitory" (temporal) nor "pliant" (flexible) fits.

6. **Choice B** is correct. The context clues are "steadfast" and "constant". The term "unswerving" would fit because it means one doesn't deviate from the course.

7. **Choice C** is correct. "Critics" typically have negative things to say and would likely have negative things to say about the play's "brevity" or shortness. Thus A, D and E can be eliminated. Choice C is the best response because its first word fits the first blank. How would the playwright "appease" the critics? By "expanding" the play, of course.

8. **Choice A** is correct. To be naïve is to be in the condition of ignorance. Ignorance is not stupidity, but simply a lack of knowledge of someone or something. All of us are ignorant about something or another. "Furtiveness" (secrecy) nor "venality" (capable of being bought) fit.

9. **Choice C** is correct. As the sun shone on the waves, the sunlight was reflected onto the white house which "mirrored" the sea.

10. **Choice D** is correct. The words "boasted" and "miraculous" and "startled' give strong evidence that the author not only "delighted" in the experience but was captivated ("in wonder") by the experience. "Awe" certainly could be used but there is no hint of fear so Choice A is incorrect.

11. **Choice B** is correct. The piece says that compared to the other three "great early Old-World state-cultures" we know the least about the Indus Valley culture precisely because we haven't deciphered the Harappan language.

12. **Choice D** is correct. The phrase "have not been totally useless" indicates that something good has been salvaged from a bad situation so the author is "somewhat encouraged" not completely discouraged or "frustrated".

13. **Choice E** is correct. Substituting each of the choices into line 14 would render only E as a possible answer.

14. **Choice C** is correct. These are "predictions" not realities, and they are predictions of the "environmental popularizers". The reality is that these predictions and those which came before them have not yet materialized.

15. **Choice D** is correct. The context of line 22 is "they do not have to face the rigors of either an ice age…or global warming". These are the "projected consequences of environmental decline".

16. **Choice D** is correct. The author is trying to drive home the point that people take action only when they are in immediate danger. Compassion for some, even most, may be a motivating factor, but fear for the overwhelming majority is a more powerful motivator. This is a "psychological fact."

17. **Choice B** is correct. The first paragraph in Passage 2 speaks of the efforts and results of Rachel Carson and the specific historical legislation that is her legacy. It is a "historical summary" that lays the foundation for the author's argument.

18. **Choice C** is correct. The author in the first paragraph makes the observation that the efforts of environmentalists have been "strikingly effective" in both the United States and Great Britain. Therefore, the rhetoric by politicians regarding the dire consequences of our present environmental path is nonsense! "The accomplishments of the environmental movement have made these pronouncements irrelevant."

19. **Choice B** is correct. People in politics tend to express themselves with extreme rhetoric. "Wickedness incarnate" might not be an unusual expression used by one party against another. The Left, in fact, is described as being "stylishly pessimistic". "Wickedness incarnate" would therefore be a mocking or "parody of the language used by people with certain political leanings".

20. **Choice B** is correct. The author of Passage 1 is doubtful of the effect, if any, that environmentalists have had on our society. Phrases like "one-sided and incomplete accounts of the state of scientific knowledge has led to projections, predictions, and warnings that, not surprisingly, have been falsified by events." This author is clearly "skeptical". Whereas, the author of Passage 2 "admires" what environmentalists have accomplished.

21. **Choice D** is correct. The author of Passage 2 would say that although the warnings were dire and maybe overstated, they did effect some positive change in the status quo and, therefore, "served a purpose in their time."

22. **Choice E** is correct. The line of thought referred to here is that of political language dominated by "images of futility, crisis and decline" despite the good that has resulted from the environmental movement. The author of Passage 1, being a "skeptic" would argue that this line of thought was of "dubious (doubtful) validity" from the beginning.

23. **Choice A** is correct. Why not trumpet the "record of success"? The author of Passage 1 would say that "fear" is a greater motivator and that "good news is less of a stimulus to action".

24. **Choice E** is correct. Both authors would agree that the environmental movement "employs exaggerated rhetoric". The results of this rhetoric they would disagree on.

Section 9

1. **Choice B** is correct. The first answer is easiest to find. If Toomer's book was written in 1923 and was being read in the 1960's, "rediscovered" certainly would be an apt description. "An interest in Black culture" would also prod or leverage or "coerce" Blacks to "read the classics of Black fiction".

2. **Choice A** is correct. The second blank is clearly associated with the phrase "In addition to.." A word which means exactly that is "supplement". Employers are also in the business of "evaluating" resumes and references.

3. **Choice E** is correct. The structure of the sentence indicates a contrast because the word "but" is used after the comma. The first half of the sentence would be the opposite of "wild" and "out of control" and parallel to "tame". The word "docile" means peaceful and fits well. "Mischievous" (prone to trouble) nor "gluttonous" (eating to excess) nor "supple" (pliable) nor "adroit" (skillful, adept) fit.

4. **Choice C** is correct. The colon indicates that what follows it will define the blank. If her "repertoire *ranged* from classical to jazz" it was clearly a *wide* range and, therefore, exhibited "noteworthy" or considerable "scope".

5. **Choice E** is correct. The term "nihilism" means an extreme form of skepticism. If the "skepticism of some ancient philosophers" helps to "elucidate" or make clear the appearance of a stronger form of skepticism, it must have laid the groundwork or predicted or "foreshadowed" its appearance. "Disseminate" means to distribute or spread.

6. **Choice E is correct.** The context clue, "debates on the issues are marred by" indicates a breakdown of communication. The word "cacophony" means lots of discordant sounds (like an orchestra warming up). If "denunciations and accusations" were flying, it certainly would be an atmosphere that would preclude (prevent) "orderly" discourse.

7. **Choice D is correct.** Clearly this passage has solely to do with Douglass' political activism with respect to both women's rights and the abolition of slavery.

8. **Choice E is correct.** "Hailing" here is used to describe the editor's comment and continues the express his "hope that it will have a powerful effect on the public's mind." This statement is an expression of "praise".

9. **Choice D is correct.** Douglass was sensitive to the plights of the disadvantaged, not only women but also slaves. Because it was uppermost in his mind, he was very aware of the negative effect that changing the name of his newspaper to *The Brotherhood* would have on women. Undoubtedly they would feel excluded. He also chose to fight for the rights of African Americans in the face of some hypocritical women.

10. **Choice D is correct.** Stanton and Anthony prevailed because it didn't make any sense to them that a movement based upon the idea of equality would have a leg to stand on if it excluded anyone.

11. **Choice B is correct.** Originally Douglass was not an advocate of equal property rights among men and women or husbands and wives because he first thought that the men were the ones who worked harder for it. After spending quite a bit of time with female political activists, he only then began to understand their point of view and agreed that the domestic responsibilities of women were just as important to the family as the men's responsibilities. This showed "he was flexible enough to change his views."

12. **Choice C is correct.** The phrase "disposition of" in the context has to do with the property of spouses. It most closely means "control over."

13. **Choice A is correct.** The author contends that Stone was willing to "advance women's rights on the backs of defenseless slave women." Clearly she allowed one cause to "supersede" or have priority over the other.

14. **Choice E is correct.** Stephen A. Douglas was "one of the architects" of a law that enabled slaveholders to reclaim their slaves. Frederick Douglass believed, therefore, that if Stephen Douglas was used to promote women's rights, it would be "exploiting Black women who were slaves".

15. **Choice C is correct.** The context tells us that this is the very reason that Douglass split with Garrison because Garrison was only willing to rely on words rather than "antislavery political action".

16. **Choice B** is correct. The effect of Douglass' political action, as indicated in lines 74-75, was to cause women's leaders to "become cool toward Douglass". Evidently, they preferred "preferred Garrison's political approach".

17. **Choice E** is correct. Although she too sided with Garrison, Susan B. Anthony's views "coincided most" with Douglass'.

18. **Choice A** is correct. The interaction between the two groups definitely helped "broaden their perspectives" because, although their agendas were not the same, the common denominator of "equal rights for all" helped them empathize with each others' causes.

19. **Choice D** is correct. The passage clearly points out that Douglass opposed any group who "neglected the rights of other groups" regardless of their objective.

Section 10

1. **Choice E** is correct. The original sentence would be correct if the "and more" was dropped. Instead, Choice E more concisely delivers the idea.

2. **Choice B** is correct. The sentence is incorrect as it stands because "duties" are being compared with "police officer". Comparing duties with duties or people with people is required by good grammar.

3. **Choice D** is correct. The original is incorrect because "winning" here is acting as an adjective since it lack a form of the verb "to be". Since this event took place in the past, the simple past "won" is appropriate.

4. **Choice B** is correct. The original sentence is too wordy, as are A, C and D. E is incorrect because "it" refers to Kaissa which was not defeated by anyone or anything. Choice B is the most succinct and grammatically correct.

5. **Choice D** is correct. The original sentence lacks consistency. "Has high motivation" and "is reasonably intelligent" are different verbs and tenses. Choice D with the phrase "is highly motivated or reasonably intelligent" gives us the consistency we are looking for.

6. **Choice A** is correct. The sentence is correct. as is.

7. **Choice B** is correct. There is a lack of agreement in the original. The pronouns "you" and "our" do not agree. If "you" is replaced with "our" it will be correct.

8. **Choice E** is correct. The original sentence exhibits a lack of parallelism. A noun and a noun construction would be consistent. Thus "leadership and awareness" is appropriate.

9. **Choice B** is correct. The original sentence contains the awkward "ing" construction "reporting". B is concise and direct.

10. **Choice C** is correct. The sentence as it stands is incorrect because "it" refers to programs. Choice C is the shortest and contains the least number of pronouns.

11. **Choice E** is correct. "For the reason that" is too long and awkward. "Because" is simple and direct.

12. **Choice D** is correct. Once again, "the reason was that" is long and awkward and "because" is the best way to express this idea.

13. **Choice D** is correct. The sentence is incorrect as is because "it" incorrectly refers to computers. The phrase "so much information" requires the word "that" to follow it.

14. **Choice E** is correct. The original sentence is incorrect because "Of all the states" modifies "the governor". Choice E is the only choice, therefore, because it is the only one which begins with a state.

Practice Test #4 - Math

Section 2

20 questions – first third - easy

1. **Choice C** is correct. She bought 1 package of 12 and 4 packages of 8. $12 + 4 * 8 = 44$

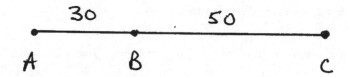

2. **Choice D** is correct. 20 more than 30 is 50. We have two pieces that are 30 and 50. The total length is 80.

3. **Choice C** is correct. Put in our own numbers here. Let $x = 5$ so $5 + 3 = a = 8$. $2x + 6 = 2 * 5 + 6 = 16$. Find one of their answers that is 16.

   A) 8 + 3 =16? WRONG

   B) 8 + 6 = 16? WRONG

   C) 2*8 = 16? Yes. Possible answer.

   D) 2*8 + 3 = 16? WRONG

   E) 2*8 + 6 = 16? WRONG

   Only C remains.

TEST SCORES OF FIVE STUDENTS

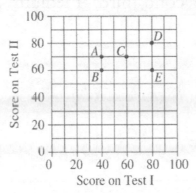

4. **Choice A** is correct. We need to find the <u>change</u> for each student.

A 70 – 40 = 30

B 60 – 40 = 20 Cross off B) since A is bigger.

C) 70 – 70 = 0 Cross off C)

D) 80 – 80 = 0, Cross off D

E) 60 – 80 = –20, Cross off E

A) has the largest change.

5. **Choice C** is correct. The 5 scores on test II are the 5 *y*-values. Those values are 60, 60, 70, 70 and 80. Looking we see that the answer should be near 70 but a little lower since the two 60's are a total of 20 below 70 and there is only one score over 70 which is 80. That is 10 above so we have 20 below and 10 above making the below a bit more for the average. Now that we know the approximate value let's find the calculator value. Add up the scores and get 340. Now divide by 5 and get 68.

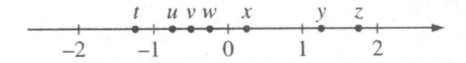

6. **Choice D** is correct. An absolute value will be positive so cross off A and B which are both negative numbers. Let's assign value for *u* and *v*. They are both negative. *v* looks like –0.5 and *u* looks like –0.75, Add them and we get –1.25. Take the absolute value and we get 1.25 which looks very much like *y*.

7. **Choice B** is correct. Use our calculator with $x = 0.5$. $1/0.5 = 2$ and $1/(0.5-1) = -2$. Adding these two answers gives us 0.

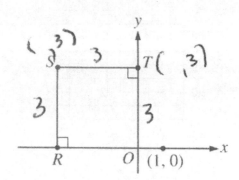

8. Choice A is correct. The figure shown is a rectangle. But RS = ST makes it a square. So all the sides are the same. Putting in the known coordinates of S (, 3) we see that T has to have the same *y*-value. That makes T 3 units above O. So all sides are 3. *k* has to be negative because S is to the left of the *y*-axis. That makes it –3.

Another Method: Since the diagram is drawn to scale we can measure with the edge of our test book. From (0,0) to (1,0) is 1 unit. We only have to look at A and B since they are the only negative answers. Is the length of ST more like 3 or 1.7? 3 it is.

9. **Choice A** is correct. Let's use their values and check the answers. The first value in the table is $f(0)=1$. Now we look at their formulas.

A) $0^2+1=1$ possible

B) $0^2+2=1$ WRONG

C) $2*0^2-2=1$ WRONG

D) $2*0^2-1=1$ WRONG

E) $2*0^2+1=1$ possible.

Now we need to pick another table value and test these two possible answers. $f(3)=10$

A) $3^2+1=9+1=10$ possible

E) $2*3^2+1=18+1=10$ WRONG.

Only A remains.

10. **Choice E** is correct. Let's put in our own numbers. $x = 5$ and $y = 10$ makes the sentence read. "How old was a person exactly 1 year ago if exactly 5 years ago the person was 10 years old?" 10 years old 5 years ago makes them 15 now. So 1 year ago they were 14. Look for 14 as the answer.

A) $10 - 1 = 14$? WRONG

B) $10 - 5 - 1 = 14$? WRONG

C) $5 - 10 - 1 = 14$? WRONG

D) $10 + 5 + 1 = 14$? WRONG

E) $10 + 5 - 1 = 14$? Possible

Only E remains.

11. **Choice B** is correct. Z needs to go to the other end of the list. The fastest way to get that to happen is to reverse the list. Making it X Y W Z. Now we need to move W to the front without moving Z. That means we need to interchange adjacent letters. Interchange Y and W making the list now X W Y Z. Almost there. Interchange X and W and the list is in order. That was three moves. So C, D and E are all wrong. We could spend a lot of time trying other moves but it is not worth the time. Remember that this is getting to be a hard problem and the smallest answer for a question asking for the *least* value is too attractive to be right. Put down B and move on to question 12.

12. **Choice D** is correct. If the box is 20 cm wide then there needs to be 5 cubes in the width. If the box is 24 cm long then there need to be 6 blocks along the length. This makes 30 blocks on the bottom layer. A height of 32 cm means there need to be 8 layers. $30 * 8 = 240$.

13. **Choice E** is correct. Let's put in our own value for n. $n = 0.5$ is a nice value. That makes $n^2 = 0.25$ and $\sqrt{n} \approx 0.71$. From smallest to largest the values are $0.25 < 0.5 < 0.71$ or E.

Last third - hard

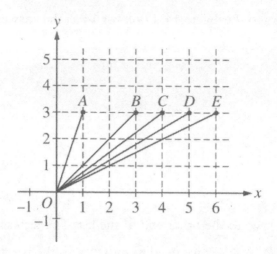

14. **Choice C** is correct. The median is the slope in the middle when they are listed in order. The lines shown have slopes in order with OA being the largest. OC has the middle slope. The line goes from (0,0) to (4,3) which is a rise of 3 over a run of 4.

15. **Choice A** is correct. Let's convert all the information to EST. The first statement tells us that there is 3 hours difference in the times and that EST is later. OK. The first plane landed at 4 P.M. PST, which is 3 hours later EST or 7 P.M. So the plane flew from noon to 7 p.m. or 7 hours. The second plane left at noon PST (3 P.M. EST) and flew for the same 7 hours. That means it landed at 10 P.M. EST

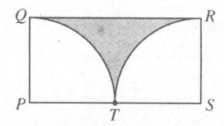

16. **Choice B** is correct. The shaded area is the area of the rectangle minus the area of the two quarter-circles. The rectangle is 1 radius high and 2 radii long making the area 2. The area of the circle is $\pi r^2 = \pi$ since the radius is 1. Two quarter-circles is $2\pi / 4$. This makes the shaded area $2 - \frac{\pi}{2}$.

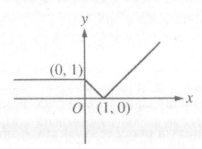

17. **Choice C** is correct. We know that $f(1) = 0$ from the given graph. So what is the value of x that we have to use to make $x + 2 = 1$? -1 is that value. So, on our new graph the point $(-1, 0)$ should be the bottom of the notch. Only C has this property so we have found our answer.

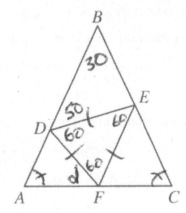

Note: Figure not drawn to scale.

18. **Choice B** is correct. Figure *not* drawn to scale. Be careful! The top angle is given as 30°. Write it in. The big triangle is isosceles (AB = BC) so mark the angles congruent. The little inside triangle is equilateral so mark all three of those angles as 60°. The measure of <BDE is 50°. Mark that one also. We are trying to find the measure of <DFA which we should mark as size *d*. Your diagram should now look like the one on the right. Find the measure of angle A. Angles A and C together add up to 150° so they are 75° each. Write 75 in by angle A. We also have a 50°, 60° and unknown that add to 180°. So the unknown is 70°. Mark that one also. $\triangle ADF$ has angle sizes 75°, 70° and d°. So $d = 35$ will give us 180° for that little triangle.

19. **Choice A** is correct. We need to find the *different* one. If we cross multiply each proportion we should see some patterns.

A) $ac = fb$

B) $fa = cb$ different products so they are not equivalent. But which one is different?

C) $cb = af$ This is like B so A is the different one. Let's look at the others just to be sure.

D) $af = cb$ Again the same as B.

E) $af = bc$ And so is this. We have it!

20. **Choice E** is correct. We are looking here for a *can* be not a *must* be. All we need to do is find values for x and y that make zero for the answer and that statement is correct. In each of these problems we are only using positive integers. No fractions and no negatives. ☺

I. $ab - b = 0$ If $a = 1$ then b can be any number and the statement is true. This means we cross out B and C.

II. $(a + b)(b) - b = 0$ This looks confusing. Maybe we can do something like I and make the $a + b = 1$ so it will disappear. But we have to use numbers from 1 up. 1 plus anything positive is bigger than 1. Guess we can't do that here. Perhaps we should reserve judgment on this and look at III.

III. $a(a + b) - (a + b) = 1$ Make $a = 1$ as we did in I. That makes it $1(1 + b) - (1 + b)$. Any value of b makes this true. Cross out A and D because they don't contain III. Only E remains so we didn't have to worry about II after all and it was good we didn't spend too much time on it.

Section 4

8 questions – first third - easy

1. **Choice E** is correct. If $z = 2$ then $y = 3(2) = 6$ and $x - 6 = 8$.

2. **Choice A** is correct. "Todd is older than Marta but younger than Susan" means he is between the girls in age. Marta is also the youngest which makes them, from youngest to oldest, Marta, Todd and Susan.
$m < t < s$

3. **Choice B** is correct. To find the average we need to add both the regions to find the total and then divide by 2. The total is given as 5 so the answer is 5 divided by 2.

Second third - medium

4. **Choice E** is correct. Let's understand the formula. $n^2 + 1$ means we square the starting number and then add 1. Start with 1. $1^2 + 1 = 2$. $2^2 + 1 = 5$, $3^2 + 1 = 10$ and so on. Each number is one more than some perfect square. If we continue this list we get 17, 26, 37, 50. Bingo! 50 is answer E.

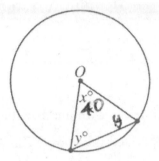

Note: Figure not drawn to scale.

5. **Choice D** is correct. The little triangle in the circle is isosceles since two of the sides are both radii. So the base angles are congruent. $180° - 40°$ is $140°$ for both of them. That makes them $70°$ each.

6. **Choice A** is correct. Aside from 1 and the number shown, what are other factors of the given numbers.

   A) 11 only. This I our answer but let's check the others to show the pattern.

   B) 2, 4, 5, 10, 25 and 50 all divide 100.

   C) 3, 9 and 27 all divide 81.

   D) 2, 4, 8, 16 and 32 all divide 64

   E) 33 is not a perfect square so it can't be a "simple square."

Last third - hard

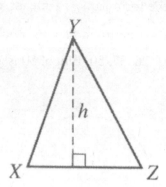

7. **Choice B** is correct. We need to substitute our own numbers here. We also need to be wise enough to put in "nice" numbers so we don't get complicated fractions. XZ is $\frac{6}{7}$ of h means we will have to multiply by a crazy fraction. Make $h = 7$ and then the multiplication is easy and $XZ = 6$. The area of $\Delta XYZ = \frac{1}{2}bh = 0.5(6)(7) = 21$. Examine their answers to see which gives us 21.

A) $\frac{49}{3} = 21$ WRONG

B) $\frac{3(49)}{7} = 21$ possible

C) $\frac{3(7)}{7} = 21$ WRONG

D) $\frac{6(49)}{7} = 21$ WRONG

E) $\frac{12(49)}{7} = 21$ WRONG

Only B remains.

© 2009 Master Learning Strategies Inc.

8. **Choice B** is correct. We need to simplify at least the side with all the exponents. We must remember the multiplication rule for exponents. There is no addition or subtraction inside the parentheses so we just multiply the exponents. Half of 6 is 3 so the exponent of a is 3. One-third of 6 is 2 so the exponent of b is 2. Now the equation is $a^3 b^2 = 432$. Now we need to find out what the value of ab is. There are two ways we can do this. Look at their answers and try to guess the values of a and b, Then check to see if it works. OR Try to separate 432 into a square and a cube to find a and b.

Guess and Check:

A) $ab = 6$. $a = 1$, $b = 6$ gives $1^3 * 6^2 = 36$. No. $a = 2$, $b = 3$ gives $2^3 * 3^2 = 72$. No. $a = 3$, $b = 2$ gives $3^3 * 2^2 = 108$. No. $a = 6$, $b = 1$ gives $6^3 * 1^2 = 216$. No. Cross off A.

B) $ab = 12$, $a = 1$, $b = 12$ gives $1^3 * 12^2 = 144$. No. $a = 2$, $b = 6$ gives $2^3 * 6^2 = 288$. No. $a = 3$, $b = 4$ gives $3^3 * 4^2 = 432$. YES. Mark down B.

Factor 432: 432 is even so divide by 2. $432 = 2 * 216$. 216 is even so divide by 2. $432 = 2 * 2 * 108$. 108 is even so divide by 2. $432 = 2 * 2 * 2 * 54$. Even again. $432 = 2 * 2 * 2 * 2 * 27$. 27 isn't even but it can be divided by 3. The resulting 9 can be divide by 3 again so we get $432 = 2 * 2 * 2 * 2 * 3 * 3 * 3$. Written as powers it would be $432 = 2^4 * 3^3 = a^3 b^2$. We can see from inspection that if $a = 3$ then we have an even number of factors left over for b. This makes $b^2 = 2^4 = 16$ or $b = 4$. So $ab = 3 * 4 = 12$

---

10 questions – first third - easy

9. **Choice 990** is correct. To have a factor of 10 it must have a 0 on the end. Since we want as large a number as possible we use 9's in the other places. Just be careful not to have four digits. The problem asks for a three digit number.

10. Choice 30 is correct. How many groups of 20 people make a total of 150 people. That would be 7.5 groups. Each group needs 4 pounds of beans so we multiply $7.5 * 4 = 30$

11. **Choice 8, 10 OR 12** is correct. Pick an even number so that adding a bit of that number puts it above 10. Start with 10. 10 plus 50% of 10 is $10 + 5 = 15$. Is that between 10 and 20? Yes. We have found a number. Move on.

    Math Method: $10 < n + 0.5n < 20$ or $10 < 1.5n < 20$. Divide all three expressions by 1.5 and get $6.66 < n < 13.33$. What even integers fall in this range? 8, 10 and 12.

Second third - medium

12. **Choice 3400** is correct. This lot is a rectangle. If one side is 40 then so is the other. Now we need to find the length of the two missing sides. The perimeter is 250 meters so and $250 - 80 = 170$. That means each side is half of it or 85. What is the area? $lw = 85 * 40 = 3400$

13. **Choice 450** is correct. Cheep bulbs cost $1 for c bulbs.. Expensive bulbs cost $2 for e bulbs. So $\$1c + \$2e = \$600$. More of the cheep bulbs were ordered. In fact there are twice as many cheep bulbs so $c = 2e$. That makes $c + 2e = 2e + 2e = 600$ or $4e = 600$ or $e = 150$. 150 expensive bulbs and twice as many (300) cheep ones. That's 450 in all. Let's check to see if our arithmetic is correct. 150 expensive bulbs at $2 each is $300. 300 cheep bulbs at $1 each is $300. That adds to $600 and we are correct.

14. **Choice 1/2 OR .5** is correct. Substitute the second equation into the first so it becomes $4(x + y)(20) = 40$ or $80(x + y) = 40$. That means $(x + y)$ is small. 80 times what gives 40? Calculator gives me an answer of 2. But I made a mistake. I divided the wrong way. The answer is $40 / 80 = 0.5$. Having the answer make sense can add points to your score.

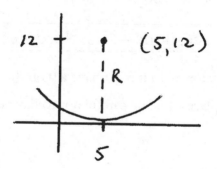

15. **Choice 12** is correct. Draw a picture of a circle just hitting the x-axis once and having the center be at $(5,12)$. Where can you measure the radius? From the center down to the x-axis. This is the y-coordinate of the center or 12.

Last third - hard

16. **Choice 5/11, .454 OR .455** is correct. To find the top of the fraction we need to find 40% of the total voting-age population. This is $40\% * 2500 = 1000$. To find the bottom we need to find the total registered voters, which is 2,200. Use our calculator to find the fraction $1000 / 2200 = 0.454$ Don't worry about rounding off.

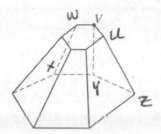

17. **Choice 8** is correct. Since there are 11 *other* vertices, there are 11 line segments to be drawn. We need to find out how many of them are not edges. We might leave some out if we try to count them directly. How about counting the ones that *are* edges and subtracting from 11. VW is an edge as is VU. Anything else connecting the top vertices won't be an edge. So we have two edges so far. What about connecting V with a vertex on the bottom. Only VY appears to be an edge. That makes a total of 3 edges out of the 11 segments. So 8 segments are *not* edges.

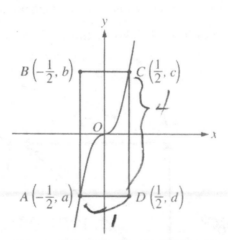

Note: Figure not drawn to scale.

18. **Choice 16** is correct. First the rectangle. Since the x-coordinates of the corners are $-\frac{1}{2}$ and $\frac{1}{2}$ the width of the rectangle is 1. The area being given as 4 means that 1*length = 4. So the length is 4. What does that mean coordinate c has to be? $c = 2$ should make it correct. Now we know that when we put $\frac{1}{2}$ in as the x-coordinate we get 2 as the y-coordinate. Our equation is $y = p(x)^3$. Plugging in our values we have $2 = p\left(\frac{1}{2}\right)^3 = p\left(\frac{1}{8}\right)$. Multiply both sides by 8 and we get $p = 16$

© 2009 Master Learning Strategies Inc.

Section 8
16 questions – first third - easy

.1 **Choice D is correct.** Both sides of the equation can be divided by 3. Doing that gives us $n - 4 = 6$. Which answer is "4 more than 6?"

2. **Choice D is correct.** With each type of stone there are 3 types of metals. So there are 4 threes or 12.

3. **Choice B is correct.** The sum of $3a$ and the square root of b can be written as $3a + \sqrt{b}$. Let's eliminate any left side that doesn't look like this. Cross off A, D and E. Now for the other side. The square of the sum means that first we add, to get a sum, and then we square the result. In B the order is adding then squaring the result. Just what we want. In C the order is square the numbers and then add. This order is backwards. Cross off C. Only B remains. Some of the other might turn out to be an equivalent expression but it is not exactly what the written sentence said so they would not be the SAT answer. Actually none of the expressions are equivalent but we didn't need to know this to find the answer that the SAT writers consider correct.

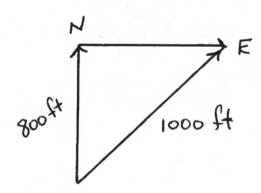

4. **Choice E is correct.** Draw a little circle to represent the 1,000 foot range. Go up (north) 800 feet (almost to the top) and then right (east) until we hit the max range circle. Now which way can we walk and still stay in the circle?

I. Due north (Up)? No. We go outside.

II. Due south (Down)? Yes. This is fine.

III. Due west (Left)? Yes. This goes back.

II and III are possible so E is the answer.

5. Choice A is correct. Cross multiply and get $ax = 8x$. We can read the value of a from this equation.

Second third - medium

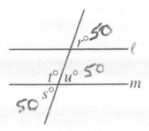

Note: Figure not drawn to scale.

6. **Choice A is correct.** "Figure *not* drawn to scale." Be careful! With parallel lines cut by a third line all the big angles are congruent, all the little angles are congruent, and a little angle and a big angle add to 180. $s + t$ is a little and a big added. The is 180. u is a little angle the same as r so they are both 50. That makes

$s + t + u = 180 + 50 = 230$

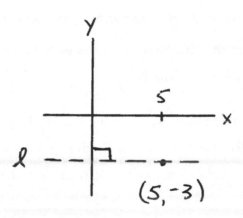

7. **Choice C is correct.** Draw a quick sketch of the axes. Locate point $(5, -3)$ and draw line l perpendicular to the y-axis. We have just drawn a horizontal line so all the y-coordinates of line l are the same. They are all -3. That makes the equation $y = -3$ or choice C.

8. **Choice E is correct.** Use their numbers to find b. 300 is the number of units produced which is x. $1,900 is the profit so it is $p(x)$. Plug in for $1900 = 17(300) - (10(300) + b)$ or $1900 = 5100 - (3000 + b) = 5100 - 3000 - b$. Be sure to be careful about the negative sign in front of the b. Now we have $1900 = 2100 - b$. We have to subtract 200.

9. **Choice E** is correct. CANNOT in the directions just means we have to find an example where it could work. Let's try to find examples.

A) $1*1 = 1$ Cross off A

B) $2*2 = 4$ Cross off B.

C) $5*5 = 25$ Ends in a 5. Cross off C.

D) $6*6 = 36$ Ends in a 6. Cross off D

E) This has to be the answer. Can you find a number so that when you square it you get an 8 on the end? It can be shown that you can only get 0, 1, 4, 5 and 9. But you didn't have to know this. Just that we showed A through D as wrong so E was the answer.

10. **Choice B** is correct. The problem asks "Which of the following *could* be ..." Only one answer will fit all the conditions although there might be lots of other numbers not shown that also work. Let's check their answers.

A) $\frac{1}{4}*10$ is not a whole number of marbles. Cross off A

B) $\frac{1}{4}*12 = 3$ and $\frac{1}{6}*12 = 2$. Both work. We have our answer. We should stop and go on to the next problem. But just to show it is correct. here are why the other numbers don't work. 18 and 30 don't divide evenly by 4 and 20 doesn't divide evenly by 6. Case closed!

11. **Choice D** is correct. Use our own numbers here. Let the sum of the prices be $36. If there are 4 prices that means the average price is $9. OK. What does the problem say? The sum of the prices ($36) is divided by the average of the prices ($9). The result is k. $(36/9 = 4)$ What does the 4 represent? It is the number of prices.

Last third - hard

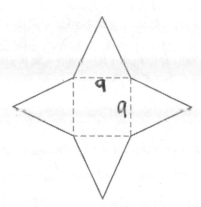

12. **Choice D** is correct. The area of the dotted square is 81 so each side is 9. the perimeter of the triangle is 30 so the two solid lines must have a total of 21. There are four triangles that are all the same. So, there are four 21s which totals to 84.

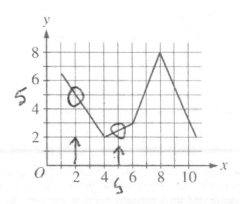

13. **Choice B** is correct. $g(2)$ is the y-value when the x-value is 2. Looking at the graph above the 2 we see that the y-value is 5. So, $k = 5$. Many people stop here. But the question asks for $g(5)$. Looking at the graph above 5 we see about 2.5 for the y-value. Now we have the answer.

14. **Choice E** is correct. How small can xy be? Since y can be negative we can get the lowest value by using $y = -1$ and $x = 8$. That makes $xy = -8$. There is only one range that has -8 as a value. E is that answer.

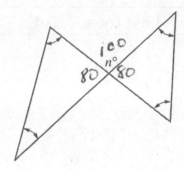

15. **Choice B** is correct. Let's put in our own value. $n = 100$ should be easy to use. So that makes both unmarked angles in the triangles 80°. We don't know what the two marked angles in the left triangle are, but we do know they add to 100°. This makes the triangle have 180°. The other triangle is the same. The sum of the four angles is 200°. Now we check their answers.

A) $100 = 200$ WRONG

B) $2*100 = 200$ possible

C) $180 - 100 = 200$ WRONG

D) $360 - 100 = 200$ WRONG

E) $360 - 2*100 = 200$ WRONG

Only B remains

16. **Choice C** is correct. Put in our own numbers here. Let's be smart and use a number we can take one-third of twice. Pick $t = 9$ as the first term. The second term is 3 more than one-third of 9 or $3 + \frac{1}{3}*9 = 3 + 3 = 6$. Now the third term is in the same pattern. $3 + \frac{1}{3}*6 = 3 + 2 = 5$. The question asks "What is the ratio of the second term to the first term. That is 6 / 9 or 0.666.

A) $\frac{9+9}{3} = 6 = 0.666$ WRONG

B) $\frac{9+3}{3} = 4 = 0.666$ WRONG

C) $\frac{9+9}{3*9} = 0.666$ possible

D) $\frac{9+3}{3*9} = 0.444 = 0.666$ WRONG

E) $\frac{9-2*9}{3} = -3 = 0.666$ WRONG

Only C remains

Practice Test #5 - Verbal

1. **Choice A** is correct. The first blank is easier to find. Americans with disabilities would certainly need laws to "ensure" that they had equal rights. "Guarantee" is really the only possible answer. "Lobby for" means to fight or persuade those in legal authority.

2. **Choice A** is correct. What follows the colon defines what fits the blank. "Heterogeneous" means mixture, as opposed to "homogeneous" which means the same. "Motley" is synonymous with "heterogeneous".

3. **Choice C** is correct. The second blank is defined by the phrase "a great deal". Both A and C are possibilities. The first blank should parallel the second because there is no context clue to reverse the relationship. "Copious" means plenty as in cornucopia.

4. **Choice A** is correct. The context clues here are the words "purportedly" and "on the contrary". "Purportedly" means supposedly and calls into question or doubt the actions of the colonial government. "Dubious" means doubtful. "On the contrary" indicates that the second blank is opposite of "humanitarian" which means thinking of others needs. "Self-serving" would fit the bill.

5. **Choice E** is correct. A "composite", as the context indicates, is a combination of many different kinds of things. An "amalgamation" is just that. "Conflagration" (huge fire) nor "distillation" (condensation) nor "concordance" (dictionary) nor "aberration" (wandering, exception) fit.

6. **Choice E** is correct. A dilemma is a two-pronged problem. Clearly Moraga had a lack of facility with English and used both languages in her title. This illustrates the author's point – "difficulty in narrating in one language when one has lived in another."

7. **Choice D** is correct. Choice D is the closest example of one growing up in one culture and trying to express oneself in a second language to a second cultural audience.

8. **Choice B** is correct. Although today's computers may have surpassed HAL in some ways, the author is clearly "appreciative" of the forward thinking of the author and producer with respect to computers.

9. **Choice A** is correct. In line 6 the author says, "Surprisingly, in some ways computers have surpassed…" HAL and gives this example at the end of the piece to illustrate the "superiority of current computers."

© 2009 Master Learning Strategies Inc.

10. **Choice A** is correct. To be counted "for the purposes of (political) representation" and, yet, not be able to vote is the height of "incongruity". Women were "free while having no political rights".

11. **Choice E** is correct. Lines 18-19 "give examples of political activities" and nothing else. They didn't "alter the course of the Revolution" (A) or "point out the only activities available to women" (C). E is the best response.

12. **Choice B** is correct. "Loyalist women" are mentioned to point out that this was a "universal" issue and not just one on the side of the Colonists.

13. **Choice C** is correct. The author is pointing out here that women didn't necessarily have to be at odds with or incompatible or separated from their husbands in order to have opposing political views. Such is the case today.

14. **Choice D** is correct. The term "naturally" here is clearly a trait which is portrayed as in-born or inherent—not something which is learned by experience. "Innate" has exactly that meaning.

15. **Choice C** is correct. Lines 50-51 indicate that John Adams had second thoughts about his wife's point of view before "coming to his senses" so to speak. A "glimpse" is an apt description of a brief second thought regarding someone else's opinion.

16. **Choice D** is correct. The context clues in the final sentence are "ludicrous" (ridiculous) and "threatening" (frightening). Choice D fits perfectly.

17. **Choice C** is correct. The term "rival" here means "is equivalent to" or is "the same as."

18. **Choice E** is correct. Lines 6-13 clearly show a number of examples of different kinds of play of different kinds of animals.

19. **Choice E** is correct. Line 26 points out the "physiological" (physical) development in "their muscle fiber and the parts of their brains regulating movement."

20. **Choice D** is correct. The principle illustrated in lines 43-46 is that play is not just some kind of fun but essential in the development of "skills" the adult will need to survive. A monkey will need to escape the attacks of animals that prey upon them by running up and down a tree. This is a good example of what the author is saying.

21. **Choice B** is correct. Line 51 is preceded by "young animals may be learning the limits of their strength and how to control themselves *among others*." The key here is the interaction of one animal with others. B is the only choice with such interaction.

22. **Choice D** is correct. The "theory" is that play has a definite purpose while the "opinion" is that play may be a diversion or "just for fun" and not purposeful at all.

23. **Choice E** is correct.

Section 4

1. **Choice B** is correct. Speaking or writing in the *active* voice, that is, when the subject performs the action is indicative of writing well. Choices A, D and E are incorrect because the *passive* voice is used, that is, someone or something other than the subject performs the action. B is correct. because it is active. Mr. Chung is the subject of both clauses.

2. **Choice E** is correct. The "strongest" and the "most peaceful" are contrasting characteristics. The clauses should therefore be joined by the contrasting conjunction "yet".

3. **Choice C** is correct. The original sentence is incorrect because "most new residents" modifies "winding streets" while it should modify the subject of the sentence, the Curtis family. This eliminates B and E. Choice D is incorrect because there is no verb.

4. **Choice B** is correct. The fact that Houston is the "third largest foreign-trade port in the United States" *despite* "being sixty miles inland" is not adequately portrayed in the original sentence. The phrase "while being" does not illustrate the contrast, "although" does.

5. **Choice C** is correct. The original sentence is incorrect because there is a lack of agreement between the singular subject "literature" and the plural pronoun "their". It should be "it". In addition, "by their speaking directly" is awkward "ing" construction. Choice C eliminates that.

6. **Choice C** is correct. Although the original sentence is not grammatically incorrect, it is not as concise as it could be. (Remember, being succinct is better than being wordy.) "Because" can replace "considering that" and "both" is redundant.

7. **Choice C** is correct. The phrase "being popular" is not only awkward "ing" construction, it is unclear what it is modifying. Story? Poem? Symphony? Choice B is incorrect because "where" refers to a time period. Choice C clarifies the relationships of description and time. D is incorrect because what follows the comma is a dependent clause. E is incorrect because it lacks a verb. "Being" and "having been" act as adjectives.

8. **Choice D** is correct. The original sentence is incorrect because the first clause lacks the verb "was". This makes the last clause dependent.

9. **Choice C** is correct. Choices A and B are incorrect because the clauses following the first commas are independent or complete thoughts and, therefore, cannot be separated by only a comma (comma splices). C does the job well.

10. **Choice A** is correct. The original sentence is correct. as is.

11. **Choice E** is correct. In order to be idiomatically correct, the construction "at once _____ **and** _____" should be used and not "**but**" since they are occurring at the same time.

12. **Choice B** contains the error. The subject is plural (Capra and Stevens) and requires a plural noun "directors".

13. **Choice D** contains the error. The adverbs "_calmly_ and thoughtfully" would correctly modify the verb "examine".

14. **Choice A** contains the error. "_I_ received an award…" not "_myself_ received an award."

15. **Choice D** contains the error. Parallel construction dictates that if the infinitive "to remain" is used then the infinitive "to move" should be used.

16. **Choice E** is correct. There is no error.

17. **Choice E** is correct. The original sentence is correct. as it stands.

18. **Choice C** contains the error. The term "whereby" means "by which" which does not work here. "Therefore" or "as a result" or "so" would be appropriate.

19. **Choice A** contains the error. The plural subject "sources" requires the plural verb "are".

20. **Choice C** contains the error. The action here clearly took place in the past and therefore the present participle "soon becoming" is incorrect. The phrase "which soon became" would be correct.

21. **Choice C** contains the error. We have a lack of agreement in verb tenses here. "Has made" is the present perfect tense while "had rented" is the past perfect. In order to be consistent, it should read "have rented."

22. **Choice C** contains the error. "Plus being" is a very awkward way to say something. The phrase "as well as" would do the job nicely.

23. **Choice C** contains the error. The subject "one" requires the pronoun "his" in order to be correct.

24. **Choice E** is correct. There is no error in the original sentence.

25. **Choice B** contains the error. Since the subject "student" is clear, it cannot be replaced by the "one" but rather, should be replaced by the pronoun "he" or "she".

26. **Choice A** contains the error. Proper idiomatic phrasing would dictate "is regarded _as_" not "is regarded _to be_".

27. **Choice B** contains the error. The singular subject "Mastery" requires the singular verb "is" not "are". BE CAREFUL !! Because the prepositional phrase "of…techniques" comes between the subject and the verb, we are apt to "hear" the verb "are" as correct.

28. **Choice D** is correct. The original sentence compares the "use of plastics" with "steel" instead of the "use of steel".

29. **Choice E** is correct. The is no error in the original sentence.

30. **Choice B** is correct. Sentence 3 is a sentence fragment as it stands because it lacks a verb. B is correct. because it provides the missing verb and is direct.

31. **Choice A** is correct. Choice B-E make meaningful grammatical revisions to the sentence. Choice A does nothing to improve it but is, in fact, superfluous.

32. **Choice C** is correct. The author has emphasized the importance of an eyewitness account. Nancy Gardner Prince "was right there…" is a critical point.

33. **Choice D** is correct. Choice D eliminates a very wordy phrase with one word.

34. **Choice E** is correct. Since the rest of the paragraph speaks of Prince's individual characteristics, E is the best response.

35. **Choice E** is correct. "Tons of things" is common vernacular or slang and should not replace "much". All the other choices would be welcome revisions.

Section 5

1. **Choice C** is correct. The word "misconception" indicates a contrasting relationship between the two blanks. Choice C is the only pair which is contrasting.

2. **Choice E** is correct. The context clue is "renowned for his improvisations" indicating that many knew of his talents. Similarly, the term "noteworthy" means the same thing.

3. **Choice D** is correct. The second blank is defined by the context clue "hunch". "Intuition" means the same thing. His "hunch" was "confirmed" or verified when Ms. Smith lost the election.

4. **Choice A** is correct. "Salutary" means remedial or benefiting health. "Alleviate" means to take away or lessen, particularly with regard to pain. "Eradicating" is close because it means to completely get rid of something but the context indicates "cannot....entirely."

5. **Choice C** is correct. To be "empathetic" is to put oneself in someone else's place. This is the best choice. "Candid" (genuine) nor "disarming" (puts at ease) fits.

6. **Choice A** is correct. Famous people often have a crowd or "entourage" of security or advisors around them. These are frequently necessary for protection, or simply, convenience when they are surrounded by an adoring public. Their job is to "interfere" with the public.

7. **Choice E** is correct. The context clearly indicates that the answer is the opposite of "light-hearted and even-tempered". The words "affability" and "equanimity" mean the same as "light-hearted" and "even-tempered". "Truculence" (cruel, savage, belligerent) is the appropriate word. " Resilience" (ability to bounce back) doesn't fit.

8. **Choice C** is correct. The context clue here is the phrase "nonspecialists who fail to comprehend its meaning." "Esoteric" language is language that only "insiders" or "specialists" understand. "Arcane" would also fit the first blank but A, D and E could be eliminated. "Hackneyed" (trite, clichéd) not "lucid" (clear) fit. "Esoteric" language would also be "impenetrable" to the "nonspecialist" or uninitiated.

© 2009 Master Learning Strategies Inc.

9. **Choice B** is correct. Clearly both passages deal with the "role that toys play in children's lives."

10. **Choice E** is correct. The author of Passage 1 would consider the last sentence unrealistic. Does the author of Passage 2 really believe that researchers should "spend more time playing with toys"? No. This claim would be "exaggerated and pretentious", that is, exaggerated in importance, for effect.

11. **Choice B** is correct. The author of Passage 2 is <u>scornful</u> of the "grandiose conclusions that the so-called "experts" have drawn…". There is nothing "apologetic" or "scholarly" or "sentimental" about his tone. He is clearly "disdainful", almost angry.

12. **Choice D** is correct. The last line of Passage 2 is written by someone who views themselves "above" or separate from this "trivial" subject. He has "lost touch with childhood realities."

13. **Choice E** is correct. The major concern of he author of Passage 1 is that of "gender." The key example she gives is that of listening to a "cassette of John Cheever's stories read by an expressive female voice." This experience was so incongruous that the author had to turn it off.

14. **Choice C** is correct. Line 8 reads "The listener is powerless against the taped voice, not at all in the position of my five-year-old daughter,…" In other words, she can be an "active participant" when someone is reading to her, whereas, if it's a tape, she has no such control. Choice A may seem to be close but the author gives no evidence of this observation.

15. **Choice D** is correct. The author of Passage 1 believes that "gender usually shapes and individual's use of language" and that is precisely why she explains in the next line that she says, "When I read a male writer, I simply adjust my vocalization to the tone of the text."

16. **Choice E** is correct. The parallel here is that a female is reading something which is written by a male and, therefore, "heard" in a male voice. "A song written by a female and normally performed by a female vocalist sung by a man" will have the same effect.

17. **Choice A** is correct. The context clue here is "the right neutrality" which describes "a clear medium". Something that is neutral does not "interfere" with what is being done or communicated.

18. **Choice B** is correct. The final line of Passage 1, "I find myself wavering, questioning the fixity of my assumptions" indicates that the author is open to a different point of view than her own and is, in fact, "challenging the main argument of the passage."

19. **Choice B** is correct. The author of Passage 1 would most likely believe that there is no "exchange" at all, but rather, "one-sided, since the listener cannot communicate directly with the speaker."

20. **Choice E** is correct. The phrase "intonations, mistakes, involuntary grunts and sighs" is preceded by the phrase "…the reader's ideas, or what I _perceive_ as their ideas…" These "unconscious expressions often betray one's true opinions".

21. **Choice B** is correct. The requirement of this teacher to have the students turn in taped readings is not only practical (pragmatic) for the teacher because she can get the work back quicker, but also educationally sound (pedagogical) because it helps the students become better writers.

22. **Choice D** is correct. What the author indicates in the quotes given is not the "fairly predictable errors" or "students being overly critical of their own work" but how 'reading aloud makes students more aware of their prose."

23. **Choice C** is correct. The term "staged pleas" indicates that the teacher is not unaware of the possibility that the students may have the ulterior motive of influencing her for a better grade.

24. **Choice C** is correct. The example of the daughter, as mentioned before, shows the "contrast with a passive experience" and the husband illustrates the beauty of the "shared experience."

Section 8

1. **Choice E** is correct. The first blank is easy to answer. If someone wrote something only to find that there were "several typographical errors", he or she would obviously be upset. Choices B, C and D can clearly be eliminated. An editorial would not be "authenticated" (verified) by errors but would be "marred" (defaced or scarred) by them.

2. **Choice D** is correct. The context implies that something needs to _counteract_ or _make up for_ the "loss of natural wetlands". This only leaves choices B and D as possible answers. Clearly they would not want to "surrender" more wetlands but "establish wetland refuges", choice D.

3. **Choice D** is correct. Again, what follows the colon defines the blank. If something "helps treat coughs etc…" it must have "curative" properties. Nothing else fits and all are self-explanatory.

4. **Choice C** is correct. The first answer is easier to get. A scientific organization would be upset, to say the least, if a newspaper "prominently covered a psychic" under any circumstances because they would likely not consider psychics worthy of media attention. "Denounced" is really the only possible choice; "neglecting", of course, fits the second blank well.

5. **Choice C** is correct. The key phrase here is "seem merely _____ but they are actually _____". This indicates that the color's and patterns may seem purposeless, to the uneducated, but actually have a purpose. The second blank is easier to find. Clearly the context is indicating that the colors are an "aid" to survival. The phrase "instrumental in" would denote that meaning. This choice really eliminates all of the other choices. The term "decorative" would follow the phrase "seem merely" well.

6. **Choice D** is correct. The term "winnow" is usually used to describe the process of separating the wheat (grain) from the chaff (useless part of the harvest). This is the perfect word to indicate any process of separating the good from the bad. "Supplant" (replace) nor "finagle" (manipulate) fit. The other words are self-explanatory.

7. **Choice D** is correct. Since the entire passage is in the third person, it is not Mulcahy himself. In addition, it must be someone very close to him because he knew not only his outward expressions but his innermost thoughts and reactions to his firing.

8. **Choice A** is correct. By firing someone who has "challenged you openly at faculty meetings" certainly lacks subtlety and tact. This is precisely why Mulcahy was "blind-sided" by the firing. The action was so "overt" that Mulcahy and other members of the faculty would have felt that it was "vindictive" (vengeful) and "unwise" because it would be so obvious.

9. **Choice E** is correct. Lines 22-23 give a list of Mulcahy's objections and do "range from the trivial to the serious". There is no evidence in the passage to support any other response.

10. **Choice C** is correct. Of course, a scrambled egg cannot be "unscrambled" so this is just a "witty play on words".

11. **Choice E** is correct. The key context phrase here is "pity, mingled with contempt". This phrase indicates that someone can have very different feelings and express them both at the same time. "Pity" would indicate "condescension" and "contempt" would indicate "scorn".

12. **Choice A** is correct. Given the context this is the obvious answer.

13. **Choice B** is correct. The term "progressive" frequently is used as a euphemism for "liberal" or "forward-thinking". None of the other choices has any support in the passage.

14. **Choice B** is correct. Clearly from the context, Dudley and Wilkins State have characteristics which are opposite that of Jocelyn and, therefore, "less progressive".

15. **Choice D** is correct. In religious language this phrase has the same sentiment as "love the sinner and hate the sin", that is, the ability to separate a person from their action. Choice D describes this principle perfectly.

16. **Choice E** is correct. In the context the term "flatly" means clearly or unquestionably. "Unequivocally" means exactly that. "Tautly" (tightly) nor "unemphatically" (without emphasis) fit.

17. **Choice A** is correct. After a list of his very impressive accomplishments in the academic arena, the phrase "yet having the salary and rank of only instructor" indicates clearly that "he has not received the recognition and rewards he deserves."

18. **Choice E** is correct. The main point of the passage deals with the surprise Mulcahy felt over his firing. "Despite his intelligence, he is naïve" with respect to college politics. No other choice is supported by the text.

19. **Choice D** is correct. The key context clue here is the last sentence. "…that ferocious envy of mediocrity for excellence…that is the passion of jobholders" indicates his belief that those less intelligent than he is are "resentful"and judge him, as a result.

Section 10

1. **Choice B** is correct. The sentence is incorrect as is because "Before signing up" modifies "schedules" instead of "students". B is the only choice with "students" in the proper position.

2. **Choice B** is correct. The original sentence is very awkward, particularly with the "ing" construction "its being". Choice B is the most concise, grammatically correct response.

3. **Choice C** is correct. The original sentence is incorrect because it begins with "We" as the subject and changes midstream to "anyone". It is also very wordy. Choice C appropriately maintains the subject "we" and succinctly communicates the idea.

4. **Choice D** is correct. The action begins in the past but, since it has a continuing effect, the present participle "causing" is appropriate. However, the phrase following the comma should be an appositive (two adjacent nouns having the same referent) and cannot begin with "this". Choice D is the best response.

5. **Choice B** is correct. The original sentence is incorrect because the pronoun "they" is used to modify "contract". Choice B puts the elements of the sentence in proper relation and smoothly communicates the idea.

6. **Choice B** is correct. The phrase "of which" is an inappropriate conjunction. The two clauses in the sentence can stand alone (independent) and should, therefore, be joined by "and" or a semicolon.

7. **Choice A** is correct. The sentence is correct. as is.

8. **Choice D** is correct. The pronoun "they" here is confusing. To what does it refer—colleges, women or people? A and B are therefore eliminated. C is incorrect. Because we need to have two complete thoughts to join with "and". Choice D is the best answer.

9. **Choice B** is correct. The phrase "and they" is awkward because there is no need to introduce this pronoun; the Navajo are already the subject and "they" becomes redundant. Choice B makes the connection between the two tribes by connecting both the migration with the similar language. Choice A is incorrect because "they" here incorrectly refers to the Apache. C and D are problematic for the same reason. E is incorrect because "A migration" modifies "Navajo".

10. **Choice E** is correct. The sentence is incorrect as is because there is a lack of parallelism. "…either _to please_" should be followed by "_to influence_". E communicates the idea nicely.

11. **Choice E** is correct. A lack of parallelism, again, is the problem here. "…inflation and… " should be followed by a noun. The "loss of faith" works well.

12. **Choice A** is correct. The sentence is correct. as it stands.

13. **Choice E** is correct. We see a lack of parallelism here again. The "number of alligators" should be compared to the "number of Gila monsters and should continue with "alligators" in the final phrase.

14. **Choice D** is correct. The phrase "particularly that of the heliograph" should follow immediately after the initial phrase "Many of the instruments" because that's what it modifies.

Practice Test #5 - Math

Section 3
8 questions – first third - easy

1. **Choice A** is correct. To find out what one pound makes, divide both things by 25. At this rate 1 pound of flour makes 300 / 25 = 12 rolls. This is our answer.

2. Choice E is correct. $2 * \frac{x}{y} * y^2 = 2 * xy = 2 * 10 = 20$

3. Choice B is correct. We solve these problems by looking at the boundaries. The boundary for x is 8. That makes the boundary for y as 22. Cross off A and E. If $x = 30$ then $y = 0$. So which of the remaining answers are true if $y = 0$?

   B) $0 < 22$ possible

   C) $0 = 22$ WRONG

   D) $0 > 22$ WRONG

   Only B remains

Second third - medium

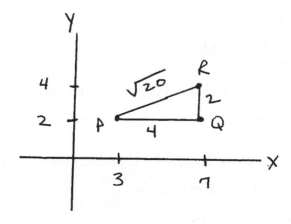

4. **Choice C** is correct. Draw a quick sketch. From P to Q is from 3 to 7 on the x-axis. That makes that side of the triangle 4. Write it in. From Q to R is from 2 to 4 on the y-axis. So that side is 2. The third side is the hypotenuse of a triangle. The perimeter is 4 + 2 + the hypotenuse. What is the hypotenuse? The Pythagorean Theorem says $c^2 = a^2 + b^2 = 4^2 + 2^2 = 16 + 4 = 20$. That makes the hypotenuse $\sqrt{20}$ and the perimeter $6 + \sqrt{20}$

5. **Choice D** is correct. The expression given is very much like a formula math teachers ask you to memorize. (The formula is $a + (n-1)d$ but do you remember what the letters stands for, what it gives you, and when you can use it? Let's reason the problem out.) The description say we find each term by adding 9 to the one before. The first term is 8. We add 9 and get 17. We add 9 again and get 26. For the third term we have added two 9s to 8. For the fourth term we add a third 9 to get 35. Then we add a fourth 9 to get the fifth term 44. So, each time we have added one less 9 than the term number. So term 12 will be 11 9s added to 8. What is $8 + (26-1)9$ tell you to do? Add 25 9s to 8. So it has to be the 26th term. By the way, that is the n in the formula.

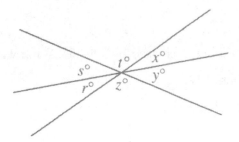

6. **Choice A** is correct. Because of the vertical angles formed we know three facts. $t = z$, $s = y$ and $r = x$. We also know that $t + s + r = 180$ since those three make a straight line. Look at their answers.

A) We only know 2 of the 6 angles.

B) We know 4 of the 6 angles and can get the other 2 from the last 180° equation.

C), D) and E) are the same as B.

Last third - hard

7. **Choice C** is correct. Use our own numbers here. The sum of two numbers that differ by 1 (Choose 9 and 10) is $t = 19$. Look at their answers to find our larger number of the pair, 10.

A) $\frac{19-1}{2} = 9 = 10$ WRONG

B) $\frac{19}{2} = 9.5 = 10$ WRONG

C) $\frac{19+1}{2} = 10$ possible

D) $\frac{19}{2} + 1 = 10.5 = 10$ WRONG

E) $\frac{2*19-1}{2} = 18.5 = 10$ WRONG

Only C remains

8. **Choice A** is correct. The total number of siblings in the original class was $3*0+6*1+2*2+1*3=13$ Since there are 12 students in the class, the average number of siblings was $13/12 \approx 1.08$. When the new student came the new average is equal to the median. With 13 students now in the class, the median is the number with 6 below so it is the 7th number in the list. That student will have 1 sibling. So we need to make the average also equal to 1. With 13 students there has to be 13 siblings. Before the new student entered the class there were already 13 siblings. So, the new student did not add any siblings.

---

10 questions – first third - easy

9. **Choice 2/5 OR .4** is correct. Solve the equation for x. $x-3=4$ so $x=7$. Now put 7 into the fraction. $(7-3)/(7+3) = 4/10 = 0.4$

10. **Choice 128** is correct. Twice a number decreased by 3 is 253. What was twice the number? 256. If twice the number is 256, what is the number? 128.
    Math Method: $2x-3=253$ and solve for x.

11. **Choice 2400** is correct. Find the White Low-tops. 5500 – 1500 = 4000. Find the Total White. 3600 + 4000 = 7600. Find the Total Black. 10000 – 7600 = 2400

Second third - medium

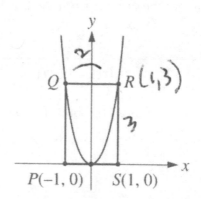

12. **Choice 3** is correct. PS = 2 = QR. If the perimeter is 10 then the two vertical sides total 6. So, they are 3 each. This makes the point R (1, 3). Substitute this point into the given equation $y=ax^2$ to get $3=a(1)^2=a$.

13. **Choice 8/3, 2.66 OR 2.67** is correct. Substitute their numbers into the problem. $2b+b=2+2*3$. Simplify to get $3b=8$ and divide both sides by 3 to get 2.66

© 2009 Master Learning Strategies Inc.

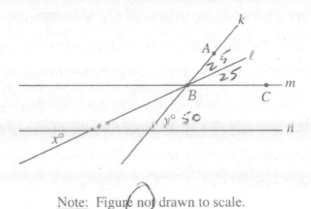

Note: Figure not drawn to scale.

14. **Choice 22.5 < x < 27.5** is correct. Be careful! Put in an acceptable value of *y* and see what we get. Choose 50°. Two parallel lines cut by a third line (*k*) means the small angles are the same size. So <ABC is also 50°. But we are told that line *l* bisects this angle making them both 25°. So all the very little angles at point B are 25°. The angle next to *y* is 130° by subtraction. So what is the third angle of that little triangle between the parallel lines? 180 – 130 – 25 = 25. Looks like that is also the value of *x* since those two are vertical angles.

15. **Choice 24** is correct. To pick the experience plumber we have 4 choices. With each of them we have 4 ways to pick the first trainee. That gives us 16 ways to pick the first two. For the last person we have a choice of 3 trainees left. That makes a total of 48 ways to pick the three men. But that method implies that the order in which we pick the trainees is important. How many ways can e mix-up two people? 2. So we divide our 48 ways by 2 and get the correct answer.

Last third - hard

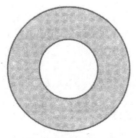

Note: Figure not drawn to scale.

16. **Choice 10** is correct. The small circle has an area of $\pi r^2 = 36\pi$. That makes the big circle have an area of $36\pi + 64\pi = 100\pi$. That makes the radius 10.

17. **Choice 8** is correct. It doesn't seem to matter what the vales of the variables are. There is only one answer. Let's put our own values in here. The value all have to be different, prime and larger than 2. Let's not get too big. $p = 3$, $r = 5$ and $s = 7$ will do. That makes $n = 3 * 5 * 7 = 105$. What are the numbers that divide evenly into 105? Here is the list. 1*105, 3*35, 5*21 and 7*15. That is a total of 8 numbers.

   Additional Note: The list was generated systematically. Once the first number got larger than the second number we could stop looking since if we did find a large number that worked, the other number would have been smaller and already found.

18. **Choice 70** is correct. We need to find the values of the constants. We know 2 time and height pairs. At 2.5 seconds the height is 106 feet. Putting those in we have $h(2.5) = c - (d - 4 * 2.5)^2 = 106$ Squaring gives us

   $106 = c - (d^2 - 20d + 100)$ or

   $106 = c - d^2 + 20d - 100$.

   We also know that the height is 6 at time 0.

   $h(0) = c - (d - 4 * 0)^2 = 6$. Simplifying gives us

   $c - d^2 = 6$

   Put this into our first equation and we get $106 = 6 + 20d - 100$

   $200 = 20d$

   $d = 10$.

   But $c - d^2 = 6$ so

   $c - 100 = 6$

   $c = 106$.

   Now the final equation becomes

   $h(x) = 106 - (10 - 4x)^2$.

   Put in $x = 1$ and we get $h(1) = 106 - (10 - 4 * 1)^2 = 106 - 36 = 70$

Section 7
20 questions – first third - easy

1. **Choice C** is correct. All of the answers given are positive integers. We only need to check which ones are divisible by 3. Since we want the largest we should start with the largest answer. Is 59 divisible by 3? Using the calculator we see $59 / 3 = 19.666$. It didn't come out even. Is 58 divisible by 3? Using the calculator we see $58 / 3 = 19.333$. It didn't come out even. Is 57 divisible by 3? Using the calculator we see $57 / 3 = 19$. We have found our answer.

2. **Choice D** is correct. We can use the same two dotted lines for the X as we see in the example for the H. we have to be able to see how the letter will change as we flip it is some direction.

3. **Choice D** is correct. We should use our own numbers here. If Bobby did 6 chores he would get $12 from chores pus $10 from his allowance. This gives him $22. Now plug in $n = 6$ and test their answers to get $22.
   A) 10 + 6 = 16 = 22 WRONG
   B) (10 + 2)*6 = 72 = 22 WRONG
   C) 10*6 + 2 = 62 = 22 WRONG
   D) 10 + 2*6 = 22 possible
   E) (10 + 6)*2 = 32 = 22 WRONG
   Only D remains

4. **Choice C** is correct. The area of Figure A is 26 and counting gives us 13 squares. Each one has to be 2 in size. Figure B has the same size little squares and has 8 little squares. 8*2 = 16

5. **Choice B** is correct. We need to look at the graph and find each persons increase.
   A) Went down. No increase
   B) Went up from 150 to 250. Increased 100
   C) Went up from 225 to 250. Increased 25
   D) Went down. No increase
   E) Went up from 250 to 300. Increased 50
   The largest of the 3 increases is 100 by Goldberg.

6. **Choice D** is correct. To find the average we need to add the values and divide by how many values we have. We have 5 values. Adding up the numbers we get 40 plus whatever x is. We should test their answers to see which one will give as the answer whatever we put in for x. Start with C.

C) $(40 + 9) / 5 = 9.8 = 9$ WRONG. Move higher

D) $(40 + 10) / 5 = 10 = 10$ Right. Here is our answer since the average (10) is the value we put in for x.

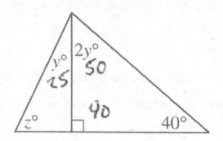

7. **Choice C** is correct. Write in the values they give us. The right angle is 90°. The third angle in that same triangle is marked as $2y°$ but we can get the value of 50 by subtraction. $180 - 90 - 40 = 50$. So $2y = 50$ or $y = 25$. Write that in the other place that y is shown. We now can get z by subtraction. $180 - 90 - 25 = 65$

Second third - medium

---

8. **Choice C** is correct. Let's test there values.

   I. 13 is odd so twice 13 or 26 is printed. Cross off B since it doesn't include I. A, C, D and E remain

   II 26 is even so it is printed. Cross off A and D since they don't include II. C and E remain.

   III. 52 is even so 52 is printed not 26. Cross off E since it includes III. Only C remains.

9. **Choice A** is correct. Choose our own numbers here. $m = 2$ and $s = 17$ makes the problem read "How many seconds are there in 2 minutes and 17 seconds?" There are $120 + 17 = 137$ seconds. Now test their answers.

   A) $60 * 2 + 17 = 137$ possible

   B) $2 + 60 * 17 = 1022 = 137$ WRONG

   C) $60(2 + 17) = 1140 = 137$ WRONG

   D) $(2 + 17) / 60 = 0.316 = 137$ WRONG

   E) $2 / 60 + 17 = 17.033 = 137$ WRONG

   Only A remains.

10. **Choice D** is correct. Let's check each of their answers.

A) $(2*0-2)(2-0)=-2*2=-4=0$ WRONG. Cross our A and E.

B) $(2*1-2)(2-1)=0*1=0$ 1 works so cross out C since it doesn't have 1 as an answer.

D) $(2*2-2)(2-2)=2*0=0$ 2 also works so cross out B since it doesn't include 2.

Only D remains

11. **Choice C** is correct. It is going to be hard to find numbers for x and y that will make $x^3 = y^9$ true. Let's find numbers that make the answer true and see if they make the above expression true.

A) $y=4$ so $x=\sqrt{4}=2$ Does $2^3=4^9$? WRONG

B) $y=2$ so $x=2^2=4$ Does $4^3=2^9$? WRONG

C) $y=2$ so $x=2^3=8$ Does $8^3=2^9$? Yes. This should be our answer. But we will check the others just for completeness. If we were pressed for time we should stop here.

D) $y=2$ so $x=2^6=32$ Does $32^3=2^9$? WRONG

E) $y=2$ so $x=2^{12}=4096$ Does $4096^3=2^9$? WRONG

Only C remains

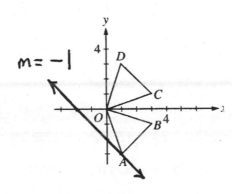

12. **Choice E** is correct. A negative slope goes down from left to right. It goes down the same amount it goes over. Let's check their answers

A) $\overline{OA}$ Down 3 over 1. Too steep. WRONG

B) $\overline{OB}$ Down 1 over 3. Too flat. WRONG

C) $\overline{OC}$ Positive slope. WRONG

D) $\overline{OD}$ Positive slope. WRONG

E) $\overline{DC}$ Down 2 over 2. Perfect!

Only E remains.

13. **Choice A** is correct. We have to understand what the sentence "If each number satisfies <u>exactly</u> one of the conditions." means. It means that one of the numbers we see will be odd. It will <u>not</u> be a multiple of 5 and it will <u>not</u> be Kyle's birthday. Let's look at the answers.

A) 13 is odd and not a multiple of 5. 20 is the multiple of 5 and not odd. 14 would be the birthday and it is not odd and not a multiple of 5. Possible.

B) 25 is both odd and a multiple of 5. WRONG

C) 15 is both odd and a multiple of 5. WRONG

D) 15 is both odd and a multiple of 5. WRONG

E) 21 is odd and not a multiple of 5. 30 is a multiple of 5 and not odd. That leaves 34 as the birthday. No month has 34 days so this is WRONG

Only A remains.

Last third - hard

---

14. **Choice C** is correct. We need to get ride of the square root symbol. The way to do that is to "square both sides."

$$\left(\sqrt{x+9}\right)^2 = \left(x-3\right)^2 \text{ Remember to FOIL the right}$$

$$x + 9 = x^2 - 3x - 3x + 9 \text{ Simplify!}$$

$$x + 9 = x^2 - 6x + 9 \text{ Subtract 9}$$

$$x = x^2 - 6x \text{ This is answer C.}$$

15. **Choice E** is correct. There are too many to count to do this directly. Let's get it by subtraction. From 1 to 100 there are 100 numbers. How many are the square of an integer? 1^2, 2^2, 3^2, all the way up to 10^2. This makes 10 of these squares. The rest are <u>not</u> squares. $100 - 10 = 90$.

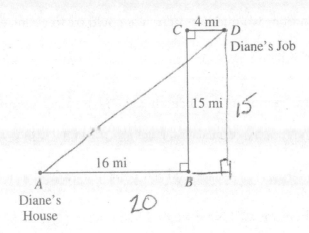

16. **Choice C** is correct. Diane travels 35 miles to work. If she could go straight there it would be the hypotenuse of a right triangle that has legs of 15 and 20. The answers that the SAT writers give us are all nice integers. That means that this hypotenuse must also be a nice integer. Remember that the SAT writers love certain size right triangles. 3, 4, 5 is one of them. 15 and 20 as the legs are 3*5 and 4*5 so the hypotenuse must be 5*5 or 25. If we didn't remember we could just use the Pythagorean Theorem and get $c^2 = 15^2 + 20^2 = 225 + 400 = 625 = 25^2$ so $c = 25$. Now back to the problem. She does travel 35 but the direct distance is 25. That would be a savings of 10 miles.

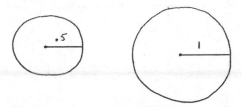

17. **Choice D** is correct. We need to find the areas. πr^2 A small radius of 0.5 gives $0.25\pi \approx 0.785$. A large radius of 1 gives $1\pi \approx 3.14$. Large over small gives $3.14/0.785 = 4$

    Geometry Method: Similar figures have proportional measures. The ratio of areas is the square of the ratio of the linear measures. The ratio of the volumes is the cube (third power) of the ratio of the linear measures. In these similar circles the ratio of the radii is $2:1$. So the ratio of the areas is $2^2 : 1^2 = 4:1$

18. **Choice B** is correct. The sum of these numbers would start out with $-22 + -21 + -20 + \ldots$ As we start adding them the sum keeps getting further and further below 0. We need some positive numbers to bring the sum back up so we can get the final sum equal to 72. Continuing to 22 gives $-22 + -21 + \ldots + 21 + 22 = 0$ because each negative number is balanced by its corresponding positive number. Tack on 23 and 24 and the sum becomes 47. Close! Add 25 and the sum is not 72. Right where we want. The last number added was 25 so that is our value of x.

© 2009 Master Learning Strategies Inc.

19. **Choice A** is correct. Plug in our own numbers here. We could try to get nice numbers or we could let the calculator do the walking. A little manipulation first. $x^{\frac{-4}{3}} = k^{-2}$ becomes $x = \left(k^{-2}\right)^{\frac{-3}{4}}$ when we raise both sides to the $-\frac{3}{4}$ power. In the same manor $y^{\frac{4}{3}} = n^2$ becomes $y = \left(n^2\right)^{\frac{3}{4}}$. Since we are using the calculator we really don't have to simplify the exponents. Now we pick values of n and k and se what x and y become.

$k = 4$ means $x = \left(4^{-2}\right)^{\frac{-3}{4}} = (4\wedge(-2))\wedge(-3/4) = 8$ and $n = 9$ means $y = \left(9^2\right)^{\frac{3}{4}} = (9\wedge 2)\wedge(3/4) = 27$

Oh look. We got nice numbers anyway! Now we find their value. $(xy)^{\frac{-2}{3}} = (8*27)\wedge(-2/3) = 0.02777$

A) $1/(4*9) = 0.02777$ Possible.

B) $4/9 = 0.444$ WRONG

C) $9/4 = 2.25$ WRONG

D) $4*9 = 36$ WRONG

E) 1 WRONG

Only A remains.

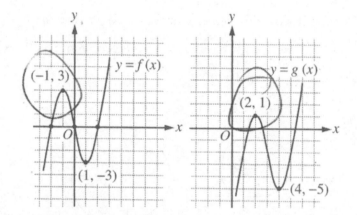

20. **Choice E** is correct. Here the second graph has exactly the same shape as the first graph. The first graph has been moved to the right and down. The point $(-1,3)$ has been moved to the point $(2,1)$. It has been moved 3 to the right and down 2. In the $g(x)$ equation the h being added before finding the $f(x)$ value has the effect of sliding the graph left and right. Adding on after finding the $f(x)$ value as the k is done has the effect of sliding up and down. The easiest to find is k. $k = -2$ because the graph went *down* 2. The left and right sliding can be confusing. The value of h is either 3 or -3. I never remember which slides it right. Let's test to see. Suppose $h = 3$. Then $g(x) = f(x+3) - 2$. The test is if the point $(2,1)$ is on this graph.

$g(2) = f(2+3) - 2 = f(5) - 2 = 5^3 - 4*5 - 2 = 103$ Oops. A little off. Try $h = -3$ Then $g(x) = f(x-3) - 2$ and wee test again.

$g(2) = f(2-3) - 2 = f(-1) - 2 = (-1)^3 - 4*(-1) - 2 = 1$ Super. Does it also have the point $(4,-5)$? Test.

$g(4) = f(4-3) - 2 = f(1) - 2 = 1^3 - 4*1 - 2 = -5$. Good again. To review $h = -3$ and $k = -2$. That makes $hk = 6$

Section 9
16 questions – first third - easy

.1 **Choice B** is correct. The probability is the number of red cars over the total cars or $6/10 = 0.6$ $3/5$ is also

0.6.

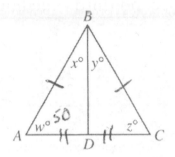

Note: Figure not drawn to scale.

2. **Choice A** is correct. Let's put in our own values for the angle sizes. $w = 50$ is a good start. Isosceles triangles

have congruent base angles. So $z = 50$ also. Write that in the diagram. $\overline{BD}$ is a median. (Hits the midpoint)

In an isosceles triangle the median from the vertex angle is also an angle bisector and perpendicular to the

base. This makes both the angles at D 90°. Write those in. We can find x by subtraction from 180°. $x = 40$

and so does y by the same method. Now we can test the SAT answers. Remember we are looking for

something that CANNOT be concluded.

A) 50 = 40? We found it right off. Put down A and move on.

3. **Choice B** is correct. $0.30 * m = 40$ so m is bigger than 40. $40/0.3 = 133.33$. $0.15 * 133.33 = 19.999$ choose 20 and

move on.

Another Thought: 15% is half of 30% so the answer should be half of 40. And it is. On easy problem the

right answers seem right.

4. **Choice E** is correct. Pick our own number for n. $n = -10$. Test their answers to find a positive number.

A) $-10/2 = -5$ WRONG B) $2(-10) = -20$ WRONG

C) $-10 + 2 = -8$ WRONG D) $-10 - 2 = -12$ WRONG

E) $2 - (-10) = 8$ Possible. Only E remains.

5. **Choice D** is correct. How do we get 1.2 to be a nice number by multiplying? Multiply by 10 to move the decimal point. (If you saw that we could use 5 you are ahead of the game. But back to using 10.) $1.2:1$ multiplied by $10/10$ gives $12:10$. Is that one of the answers? No. But if we cut them both in half we get $6:5$ which is there. That's what we would have gotten if we had used 5 as the multiplier as you suggested in the beginning.

Second third - medium

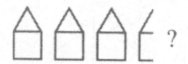

6. **Choice D** is correct. There are three full symbols and one half symbol. That makes three 5's and a half of a 5 or $3.5*5 = 17.5$

7. **Choice B** is correct. Use their answers and see if we can find the one they want.

A) $9 - b^2 = 7$ so $b^2 = 2$. That makes $b \approx 1.4$ which is *not* an integer. WRONG

B)) $16 - b^2 = 7$ so $b^2 = 9$. That makes $b = 3$ which is an integer. SUCCESS!

Mark B and move on.

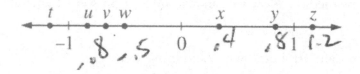

8. **Choice C** is correct. Give approximations for the values of each point. Now use our calculator to find $\left|-0.8 - (-0.5)\right| = \left|-0.3\right| = 0.3$ This is closest to *x*.

9. **Choice D** is correct. Let's use our own number here. $n = 7$. 7 increased by 5 is 12. 12 multiplied by 5 is 60. 60 decreased by 5 is 55. 55 divided by 5 is 11. Now check their answers.

A) $7 - 5 = 2 = 11$ WRONG

B) $7 - 1 = 6 = 11$ WRONG

C) $7 = 11$ WRONG

D) $7 + 4 = 11$ Possible

E) $5(7 + 5) = 60 = 11$ WRONG

Only D remains.

© 2009 Master Learning Strategies Inc.

10. **Choice B** is correct. Philip uses $4*6 = 24$ inches of masking tape for each poster. If he put up 10 posters then $n = 10$. The problem asks how many *feet* of masking tape are left after putting up the posters. We need to convert the 24 inches to feet. That would be 2 feet. So he used $2*10 = 20$ feet of tape for all 10 posters. That means he had $300 - 20 = 280$ feet left.

A) $300 - 6*10 = 240 = 280$ WRONG

B) $300 - 2*10 = 280$ Possible

C) $300 - 10 = 290 = 280$ WRONG

D) $300 - 0.5*10 = 295 = 280$ WRONG

E) $300 - 0.25*10 = 297.5 = 280$ WRONG

Only B remains.

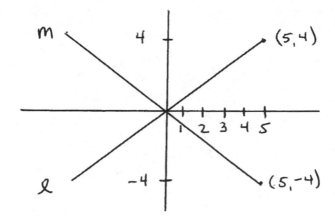

11. **Choice B** is correct. Draw a quick sketch. The problem doesn't say exactly where line m is so make it go through the Origin. It has a slope of $-\frac{4}{5}$ so make it go down. The point $(5,-4)$ would make the line go down 4 over 5 from the origin. That point is on the graph. The reflection about the x-axis means from each point we go perpendicular to the x-axis and then continue the same distance on the other side. So from $(5,-4)$ we would go up 4 to get to the x-axis. Now move up the same 4 units and we get to the point $(5,4)$. This is a point on the other line. $(0,0)$ is on the x-axis so it is also on the reflection. The question asks the slope of line l. What is the slope from $(0,0)$ to $(5,4)$? Up 4 over 5.

Last third - hard

12. **Choice A** is correct. The problem asks for the value of p. Use their values and check.

A) $p = 0$ so $n = 3*0 = 0$ Does $n = p$? Yes. Done. If we have time later we could come back and check to see that the others are wrong.

B) $p = 0.333$ so $n = 3*0.333 = 0.999$ Does $n = p$? WRONG

C) $p = 1$ so $n = 3*1 = 3$ Does $n = p$? WRONG

D) $p = 3$ so $n = 3*3 = 9$ Does $n = p$? WRONG

E) we found a value so this is WRONG

Math Method: Combine the equations and get

$3p = p$ Subtract p and get $2p = 0$ or $p = 0$

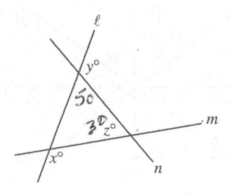

Note: Figure not drawn to scale.

13. **Choice D** is correct. Write in the known value of 30 for z. It would seem that we are missing a lot of information about the diagram and that is what makes this problem hard. But all the answers given are numbers. It must work out the same no matter what the other angles are. Put in our own number 50 next to y as the start. What else can we now put down? $y = 130$ by subtraction. Write that in as well. The other angle in the triangle is 100° by subtraction. That lets us find $x = 80$. That makes the value of $x + y = 80 + 130 = 210$ Write that down and give ourselves a pat on the back for getting it so quickly.

(A)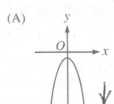

(B)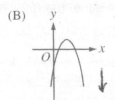

(C)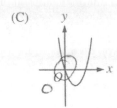

(D)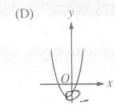

(E)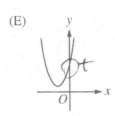

14. **Choice E** is correct. $f(x) = x^2 + bx + c$ has branches that point up because the number in front of x^2 is positive. (The number is actually 1 even though we don't write it.) Cross off A and B since they point down. C, D and E are left. Now to look for another clue. What happens when $x = 0$? Plug in and see.

$f(0) = 0^2 + b*0 + c = c$ So the graph crosses the y-axis at c. What do we know about c? From the problem we know it is a *positive* constant. That means the graph should hit the y-axis at a positive number. D hits at a negative value and C hits either at 0 or just below. Cross them both off. Only E remains.

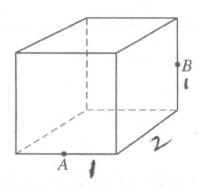

15. **Choice D** is correct. This is a three-dimensional distance problem. The formula is just like the Pythagorean Theorem for two dimensions. Just add another square. The three perpendicular lengths are 1 to the right, 2 back and 1 up. $d = \sqrt{1^2 + 2^2 + 1^2} = \sqrt{6}$ Write down D and go to the last problem on the test.

16. **Choice C** is correct. This is a "follow the rules" or "function" type of problem. Just put in their answers and see which one works. We will be calculating two values for each of their answers. We will find the answer when the two values we find are both the same. $f(x) = f(x-2)$

A) $x = 1$; $f(1) = 1^2 - 1 = 0$;

$f(1-2) = (-1)^2 - (-1) = 2$ $0 = 2$ WRONG)

B) $x = 0.5$; $f(0.5) = 0.5^2 - 0.5 = -0.25$;

$f(0.5-2) = (-1.5)^2 - (-1.5) = 3.75$ $-0.25 = 3.75$ WRONG

C) $x = 1.5$; $f(1.5) = 1.5^2 - 1.5 = 0.75$;

$f(1.5-2) = (-0.5)^2 - (-0.5) = 0.75$ $0.75 = 0.75$ Right. We are done but here are the rest just for completeness

D) $x = 1.2$; $f(1.2) = 1.2^2 - 1.2 = 0.24$;

$f(1.2-2) = (-0.8)^2 - (-0.8) = 1.44$ $0.24 = 1.44$ WRONG

E) $x = 3$; $f(3) = 3^2 - 3 = 6$;

$f(3-2) = (1)^2 - (1) = 0$ $6 = 0$ WRONG

Practice Test #6 - Verbal

Section 2

1. **Choice D** is correct. The context of the sentence makes the second blank easier to answer. If the island is "secluded" their "quiet way of life" will be upset by commercial development of any kind. This immediately eliminates A, C and E. Both "harm" and "disturb" will work but "waning" (decreasing or lessening) clearly does not fit the first blank, whereas, "encroaching" (creeping closer) does.

2. **Choice E** is correct. The first blank here is easier to answer. A jungle is not "often protected by" or "often located in" or "often surrounded by" anything. Choices C and E are the only possible answers but E is by far the best fit.

3. **Choice C** is correct. The context indicates that an "abundance" of information is given in the recent book. "Surfeit" means exactly that. "Modicum" (modest amount) nor "discrepancy" (difference) nor "deficit" (lacking) nor "juxtaposition" (adjacent to) fit.

4. **Choice B** is correct. The context of the sentence indicates that the two blanks will be opposite of one another. "Phlegmatic" and "apathetic" mean the same thing---uncaring. "Empathetic" and "compassionate" are also synonyms. "Vigilant" (watchful) and "reputable" (trustworthy) have no connection with each other and don't fit at all. "Penurious" (stingy) and "frugal" (careful with money) are essentially the same. Choice B is the best response because "conciliatory" (willing to forgive or reconcile) would certainly be an attribute opposite of "confrontational".

5. **Choice C** is correct. A number of the choices are possible fits so the context becomes very important. The clause which follows the colon defines the blank. "...so common that they seem humdrum." is the context clue. "Flabbergasted" (awestruck), "miffed" (upset), "wary" (cautious) and "embittered" (angry) can all fit the first part of the sentence but none fits the second part. The term "jaded" literally means "worn out" but frequently is used to mean "cynical". It is the perfect word in this context because we are all so "worn out" by technological advances, particularly in the computer industry, that they have become "humdrum" or commonplace.

6. **Choice D** is correct. Passage 1 suggests, "Science fiction's most important use...is as a means of dramatizing social inquiry..." The author of Passage 2 opines, "Younger readers of science fiction...absorb both scientific and humanistic elements from their readings." Both of these statements indicate that science fiction is "socially useful".

© 2009 Master Learning Strategies Inc.

7. **Choice E** is correct. Line 3 of Passage 1 states directly, "…most of the science is wrong" and the first line of Passage 2 says, "Much of the science in science fiction is hokum (pretentious nonsense, bunk)". This clearly indicates that there is no "attempt to reflect scientific reality" in science fiction.

8. **Choice C** is correct. The author of Passage 1, as indicated in lines 3-6, believes that there is very little, if any, "scientific benefit" that comes from science fiction. On the other hand, the author of Passage 2, in line 14 says, "…there is a general respect for science and some appreciation of its methodology" in the genre. Therefore, science fiction "values scientific thought".

9. **Choice B** is correct. As indicated above, each author believes that science fiction provides some kind of social usefulness. Exactly what and how much may be in dispute between these two authors. Their attitudes can best be described as "qualified appreciation."

10. **Choice B** is correct. The key context clue here is the word "ancillary" which means auxiliary or supplementary or subordinate. If other senses are thus compared to sight, then sight must be, for human beings, our "… primary means of knowing about the world."

11. **Choice C** is correct. The "principles of phenomenology" are illustrated in the last paragraph. The example of Fido and the author sitting on the terrace and seeing the same things is contrasted with Fido "believing the scents of the garden behind us" illustrates the differences between the "ways and means of knowing about something."

12. **Choice C** is correct. The context, again, indicates how differently dogs and humans "know" things. The author is describing his "180 degree view" of things and contrasting that with Fido's perspective. Clearly Fido's "perception of the world" is what we don't know about and can't know because of our phenomenological limitations.

13. **Choice D** is correct. The author in line 43 emphasizes the difference between "that" and "how" by italicizing the two words. There is no question is the author's mind "*that* Fido is alerted to the kitty, but not *how*". "Awareness of the presence and the *nature* of the awareness" is what is in question.

14. **Choice A** is correct. From the context, and from the discussion of the previous answers and examples, this answer is self-evident.

15. **Choice D** is correct. Line 42 states, "Garvey invited Du Bois to preside over his first public lecture...and asked permissions to submit Du Bois's name as a 'leader' of Black America…" indicating that Garvey initially respected Du Bois. However, the majority of the passage "describes the differences between the philosophies of Du Bois and Garvey".

16. **Choice C** is correct. Line 1 opens the first paragraph which deals with the tension between loyalty to one's race and loyalty to one's country which clearly had racial bias.

17. **Choice A** is correct. Du Bois's subsequent statement in line 15, "_first_ your Country, _then_ your Rights!" clarifies how his original statement seemed to have been taken by Black-Americans, that is, that he "devalued their specific concerns".

18. **Choice E** is correct. Lines 15-21 describe the author's belief that, "…the defeat of the former (Allies) would be disastrous for the 'United States of the World'". This implies that "despite American racism", which is evil, "an Allied defeat would be even worse."

19. **Choice D** is correct. Lines 20-21 state plainly that, "…the 'United States of the World'" was what he was "most loyal" to.

20. **Choice B** is correct. Line 31 indicates Du Bois's view of Garvey's philosophy and he summed it up like this, "…black skin was in itself a sort of patent to nobility. Du Bois recognized the inherent incongruity between fighting against bias and, at the same time, believing that "an entire group is inherently dignified or worthy."

21. **Choice C** is correct. The term "patent" is usually used to mean a license to the rights of an invention, solely to the inventor. In other words, it's a "guarantee" that no one else can benefit from it. That is what is meant here with respect to black skin.

22. **Choice E** is correct. As stated before, lines 41-46 suggest that Garvey initially "appreciated Du Bois's influence" whether he agreed with Du Bois's philosophy or not.

23. **Choice A** is correct. Line 59-61 precedes those of 62-66 and gives us an important clue. The passage at this point is speaking of Garvey's love for and view of Africa but then states, "…his obsession with Africa as the solution to the problems of its scattered peoples, and his refusal to allow any liberal idea to deflect his purpose differed greatly from Du Bois's." These lines, in conjunction with lines 62-66 show that both men "valued Africa" but "in a very different way" and for different reasons.

24. **Choice A** is correct. Although some may not have had the same philosophies, they can still be cordial or "courteous" to one another. That was the relationship between Garvey and Du Bois, at first. But after one gets to know the true motivation of another, sometimes that relationship can deteriorate. That's precisely what took place between these two men. Line 68 implies that Du Bois thought of Garvey as a demagogue, that is, one who incites a riot or rebellion. This would certainly be "antagonistic".

Section 4

1. **Choice D** is correct. The original sentence is not a sentence at all but a sentence fragment because it lacks a verb as it stands. It could be perfectly fine if it continued on, but it doesn't. D and E are the only answers which provide a verb for the subject "problem". E is incorrect because the word "so" (as a result) indicates a cause and effect relationship which doesn't make sense.

2. **Choice C** is correct. Because the action is in the past, the verb coming is in the wrong tense, it too should be in the past. "They" is also redundant and, therefore, unnecessary, at the beginning of the dependent clause. Choice C solves the problems nicely.

3. **Choice D** is correct. The original sentence is incorrect because the subject changes from "lab instructor" to "we". It also has the tendency to run-on. D clarifies the subject and concisely communicates the idea. E is incorrect because the timing is out of order.

4. **Choice B** is correct. The original sentence is incorrect because it is a comma splice. Both the clause before and the clause after the comma are independent, therefore, a comma is insufficient to separate them. C is incorrect because "demand" is not consistent with "exposing". D is incorrect because "although" indicates a contrast not indicated. E is simply awkward and roundabout.

5. **Choice B** is correct. The sentence is incorrect as is because there is a lack of agreement in number. It should read "…every woman reads from _her_ own unique _perspective_."

6. **Choice B** is correct. There is a lack of parallelism in the original sentence. The subject "spirit of the honor code" is followed by the two nouns "honesty" and "behavior" which should then also be followed by "responsibility in action." The phrase "and it demands" is inappropriate.

7. **Choice A** is correct. The original sentence is correct. as it stands.

8. **Choice B** is correct. The original sentence is incorrect because the plural subject "difficulties" requires the plural verb "threaten" to complement it.

© 2009 Master Learning Strategies Inc.

9. **Choice E** is correct. We have a lack of parallelism in the original sentence. In order to be correct, "to appeal and persuade" should be followed by "to educate and inform". The other problem lies with the change from the verb "to be" to the verb "to do". Therefore, the verb "was" is necessary to maintain the proper comparison.

10. **Choice A** is correct. The original sentence is clear and grammatically correct as is.

11. **Choice E** is correct. The original sentence is incorrect because "The Roman Empire" should be followed by the pronoun "its" and not "their" in order to be correct. Also, in order to avoid the passive voice, the action (attempted) should follow immediately after the subject (Roman Empire). E does this nicely.

12. **Choice C** contains the error. The adverb "serenely" should follow the verb "float".

13. **Choice A** contains the error. We have an error in tense here. Since the action is in the past ("if she had taken…than she did"), the verb "would have voted" is required.

14. **Choice E** is correct. There is no error in this sentence.

15. **Choice D** contains the error. The adverbs "*calmly* and competently" should modify examine.

16. **Choice C** contains the error. The simple past ("throw") instead of the past participle ("have thrown") is all that is necessary here.

17. **Choice A** contains the error. "Which" is a pronoun that should be used to refer to things not people. "Who" should replace "which" in order to make the sentence correct.

18. **Choice B** contains the error. Proper idiomatic English requires the construction "to prefer something *over* something else" rather "than to prefer something *more than* something else".

19. **Choice D** contains the error. The pronoun "your" cannot be used to refer to "people" as it does in this sentence. "Your" should be replaced with "their".

20. **Choice C** contains the error. The singular subject "use" requires the singular verb "*has* increased" not "*have* increased."

21. **Choice C** contains the error. Since the opening of the library is clearly in the future, the future tense "will be delayed" is required.

22. **Choice E** is correct. There is no error in this sentence.

23. **Choice C** contains the error. The word "over" is unnecessary. "…Burns vehemently protested her party's failure…" is perfectly fine.

24. **Choice A** contains the error. Proper English demands the construction "between you and me" because I cannot be a pronoun with a prepositional phrase. In this case, "between my older sister and me".

25. **Choice A** contains the error. The plural subject "people" requires the plural noun "models" in order for this sentence to be correct.

26. **Choice D** contains the error. The pronoun "it" here is a bit confusing. To what does "it" refer? Either the sentence should say "to do so" or a *specific* action should be described.

27. **Choice A** contains the error. The singular subject "insistence" requires the singular verb "is".

28. **Choice E** is correct. This sentence is grammatically correct as is.

29. **Choice D** contains the error. The word "or" should be "and" because the phrase "make a choice *between*…" already indicates one or the other. Proper construction dictates "either _____ or _____" or "between _____ and _____".

30. **Choice D** is correct. The pronoun "them" is ambiguous. Is it referring to personages, infirmities, painters or theories? It must be clarified and D does this well.

31. **Choice D** is correct. The entire passage is in the first person, therefore, sentence 7 is out of place unless it becomes a personal observation. Choice D makes it just that and allows it to fit nicely into the passage.

32. **Choice C** is correct. The sentence as it stands is a comma splice. Choice C is the only correct answer choice.

33. **Choice B** is correct. Since sentence 8 has indicated that the author has become "an authority among his peers, sentence 9 should start with the words "For example" because an excellent example of this follows.

34. **Choice A** is correct. Choices A-D are all viable possibilities but A is the best because it is the last sentence of the passage and should summarize what the entire passage was about. Choice A does this well.

35. **Choice D** is correct. There is a shift in thought between sentence 7 and 8 and, therefore, this would be the most logical place to begin a new paragraph.

| Section 5 |

1. **Choice B** is correct. The context clues here are "not to explain" and "warped". The word "distort" would describe both. The other words are self-explanatory.

2. **Choice D** is correct. The motto found on our coinage is ' E Pluribus Unum' or 'Out of the Many, One'. The idea is that the cultures and languages and creeds of many people have come together or been "absorbed" into one. The term "convergence" has the same connotation. "Eradication" means to completely get rid of and doesn't fit.

3. **Choice E** is correct. The context clue here is "not from one brilliant discovery but a lifetime of work." It was the "sum total" or "cumulative" effect of the work. "Tangential" (peripheral, insignificant) nor "premature" (early) nor "exorbitant" (expensive) nor "indiscernible" (unable to be understood) fit.

4. **Choice B** is correct. The context indicates a contrast between the two ideas in the first part of the sentence. The first blank also opposite in meaning to "openly defied". Choices A and D would be immediately eliminated. Choice B is the best among the rest. If one "suppresses" anger and resentment, he also avoids "conflict."

5. **Choice E** is correct. Again, the context indicates a contrast of sorts. The terms "actually" and "though" are the context clues. The first blank must be opposite the phrase "…for several minutes before one falls asleep." The only clear response would be "instantaneously".

6. **Choice B** is correct. The flow of this sentence indicates that there is a direct relationship between the two blanks. The only choice where this is the case is B. A "pioneer" is a trailblazer or someone who does something for the first time. When something is "implemented" it is _established or begun_. Someone who "campaigns" for something is an advocate for it and B, therefore, makes perfect sense.

7. **Choice A** is correct. The phrase which follows the comma defines the blank, as usual. The word we are looking for, then, must mean quickly or speedily. "Alacrity" means just that. "Conformity" (done like everyone else) nor "deliberation" (slowly, carefully) nor "recrimination" (accusation) nor "exasperation" (frustration) fit.

8. **Choice A** is correct. The key word here is "yet" because it indicates the opposite of "celebrates". C and D can be eliminated directly. "Delineate" (specify, clarify) doesn't work either. The term "exacerbate" means to make worse and is not an adjective that can be used of a "role". Choice A is the answer because "censure" means to harshly criticize. This term should not be confused with *censor* which means to edit or delete due to objectionable material.

9. **Choice D** is correct. It is clear from these lines that Stephens wasn't going to let the prejudice of the day inhibit her from being an artist and did so from home. (She may have simply called herself A.B. Stephens and let people think she was a man.)

10. **Choice C** is correct. The passage reveals that she was a "pragmatist" (practical) and an "activist" because she campaigned for the rights of women artists.

11. **Choice B** is correct. Choices A and C are incorrect because the opposite happened. Choice D is incorrect because there is no evidence for this in the passage. B is correct. because line 11 indicates that the Native Americans "frequently entered into competition with one another."

12. **Choice C** is correct. The key phrase in lines 5-7 is "unprecedented only in the strangeness of the visitors and their wares." This implies that the "visitors and wares" of the Europeans were "exotic" or *non-native*. The terms "reserved" (conservative) nor "arrogant" nor "capricious" (whimsical, impulsive) nor "grasping" (possessive).

13. **Choice B** is correct. The term "plastic" could either mean "pliable" or "impermanent" but since it is found in this phrase, "A plastic paradise in kitsch (low class) city" it would be closest to "artificial".

14. **Choice D** is correct. The critics would certainly describe the museum in negative terms. "Garish" (in bad taste) and "inauthentic" (unreal) would certainly fit. All the other choices are either positive (B and C) or not supported by the passage.

15. **Choice A** is correct. The last sentence of the third paragraph offers the best clues. The phrases, "The details are all based on known Roman examples from *various* places" and, they "…create an *incongruous* appearance" indicate that the "separate parts do not create a coherent (unified) whole."

16. **Choice E** is correct. Lines 38-40 state, "No one knows about its precise style and details, how many floors it had, or exactly how tall it was." This is the evidence that indicates choice E is correct.

17. **Choice C** is correct. Line 8 indicates the museum is "…a re-creation of the Villa dei Papyri.." but Pastier is quoted as saying that it is "…a faithful replica of nothing that ever existed." Some of the critics would object that it is not just a poor representation but a presumptuous one.

18. **Choice C** is correct. The sentence which follows states, " They, too, wanted the museum building itself to be unique and a work of art." Clearly, they were "in accord" with Mr. Getty.

19. **Choice A** is correct. This sentence is the opening sentence of the second paragraph which refers directly to the main idea of the first. The first paragraph deals solely with the "design of the museum building."

20. **Choice A** is correct. If "flouting conventional wisdom and refusal to conform carry many risks" and Getty went on to do just that, then Choice A is the only possible answer.

21. **Choice D** is correct. Lines 12-14 indicate that most of the controversy occurred over the design. The entire second paragraph of Passage 2 is devoted to the kind of response that Getty expected of the Art World and his delight in defying them.

22. **Choice C** is correct. Quite a bit of Passage 1 (line 21-42) deals with the details of the original building and the lack of authenticity found in Getty's replica. Getty himself does not deal with this subject at all in his piece.

23. **Choice D** is correct. Line 20 states, "…it is permissible for a museum to be a work of art.." and the trustees certainly felt that way.

24. **Choice E** is correct. The phrase "…shrillness of the cries and howls very quickly exhausts their wind." Indicates that their criticism will be "short-lived."

Section 8

1. **Choice B** is correct. If many writers were not originally from Harlem but were associated with its Renaissance, they must have "adopted" it as a home.

2. **Choice A** is correct. Contact lenses "correct" flawed vision. No other choice is reasonable.

3. **Choice C** is correct. The context would imply a contrast between the blanks. Also, an architect who "rehabilitates older buildings" would object to the destruction of them. The term "razing" means destruction and "salvageable" means able to be saved.

4. **Choice C** is correct. The term "glacial" is the adjective form of glacier. The properties of glaciers, since they are huge sheets of ice, are: icy and slow moving. "Glacial", in this case, means a figurative cold shoulder. The terms "amiable" (friendly) nor "ethical" (moral) nor "taunting" (teasing) nor "nondescript" (plain) fit.

5. **Choice D** is correct. The blank is clearly defined by the phrase "…because of the flexibility and grace…". The term "lithe" is synonymous with these.

6. **Choice A** is correct. The first blank is the easier one to find. If the museum received something that was "much-needed", then the collapse must have been averted. Choices A and B are possible answers. Choice A is best because a "reprieve" is *relief or deliverance* from punishment. An "infusion", like a transfusion, is an influx of something.

7. **Choice B** is correct. This phrase, as well as the example of a mother with her sleigh-riding son, implies a "peaceful security" that a "parental burrow" could afford.

8. **Choice C** is correct. Nothing had changed much in technological terms between the early and late 1800's. Therefore, the author's life "resembled" her grandparents' lives.

9. **Choice D** is correct. The phrase "…watching with her grandfather's eyes" can only mean "…seeing something he might have seen".

10. **Choice D** is correct. Water would move very slowly through the dense, organic soil of a bog. This reference would clearly allude to the "deliberate pace of life in Milton." Line35, "…the comfortable past asserted itself unchanged" ,would also be a clue.

11. **Choice E** is correct. The passage indicates (lines 30-34) a direct relationship between the welcome at home and the prospects of future employment or security.

12. **Choice D** is correct. The term "sunk" here implies that she is *overwhelmed* by her affection for home, probably because she missed and worried about her husband so much.

13. **Choice D** is correct. Lines 49-50 precede this and convey the idea of most living "too shallowly" in too many places. This would indicate that Susan Ward would have deep knowledge and love of the town.

14. **Choice D** is correct. The last part of the sentence states, "…they are not talking about people like my grandmother." Clearly this is a viewpoint contrary to his.

15. **Choice A** is correct. People like Susan Ward had to make the best of a bad situation and so "recreated a domestic haven" for their children.

16. **Choice B** is correct. The phrase "little baggage" is followed by "of the cultural kind" and is a metaphor for the "values of the past".

17. **Choice E** is correct. In these lines, modernists are described as having no domestic sentiment or empathy and are contrasted with people of past generations.

18. **Choice D** is correct. Obviously if modernists have no deep feelings for home, they would not have "earlier generation's attachment" to home.

19. **Choice C** is correct. Both the narrator and Susan Ward are writing about a grandparent.

Section 10

1. **Choice B** is correct. There is a lack of parallelism in the original sentence. The verb "has been driven" should be followed by "has taken refuge".

2. **Choice D** is correct. The pronoun "they" is redundant and can be eliminated.

3. **Choice B** is correct. The original sentence has very awkward "ing" construction and uses "often" too often!! Choice B is concise and grammatically correct.

4. **Choice E** is correct. A lack of parallelism is the problem in the original sentence. "Finding" is followed by "designing" and should be followed by "securing" **only** and not "*the* securing".

5. **Choice A** is correct. The original sentence is correct. as it stands.

6. **Choice C** is correct. The context of the sentence indicates a contrast between many and few but the conjunction "and" does not illustrate the contrast. The conjunction "but" should replace "and".

7. **Choice E** is correct. The original sentence is not a sentence because it is an incomplete thought. E supplies the verb which is lacking and completes the intended thought.

8. **Choice D** is correct. People or things are adopted "by" something or someone not "through" something or someone.

9. **Choice B** is correct. The word "while" indicates action concurrent with another. Clearly something couldn't be happening in the 80's and 90's at the same time. Therefore, "while" should be replaced with "and it".

10. **Choice D** is correct. Choice A is an incomplete thought. D is a much more direct and concise way of communicating the idea.

11. **Choice A** is correct. This sentence is correct. as is.

12. **Choice E** is correct. The pronoun "they" is confusing because we don't know what it refers to. It is also a run-on sentence. E nicely separates the independent clauses.

13. **Choice A** is correct. This sentence is grammatically correct as it stands.

14. **Choice C** is correct. "This being" is awkward "ing" construction. B is a comma splice and should be separated by a semicolon as in Choice C.

Practice Test #6 - Math

Section 3
8 questions – first third - easy

1. **Choice D is correct.** If you have to use the calculator to turn the fractions into decimals which are easier to compare. $1/5 = 0.2$ and $1/4 = 0.25$. A, B and C are too low and E is too high.

2. **Choice B is correct.** Test each of their points to find the one closest to the Origin. $(0, 0)$

   A) 1 unit away to the left

   B) 0.5 units away to the right. Closest so far.

   C) 0.5 right then 0.5 down. Further away than B.

   D) 0.5 right then 0.5 up. Further away than B.

   E) 1 left then 1 down. Farthest away.

   B is the closest.

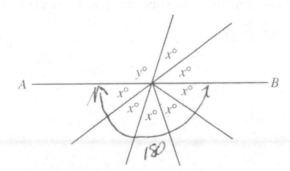

3. **Choice A is correct.** The five angles on the bottom are all the same size and total 180. That makes them $36°$ each. Two of the same size angles are on the top. That makes $y + 72 = 180$ or $y = 108$

Second third - medium

4. **Choice C is correct.** Test their answers starting with C.

   C) $6,565 = 65(100 + 11) = 6565$ Got it. Mark C and go on to the next problem.

5. **Choice D is correct.** We have to know the rules for simplifying exponents for this problem.

   $m^x * m^7 = m^{28}$ is addition. $x + 7 = 28$ or $x = 21$

   $\left(m^5\right)^y = m^{15}$ is multiplication. $5y = 15$ or $y = 3$

   $21 + 3 = 24$. Mark D and move to the next problem.

© 2009 Master Learning Strategies Inc.

HOME SALES

6. **Choice C** is correct. We need to read the graph. In 1987 there were about 156,000 home sales. In 1990 there were about 113,000 sales. This is a decrease of about 43,000. This was a 3 year drop. What is it <u>per year</u>? $43000 / 3 = 14333.33$ which is close to C. Reading the graph is never exact so our reading is not always what the SAT writers read. Close enough.

Last third - hard

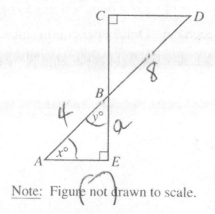

Note: Figure not drawn to scale.

7. **Choice B** is correct. CE is the perpendicular distance so it has to be shorter than the 12 from A to D. That makes answers D and E WRONG. Cross them off. We are told that $x = y$ so that makes $\triangle ABE$ isosceles as well as a right triangle. Use a as the length of BE and that makes AE that same length. Write a in the diagram for AE also. Now Mr. Pythagoras helps with his theorem. $4^2 = a^2 + a^2$ or $16 = 2a^2$ or $8 = a^2$ so $a \approx 2.8$. That gives us BE. How do we find BC. It is actually easier than finding BE. The two triangles shown are similar to each other. They both have right angles and the two vertical angles are congruent. Any two triangles that have two pair of congruent angles are similar. Can we remember $AA \sim$? Similar triangles have proportional sides. Which triangle is bigger? The top one. How much bigger? Twice as big since 8 is twice 4. So if BE is 2.8 then BC should be twice that or 5.6. That makes $CE \approx 2.8 + 5.6 = 8.4$ which is very close to answer B. Solving with those funny square root symbols would have gotten the exact answer but it is not worth the trouble since we only had to be close to find the SAT answer.

8. **Choice A is correct.** Put our own numbers in for their variables. If $d = 3$ and $c = 5$ then the problem reads: "The price of ground coffee beans is \$3 for 8 ounces and each ounce makes 5 cups of brewed coffee." So how many cups of coffee do we get for our \$3? 8 ounces times 5 cups per ounce means we get 40 cups for our \$3. That's just a few cents for each cup. Dollars per cup means we put 3 dollars on top and 40 cups on the bottom. $3 / 40 = 0.075$ which is a little over 7 cents per cup. Now to see which of their answers produces 0.075.

A) $3 / (8 * 5) = 0.075$ Possible

B) $(5 * 3) / (8) = 1.875 = 0.075$ WRONG

C) $(8 * 5) / (3) = 13.33 = 0.075$ WRONG

D) $(8 * 3) / (5) = 4.8 = 0.075$ WRONG

E) $8 * 3 * 5 = 120 = 0.075$ WRONG

Only A remains

---

10 questions – first third - easy

---

9. **Choice 120 is correct.** Cross-multiply here and get $120 = ab$

10. **Choice 6/25 OR .24 is correct.** We only have to find two more terms. Multiply to find the fourth term. $6 * 1 / 5 = 1.2$ and again to find the fifth term. $1.2 * 1 / 5 = 0.24$

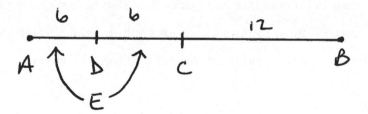

11. **Choice 1 OR 11 is correct.** Make a quick sketch. Draw AB of length 24. Now make C be the midpoint. That makes both sides 12. Now make D the midpoint of AC so both of those lengths are 6. We are now up to our last point. E is 5 from D but we don't know if it is left or right. The problem asks for one possible distance. Suppose it is on the right. Then AE is the 6 units from A to D and then the 5 more to D. Total 11. The other answer comes if we put E on the left of D. Then it is only 1 unit from A so that 5 more to D will make the 6 units in the problem.

Second third - medium

12. **Choice 39** is correct. The total of 5 numbers is 185. the average of them is $185/5 = 37$. The numbers are consecutive integers so they go up by 1. There should be 2 bigger than 37 and 2 smaller. That would make them 35, 36, 37, 38 and 39. Adding them gives me 185 so these are the correct numbers. The largest is 39.

13. **Choice 6500** is correct. This salesman's salary is $1,200 pay plus an amount based on sales to total $2,500. This means his other amount is $1,300 which we get by subtraction. The problem sys that the 1,300 is 20% of his sales. His sales must be a big number so we can take 20% of it to get 1,300. Here is the math statement. $1300 = 0.20 * s$ Divide both sides by 0.20 and get $1300/.2 = 6500$. Is this the answer? What is 20% of 6500? $.20 * 6500 = 1300$ 6500 is the answer.

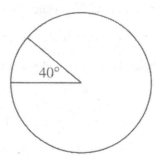

14. **Choice 5/18, .277 OR .288** is correct. 40° is $40/360 = 0.1111$ of the circle. The wedge should weigh that same fraction of the 2.5 grams. $0.1111 * 2.5 = 0.27775$

15. **Choice 2** is correct. We should remember the special factoring of $x^2 - y^2 = (x+y)(x-y)$ which gives us $(x+y)(x-y) = 10$. Put in 5 for $(x+y)$ and we have $5(x-y) = 10$ or $(x-y) = 2$ Problem finished.

Last third - hard

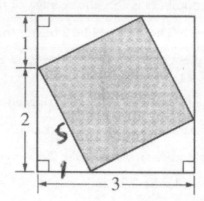

16. **Choice** 5 is correct. There are two ways to do this problem. Do it directly by finding the length of one side of the shaded square and squaring to get the area. We could also do it indirectly by finding the area of the big square and subtracting the area of the four white triangles. Here are both methods.

    Directly: We need s^2. The little white right triangle has legs 2 and 1. Mr. Pythagoras says $s^2 = 2^2 + 1^2 = 5$ We have s^2 so we are done.

    Indirectly: The big square is 3 on a side so the area is 9. Each little triangle has area $0.5bh = 0.5 * 2 * 1 = 1$. There are four of these triangles so the total white area is 4. $9 - 4 = 5$ and we have our shaded area.

17. **Choice 11** is correct. Follow the rules again. The value is the remainder after we do the division. Do the divisions and find the remainder. We only have to use positive numbers.

    $13 / 2 = 6$ R 1 $13 / 3 = 4$ R 1

    $13 / 4 = 3$ R 1 $13 / 5 = 2$ R 3

    $13 / 6 = 2$ R 1 $13 / 7 = 1$ R 6

    $13 / 8 = 1$ R 5 $13 / 9 = 1$ R 4

    $13 / 10 = 1$ R 3 $13 / 11 = 1$ R 2 Success!

18. **Choice 3/8 OR .375** is correct. When given averages always find the totals. For p students the average is 70. The total is $70p$. For n students the average is 92. the total is $92n$. For all these students $(p+n)$ the average is $86(p+n)$. While the averages are hard to work, the totals are very easy. The total of the first class plus the total of the second class is equal to the total of both classes. $70p+92n=86(p+n)$ simplify to find p/n.

$70p+92n=86(p+n)=86p+86n$

$70p+92n=86p+86n$ Move p's right and n's left

$6n=16p$ We want p on top so divide by $16n$.

$\dfrac{6n}{16n}=\dfrac{16p}{16n}$ simplifies to $\dfrac{3}{8}=\dfrac{p}{n}$ and we are done.

Section 7

20 questions – first third - easy

1. **Choice B** is correct. "exquisite" has one x and one q. They are 5 points each giving 10 points for those two letters. The other 7 letters get one point each for a total of 7 points. $10+7=17$ which is choice B.

2. **Choice B** is correct. Dividing both sides of $2x-10=20$ by 2 we get $x-5=10$ which is what we want. Of course we could have "solved for x" but that takes longer. If we hadn't seen the quick division we should have started to "solve for x" immediately so as not to waste time.

3. **Choice E** is correct. Pick our own odd number. $t=5$ is be fine. Now test their answers to get an even number.

   A) $5+2=7$ WRONG   B) $2*5-1=9$ WRONG

   C) $3*5-2=13$ WRONG D) $3*5+2=17$ WRONG

   E) $5*5+1=26$ Possible   Only E remains.

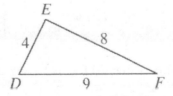

4. **Choice C** is correct. The perimeter of $\triangle DEF=4+8+9=21$. The perimeter of $\triangle ABC$ is also 21 and all three sides are the same length. That makes them each 7.

SALES OF JEANS IN 2001

5. **Choice E** is correct. The 900 "Other Brands" are 20% of the total jeans sold. This makes $900 = 0.20 * ???$

Use their answers to see which is correct. Start with C.

C) $900 = 0.20 * 3000 = 600$ WRONG and we need to go up

D) $900 = 0.20 * 3600 = 720$ WRONG but still too low

E) $900 = 0.20 * 4500 = 900$ Our answer.

6. **Choice C** is correct. 12 feet by 18 feet is 4 yards by 6 yards. That makes $4 * 6 = 24$ square yards of carpeting.

7. **Choice D** is correct. Put in their answers to test and see which is correct. Start with C.

C) $p = 4$ so $k = 4$ to have them total 8. Then $b = 3$ so the kitten and the bunny total 7. Do the bunny and the puppy total 9? $b + p = 3 + 4 = 7$ WRONG. Up or down? Try up.

D)) $p = 5$ so $k = 3$ to have them total 8. Then $b = 4$ so the kitten and the bunny total 7. Do the bunny and the puppy total 9? $b + p = 4 + 5 = 9$ Success.

If we had gone down we would have see that the bunny and puppy total would have gone down to 5. This should have made us try D next.

Second third - medium

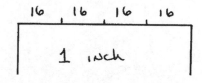

8. **Choice B** is correct. A quick sketch shows that 40 feet is between 0.5 inches and 0.75 inches in the map. A is too small for this and C, D and E are too large.

Math Method: Make a map to ground proportion. $1 / 4 : 16 = x : 40$ which can be written as a fraction also.

$\frac{0.25}{16} = \frac{x}{40}$ cross-multiply and get $10 = 16x$ and solve for $x = \frac{10}{16} = \frac{5}{8}$

© 2009 Master Learning Strategies Inc.

9. **Choice A** is correct. $(p,0)$ being one of the intersection points means that the y-value will be 0 on both graphs. Plug in their values starting with C.

C) $y = 9^2 - 9 = 72$ WRONG since it doesn't produce a 0 for y. The y-value is much too high. Use a smaller x-value.

B) $y = 6^2 - 9 = 25$ WRONG since it doesn't produce a 0 for y. The y-value is still too high. Use a smaller x-value.

A) $y = 3^2 - 9 = 0$ Good for the first equation. Now try the second. $y = -(3^2) + 9 = 0$ Works here too. We have our answer.

10. **Choice B** is correct. We need to convert everything to minutes since that is what the final answer has to be. 300 bolts per hour is $300 / 60 = 5$ bolts per minute. 450 bolts per hour is $450 / 60 = 7.5$ bolts per minute. So with both machines working we get $5 + 7.5 = 12.5$ bolts each minute. Now we use their answers to see which one is correct. Start with C.

C) $12.5 * 120 = 1500$ WRONG and too high.

B) $12.5 * 72 = 900$ Success.

11. **Choice E** is correct. For the equation to be correct, each time we put in a t value we need to get the $g(t)$ value out. We will start with some easy values to calculate. Use $t = 0$ where $g(0) = 2$ from the table.

A, B and C all give 1 when we plug in 0. Cross them all out. D and E give 2 so they are still in the running. $g(1) = 0$ from the table. Test D and E

D) $g(1) = -1 + 2 = 1$ WRONG. Cross it out. Only E remains but let's test it to make sure of our arithmetic.

E) $g(1) = -2 * 1 + 2 = 0$ Success.

12. **Choice C** is correct. This is a reading the graph problem. Look at each statement and see if it is true or false. Throw out the false ones.

A) Looking at the 2 on the bottom we see two dots above it. A 9th grader and an 11th grader. FALSE

B) How many dots are to the left of the 4? We should get 5. Is that half of 16? FALSE

C) There are 3 12th graders who travel 6 or more miles to school. There are 2 11th graders who travel 6 or more miles to school. TRUE This is the answer but we will test the others just for completeness.

D) There is a 10th grader who travels only 1 mile to school. So not ALL of the less that 3 mile travelers are seniors. FALSE

E) Two 9th graders travel 7 or more mils to school. 5 students total travel 7 or more miles to school. Is 2 half of 5? FALSE

13. **Choice A** is correct. Each number must look like 3?4 since we have very strict rules. But we may put any digit in the place of the question mark. How many digits can be used? 10, which gives us the answer.

Last third - hard

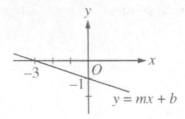

14. **Choice D** is correct. For the original line with equation $y = mx + b$, the b is -1 since that is where it crosses the y-axis. The new line is $y = -3mx + b$. It has the same $-$intercept. Cross off B, C and E since they don't cross the y-axis at -1. The slope of the old line is down 1 over 3 which makes $m = -\frac{1}{3}$. The slope of the new line is $-3m$ as read from the equation. $-3m = -3(-\frac{1}{3}) = 1$. Of the two answers left, D has a slope of 1.

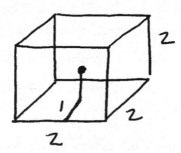

15. **Choice A** is correct. If the volume of the cube is 8 then the edge of the cube is 2. ($2^3 = 8$) So, from the middle of the cube down to the bottom is half the length of an edge. Half of 2 is 1.

16. **Choice E** is correct. Let $x = 1$ and $z = 1$. Then $y = \dfrac{5(1^3)}{1} = 5$. When both x and z are doubled we get

$y = \dfrac{5(2^3)}{2} = 20$ Multiplying by 4 best describes how to go from 5 to 20.

17. **Choice B** is correct. We only have to plug in their answers to see which one works. Start with C.

C) $V(3) = 5000 * (0.8 \wedge 3) = 2560$ WRONG and too low.

B) $V(2) = 5000 * (0.8 \wedge 2) = 3200$ Success

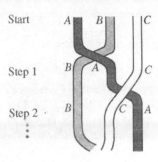

18. **Choice D** is correct. Continue the process

    Step 3 Left over gives C B A

    Step 4 Right over gives C A B

    Step 5 Left over gives A C B

    Step 6 Right over gives A B C Success

19. **Choice E** is correct. Test each of their answers looking to find something the affects what the middle

    number in the ordered list is.

    A) Doubling each number keeps them in the same order. Now the median is twice as large. WRONG

    B) Increasing each number again keeps them in the same order. But it increases the median by 10. WRONG

    C) Increasing the smallest number might keep it in the same position or, if you increased it to past the

    highest nuber then the new median is one past the old median. WRONG

    D) Decreasing the largest number runs the same risk as increasing the smallest number. WRONG

    E) Increasing the largest number only means that all the others stayed the same. What was the largest

    number is still the largest number. All the numbers are in the same places so the median is still the same.

    Success

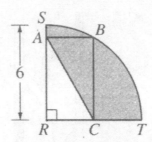

20. **Choice B** is correct. The perimeter of the shaded region is the sum of the straight lines plus the quarter-circle. The quarter circle is easy to find. It is one-fourth of the circumference of the circle.

$0.25 * 2 * 6 * \pi = 3\pi$. Cross of D and E since they have the wrong quarter circle measurement. The straight parts are a bit harder. We are told that the length plus the width of the rectangle is 8. SA + CT can be thought of as two radii minus a width and a length of the rectangle. $6 + 6 - 8 = 4$. So far we have $4 + 3\pi + AC$. How to find the AC? Lets look at the answers the SAT writes gave us.

A) $8 + 3\pi$ We already have $4 + 3\pi + AC$ so AC has to be 4 if this answer is correct? The diagram is to scale. Does it look like 4? Use the edge of your answer paper to compare the radius o 6 with the length of AC. They look the same! $AC = 6$ is a good approximation. That means that $4 + 3\pi + AC = 4 + 3\pi + 6 = 10 + 3\pi$ B is the answer.

Geometry Method: We are trying to find AC. It is a diagonal of the rectangle. In a rectangle both diagonals have the same length so $AC = RB$. But RB is a radius of the circle so it has length 6.

Section 9

16 questions – first third - easy

.1 **Choice A** is correct. We need to find a value that makes $3m - 1 > 10$. It must be one of their answers. We want m big so use the biggest value they give.

A) $3 * 4 - 1 = 11 > 10$ Got it!

2. **Choice D** is correct. Try their values starting with C

C) $a * 0 = a$ Is this always true? WRONG

D) $a * 1 = a$ Is this always true? Success

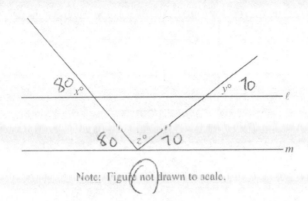

Note: Figure not drawn to scale.

3. **Choice A** is correct. Mark 80° by x and 70° by y. With parallel lines cut by a third line all the little angles are the same size. So mark the 70° and 80° where they belong next to the z. Doesn't look very difficult now! $80 + 70 + z = 180$ Subtraction gives us $z = 30$.

4. **Choice C** is correct. Mia went one direct distance and one scenic distance. A scenic distance is a direct distance plus 5 km. So Mia went a direct distance plus a direct distance plus 5 km. In math language it would be $d + (d + 5) = 35$. Solving this gives $d = 15$

5. **Choice B** is correct. The probability can be written as the time it is not red over the total time or $50 / 80$ which reduces to $5 / 8$

Second third - medium

6. **Choice B** is correct. The English "heating expenses *is directly proportional to* water temperature" gives the simple formula $h = kt$ where h is the *h*eating expenses, t is the water *t*emperature and k is a constant that we need to figure out. The first pair will help us figure this out. $24 = k * 20$ or

$k = 24 / 20 = 1.2$ which makes the formula

$h = 1.2t$.

We are now asked for the expenses when the temperature is 15.

$h = 1.2 * 15 = 18$

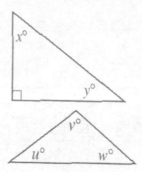

7. **Choice E is correct.** To find the average we need to find the sum of all the angles and divide by 5.

$x + y = 90$ because this is a right triangle. $u + v + w = 180$ because these are all the angles of the triangle. So

$x + y + u + v + w = 90 + 180 = 270$ which is the total of the 5 angles. The average is $270 / 5 = 54$

8. **Choice C is correct.** x^2 is a positive number. Since x is on the right side of a positive number then it is also positive. Cross off A and B since they aren't positive.

If $x = 1$ the $x^2 = 1$ and the two values would be on the same point. Cross off D.

If $x = 1.5$ then $x^2 = 2.25$ and would be on the right side of x. Cross off E.

If $x = 0.75$ then $x^2 = 0.5625$ and would be on the left side of x. It is. Now check for the cube. . $x^3 = 0.4218$ which is further left again. It is. Success.

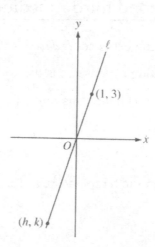

9. **Choice A is correct.** It doesn't seem to matter where on the line the point (h, k) is located since we are not told anything else about it. It could be down 3 back 1 from the Origin. That would make it $(-1, -3)$ and we are being asked to find $k / h = -3 / -1 = 3$. That is one of the given answers. It is also the slope.

10. **Choice E is correct.** Solve for m and k.

$|m-3|=5$ has two answers. $m-3=5$ is one. Solve and we get $m=8$. It works but we were told that $m<0$ so this isn't the number the SAT people had in mind. The other answer is $m-3=-5$. In this case the absolute value would make the -5 into $+5$. $m-3=-5$ means $m=-2$. That is the one they wanted.

$|k+7|=15$ also has 2 solutions. They are 8 and -22. They are found the same way as the last problem. The SAT writers want us to use the negative one here too.

Find the value they want. $m-k=-2-(-22)=20$

11. **Choice C is correct.** Going down is getting slower by half. Then going up is getting faster by doubling. Lets start with a speed we pick.

20W has a speed of 1 (We picked this ☺)

15W is twice as fast so it has a speed of 2.

10W is twice as fast again so it has a speed of 4

5W is twice as fast again so it is now 8 times as fast as 20W.

Last third - hard

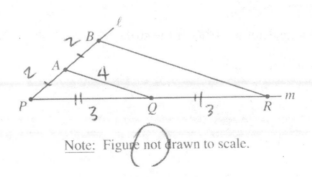

Note: Figure not drawn to scale.

12. **Choice E is correct.** Putting the info into the diagram helps. Since P, A and B are equally spaced then A is the midpoint. So each side is half of the given 4. Likewise we put in the 3's on the bottom. To find the perimeter we add up the sides. $P=2+4+3+BR$. How much is BR? The figure is not drawn to scale so we can't measure it. A geometry rule comes to the rescue here. When you connect the midpoints of two sides of a triangle then that segment is parallel to the third side and half the length of it. Since the connection of the midpoints is 4, the third side is 8. We have $BR=8$ and $P=17$.

Another Way: Don't remember that nice geometry rule? We can do it by similar triangles. The little triangle PAQ is similar to the big triangle PBR. $PB=2PA$ so all the big triangle sides are twice the small triangle sides.

13. **Choice D** is correct. Follow the function rules. $g(5) = 5^2 + 5 = 30$ and $h(4) = 4^2 - 4 = 12$.

$g(5) - h(4) = 30 - 12 = 18$

14. **Choice A** is correct. Follow the same rules as the last problem but this time we pick our own number to use. Then we check the answers. We can be cute when we pick a number. Let $m = 3$ so $h(3+1) = h(4)$ which we have already found as 12. Now to test their answers to find the 12.

A) $g(3) = 3^2 + 3 = 12$ Possible

B) $g(3) + 1 = 3^2 + 3 + 1 = 13$ WRONG

C) $g(3) - 1 = 3^2 + 3 - 1 = 11$ WRONG

D) $h(3) + 1 = 3^2 - 3 + 1 = 7$ WRONG

E) $h(3) - 1 = 3^2 - 3 - 1 = 5$ WRONG

Only A remains

15. **Choice B** is correct. The store cost plus 40% of the store cost is $28. How much is the store cost?

$c + 0.4c = 28$ Combine the c's

$1.4c = 28$ Divide both sides by 1.4

$c = 28 / 1.4 = 20$ So the store cost is $20.

Employees can purchase this sweater at 30% off the store cost. $0.30 * 20 = 6$ so they get $6 off the $20 store price. That makes the price $14.

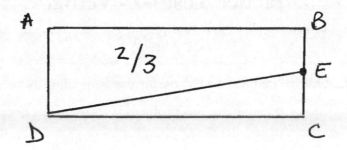

16. **Choice C** is correct. Make a quick sketch of the info. Rectangle with midpoint E on BC. The area of ABED is 2/3. The whole area has to be larger than 2/3 so cross off A. By looking at it the area isn't lots more than 2/3 so cross off E. We seem to be missing the height of the rectangle. Let's put our own height in and work out the width. Let $h = 1$ to make the arithmetic simple. Write the 1 in the diagram. ABED is a trapezoid. (One pair of sides parallel and the other not parallel.) The formula for the area of a trapezoid is not given in the front of the test. We have to remember it. In words it is half the sum of the bases times the height. $\frac{1}{2}(b_1 + b_2)h$. We know the height of 1 but what about the bases. We do know that E is a midpoint. So the bottom base is twice the top base. Make them x and $2x$ and put it into the formula.

$\frac{1}{2}(x + 2x)1 = \frac{2}{3}$ Simplify

$\frac{1}{2}(3x) = \frac{2}{3}$

$\frac{3}{2}x = \frac{2}{3}$ Multiply both sides by $\frac{2}{3}$ and get $x = \frac{4}{9}$

But this is the smaller base. The rectangle has $2x$ as its length. That means the rectangle has length $8/9$ and width 1. That makes the area $8/9$.

Practice Test #7 - Verbal

Section 3

1. **Choice B** is correct. The phrase "that was when" means the same thing as "while" and, therefore, is both redundant and awkward. Choice B eliminates this problem. C is incorrect because the passive voice is used. Both D and E are incorrect because the subject must be "Mother Teresa" not her "profound love".

2. **Choice B** is correct. The original sentence is a run-on sentence because it contains two independent clauses but does not have **both** a comma **and** a coordinating conjunction. Choice B eliminates "and they would" and makes it more concise. C, D and E are all incorrect because of awkward "ing" construction.

3. **Choice D** is correct. The original sentence is incomplete as it stands. In order to correct it one must replace "using" with "used" because we are talking about an action in the past.

4. **Choice D** is correct. The problem here is agreement in number. The singular subject "one" requires the singular verb "was" not "were". This eliminates A and C. Choice D is correct. because "something _was_ wrong" is grammatically correct. E in incorrect because the meaning of the sentence is very different than what was intended.

5. **Choice E** is correct. The original sentence is simply too wordy. B is incorrect because it changes the meaning of the sentence. We don't know if the programmers had the "least" amount of work, only "less". When writing, get to the point! E is short and to the point.

6. **Choice E** is correct. We have an incorrect comparison here. "Audiences" must be compared with "audiences" not decades as the original does.

7. **Choice A** is correct. The original sentence is grammatically correct.

8. **Choice D** is correct. The problem here is with parallelism. The phrase "_in_ poetry" should be complemented by "_in_ either…".

9. **Choice B** is correct. The phrase "is the reason why" is extraneous and unnecessary and makes the sentence awkward. Choice B communicates the idea concisely and correctly. The other choices are awkward.

10. **Choice A** is correct. The original sentence is correct. as it stands.

11. **Choice E** is correct. The phrase "since such is the case" is wordy and awkward. The simple phrase "and so" or words such as "hence" or "therefore" would do nicely.

12. **Choice C** contains the error. The past participle of write is "had written" not "had wrote".

13. **Choice C** contains the error. The phrase "more busy" is the correct one.

14. **Choice B** contains the error. The plural subject "shepherds" requires the plural verb "are".

15. **Choice B** contains the error. The pronoun "which" is not appropriate when referring to people. It should be replaced by "who".

16. **Choice E** is correct. There is no error in this sentence.

17. **Choice E** is correct. There is no error in this sentence.

18. **Choice B** contains the error. The plural subject "species" requires the plural verb "are".

19. **Choice B** contains the error. The singular pronoun "this" cannot modify "signs" as it does in the original sentence. The word "these" needs to replace it in order to be correct.

20. **Choice A** contains the error. The phrase "has to imitate" complements the later verb phrase "attempts to reveal" because they are the same tense.

21. **Choice B** contains the error. The plural subject "nations" requires the plural verb "have issued". By lifting out the phrase set off by commas, it becomes easier to see the correct agreement.

22. **Choice C** contains the error. The lack of parallelism is the problem here. The series is "familiarized young people" and "taught them" and should be "*gave* them the opportunity" instead of "they had the opportunity".

23. **Choice A** contains the error. The singular subject "Observation" requires the singular verb "shows" not "show".

24. **Choice A** contains the error. The phrase "far *away* from" should only be used when referring to actual distances between two objects. The correct phrase here should be "far from".

25. **Choice B** contains the error. Because Yellowstone continues to be a "sociological laboratory", the verb "was" should be changed to "has been" in order to be correct.

© 2009 Master Learning Strategies Inc.

26. **Choice C** contains the error. The proper phrase here is "inconsistent _with_ those he made" not "…inconsistent _to_ those…"

27. **Choice D** contains the error. When only two attributes or objects are being compared, the word "more" not the superlative "most" should be used. The word "most" should be used if three or more are compared.

28. **Choice A** contains the error. "I" is a subject and not an object as it is being used here. "Me" is an object and should, therefore, have been used here.

29. **Choice E** is correct. There is no error is this sentence.

30. **Choice A** is correct. The sentence is grammatically correct as is.

31. **Choice D** is correct. Typically when one writes, he or she is looking for the most concise way to express himself or herself. Choice D does so nicely.

32. **Choice D** is correct. If we are looking for a sentence which links sentence 10 to the rest of the paragraph, the question we need to ask ourselves is, "what does the rest of the paragraph say?" The second paragraph enumerates a series of Lou Hoover's accomplishments. A sentence linking these should refer to them in some way. Choice D is, therefore, the best answer.

33. **Choice A** is correct. The sentence as it stands is not a sentence because it is incomplete. Changing "being" to "was" inserts a verb, in the appropriate tense, which makes the sentence correct.

34. **Choice B** is correct. As the passage now stands, these sentences, because they refer to diverse events, are very disjointed. The should be linked together so the flow is smoother. Choice B is the best way to do so.

35. **Choice B** is correct. Sentence 15 deals with Hoover's advocacy for African American rights which clearly was something well ahead of its time. It was not until the Civil Rights movement of the 1960's that this topic became more prominent in political circles.

Section 4

1. **Choice E** is correct. This sentence indicates a sequence of events with the use of the words "initially" and "eventually". First, a carpet would be "drenched", then the "hallway flooded".

2. **Choice B** is correct. The key context clue here is "advantages and disadvantages". The first blank will be a positive attribute and the second a negative one. Both B and C will work for the first blank because "maintaining or retaining" body heat is an advantage. However, the nests being "vulnerable" not "immune" to predators is a disadvantage.

3. **Choice C** is correct. The blank is defined by the qualifier "pathological" and the phrase "knowing every detail". "Pathological" means abnormal. The only real possibility here is "curiosity".

4. **Choice E** is correct. The word "despite" indicates a contrast. The second blank is easier to determine. If malaria still affects millions of people per year it clearly must be uninhibited. This eliminates A and C. "Thrive", "prosper" and "flourish" all fit the second blank. The first blank must be the opposite, however, and "eradicate" is the best response since it means to completely destroy.

5. **Choice B** is correct. The word "Although" indicates a contrast in the sentence. If the movie was "condemned" by a review panel, it would be so because of something deemed harmful. The word "innocuous" (harmless) would be the appropriate antonym.

6. **Choice B** is correct. The phrase following the comma defines the blank. An "indomitable" person is one who cannot be dominated or who "prevails against all odds."

7. **Choice A** is correct. Again, the word "although" indicates a contrast. The first blank is easy to determine. If the company stayed in business *despite* something, then it must have been either "insolvent" (having liabilities in excess of assets) or "bankrupt" (out of money). It must have been afloat only by some *illegal* activity. The term "fraudulent" (deceptive, illegal) fits the bill.

8. **Choice B** is correct. The phrase "overweening pride" is the context clue and defines the blank. "Hubris" (pride) is the correct choice. "Obstinacy" (stubbornness) nor "impetuosity" (rashness) nor "valor" (courage) nor "callousness" (hardness) fit.

9. **Choice B** is correct. Both allude to the personal loss Clemens experienced.

10. **Choice B** is correct. The key clue in lines 7-11 is the phrase "a slow process of incubation" which indicates "gradual development".

11. **Choice E** is correct. The author of Passage 2 would say that the personal losses enumerated in Passage 1 help Clemens "transform them into a culminating work of art". Choice E is, therefore, the best response.

12. **Choice D** is correct. The author of Passage 1 would disagree with the conclusions of the author of Passage 2. Lines 5-11 indicate that "public events" influenced Clemens more.

13. **Choice E** is correct. This passage is a "personal account" of an experience of a neurologist. It is also inductive. That is, when one takes a specific incident and makes "general observations" as opposed to a deductive approach going from general to specific.

14. **Choice C** is correct. The term "strongly" here suggests "the difficulties he had to overcome" or else he would not have used the term at all.

15. **Choice A** is correct. The author's remarks here are "conjecture" (hypothesizing) because he indicates in line 22 "...of which I know nothing..." that the mechanics of what takes place in the brain is beyond his understanding.

16. **Choice D** is correct. The imaging techniques were "crude" or lacking in detail or "underdeveloped".

17. **Choice E** is correct. The parenthetical statement illustrates what preceded it, namely, "most have occurred by themselves, unconsciously...". "Unconscious adaptation" is being described here.

18. **Choice D** is correct. Although the surgeon suggests that there are some general rules or guidelines for all, how one learns to cope is an individual thing.

19. **Choice C** is correct. Line 39 clearly indicates that the therapist assumes that "all neurologists are aware" of the adaptability of the nervous system.

20. **Choice D** is correct. The term "richness" is followed in the text by the descriptor "endless diversity". This defines "richness" as "variety".

21. **Choice A** is correct. The author mentions here that he is a physician because he had just given the perspective of a physicist and he wanted to contrast their points of view.

22. **Choice B** is correct. Lines 49-54 include the idea of "growth and evolution" as positive things which can come out of disease and that's why we can redefine the "norm".

23. **Choice C** is correct. In these lines the author speaks of "radical adaptations" that can occur in the brain which argues against those who believe that the brain is "inflexible and unchanging".

24. **Choice E** is correct. The main point of the passage is that the brain adapts to each individual's needs dependent upon the "abnormality". This implies a "virtually limitless" ability to adapt.

Section 6

1. **Choice D** is correct. The construction of the sentence indicates a direct relationship between the two blanks. If her career spanned the years 1929-1994, clearly that was a "lengthy" one by anyone's estimation. The term "lasted" fits the second blank perfectly.

2. **Choice C** is correct. If recent date of a "phenomenal" dive were recorded, it would be strong evidence that such whales are "among the sea's deepest divers". It would, therefore, "confirm" (validate) these "speculations" (hypotheses).

3. **Choice D** is correct. The second blank is easier to determine. "Wild" (uncontrolled) is in series with this blank and "impulsive" would be the best synonym. The first blank would be opposite this. To live circumspect or "circumscribed" lives would be ones of upright living.

4. **Choice E** is correct. The phrase "new evidence" indicates a contrast or shift in the flow of the sentence. A and B can be eliminated immediately. The second blank must be the opposite of "declining" and can only be "thriving", Choice E.

5. **Choice E** is correct. The phrase following the comma defines the blank. Management was interested in the "near" rather than the "far" consequences. The term "myopic" (near-sighted) fits best. "Irresolute" (not determined) nor "officious" (hard-working) nor "rancorous" (argumentative) nor "punctilious" (attentive to detail) fit.

6. **Choice C** is correct. After reading his book and seeing the pictures one would quite naturally "conjure up" or "imagine" Flaubert in that setting.

7. **Choice A** is correct. The term "affected" means abnormal. The description of Flaubert, head-shaven, dressed in a tarboosh, reading poetry in a temple and being bored, certainly seems like an "affected manner".

8. **Choice A** is correct. If something is "broken down to a bare minimum", everything that is extraneous is stripped away and only the essential elements are left. The point in this passage is to "accentuate selected information" so that it is "easier on the eyes".

© 2009 Master Learning Strategies Inc.

9. **Choice C** is correct. The phrase "maps of perception" in line 8 is immediately followed by a colon, indicating that what follows the colon is an explanation of that peculiar phrase. "…how perception filters and maps…torrents of information…" is a "model of how humans process what they encounter."

10. **Choice E** is correct. The purpose of the first paragraph of any passage is to establish the topic and set the tone of the passage. Lines 4-10 give specific examples of "different kinds of resistance" to the story of Black women.

11. **Choice A** is correct. The first sentence of the second paragraph is a straightforward declaration or "assertion". It is not an apology or criticism or anything else.

12. **Choice D** is correct. The chemical analogy is used to indicate and "interaction which produces a unique perspective." Line 19 and 20 suggest a "combination, not just a mixture" meaning that the ingredients don't remain separate but are "transformed" or make something new (unique).

13. **Choice B** is correct. If anything is seen as "threatening" or makes people "feel nervous and guilty", anything which diminishes these feelings would be viewed as "calculated self-interest".

14. **Choice D** is correct. The phrase "sad situation" begins the fourth paragraph and goes on to describe the erroneous idea that unity and loyalty depend upon absolute homogeneity (line 34). Choice D is, therefore, the best response.

15. **Choice E** is correct. Lines 37-39 indicate the position someone would take who believed they have the higher moral ground. This tone would be considered "admonishing". No other choice applies.

16. **Choice A** is correct. Brown indicates in lines 49-50 that listening to millions of voices at once can be confusing but silencing even one would be dangerous. This clearly indicates "multiplicity and inclusion".

17. **Choice B** is correct. The author indicates in line 3 that government offices are "readily moved to wrath" and so, does not mention the name of the department. Fear of "repercussions" is his reason.

18. **Choice C** is correct. Line 21 is preceded by a description of a number of higher ranking officials coming and going. Akakyevitch, on the other hand, is the "perpetual" clerk who is "always seen in the same place, at the very same duty". This indicates that the people in the office "could not imagine" anyone else replacing him or Akaky acting any other way than he did.

19. **Choice D** is correct. The phrase "simple fly" is preceded by the phrase "took no more notice of him". This indicates that he is "easily overlooked".

20. **Choice A** is correct. The phrase "without even saying" implies that these statements are civilities which would be "typical" in an office of any governmental department.

21. **Choice C** is correct. The word "stories" in this context would simply mean lies. The word "fabrication" is a fancy word for lie.

22. **Choice A** is correct. The is not a lot of evidence for the author's attitude toward the young clerks. We must, therefore, do our best to eliminate choices. There is no mention of "their disrespect for supervisors" nor of their "laziness" nor "their lack of challenge". This leaves only A and E as possibilities. Although neither is explicitly clear, it seems that the tone is one of compassion toward Akakyevitch. The "I am your brother" remark of the new clerk and the good-natured director who was "anxious to reward him" would be evidence of this.

23. **Choice E** is correct. See the previous answer.

24. **Choice E** is correct. Because the different assignment completely threw Akaky for a loop, it can be inferred that he feared greater responsibility. No other choice is supported by the text.

Section 9

1. **Choice B** is correct. If traffic congestion is a problem, the solution must somehow try to reduce it. The term "alleviate" means to lessen and is the best response. The other choices are self-explanatory.

2. **Choice D** is correct. The term "though" indicates a contrast. The answer must be the opposite of "quite disturbed" which would be "serene" (peaceful).

3. **Choice B** is correct. The flow of this sentence indicates a contrast, thus, the first blank will be the opposite of the second. The second blank is easier to find. What would we expect rulers would "usually" do with respect to expressing their personal thoughts? We would expect them to be secretive or to "play their cards close to the vest". The word that jumps off the list of the second choices is "reserved". No other word fits at all. Is "forthrightness" the opposite of "reserved"? Absolutely.

4. **Choice E** is correct. The key clue here is the word "but", which indicates a contrast. The second blank should be easier for us to find. Insufficient rainfall would have a very adverse affect on the land. The best and only real possibility is that the land was "denuded" (stripped). Although "despoiled" and "debilitated" are negative terms, neither would be used to describe land. The term "imprudent" (unwise) would be a perfect fit in the first blank.

5. **Choice A** is correct. The key word here is "usually" and sets up a contrast. If cathedrals "usually" take a very long time to build, no one would expect this one to be built *quickly*. The phrase "with dispatch" means speedily. The word "presumption" (audacity, assumption) nor "durability" (long lasting) nor "deliberation" (slowly, carefully) nor "reverence" (sacredness) fit.

6. **Choice B** is correct. The word "eclectic" (combination of diverse things) is a key clue, and is synonymous with the answer considering the diversity of the description of the clothes.

7. **Choice E** is correct. Both of the lines cited illustrate the professional artists with which the authors had direct personal experience. "Range" or "appreciation" or "views of quality" are not mentioned in the passages.

8. **Choice D** is correct. The evidence for this answer is found in the text. In lines 14-16, the author of Passage 1 states "A songwriter makes nothing until a song is marketed in the form of a recording for sale to the public." The author of Passage 2 in lines 64-66 indicates "…fans still went out and bought records…" Both agree that "commercial sales are necessary."

9. **Choice A** is correct. The "gamble" is defined in the next line when the author speaks of "marketing" and "sales". It must be a "financial" gamble.

10. **Choice A** is correct. Though both agree commercial sales are their "bread and butter", they disagree on the effect of free downloading. The author of Passage 2 believes that in the "long run", free downloading will lead to greater popularity and greater commercial sales. Thus, he would consider author 1 "shortsighted".

11. **Choice C** is correct. Here the author relates a very *practical* result of free downloading. If he does not receive the royalties he deserves, he must get a "regular" job and will not have the time to be creative and write more songs. The word "pragmatic" means practical.

12. **Choice D** is correct. An example of the author's "fear" is found in the very same sentence. "…the seventeen year old songwriter looking forward…". Choice D is the obvious response.

13. **Choice E** is correct. The main thrust of Passage 1 is that free downloading is a practice which is akin to thievery and should be stopped. So, he is "arguing against this practice." None of the other choices are supported by the text.

14. **Choice D** is correct. The quotation marks indicate the pretense of accepting the opposite point of view of the author and show that he is not inclined to believe that point of view.

15. **Choice C** is correct. The phrase "pretty decent creative work" is followed a list of some of the most powerful and creative minds throughout all of history. The author is obviously using "ironic understatement" here.

16. **Choice E** is correct. The author of Passage 2 does not believe that Napsterians are stealing, so this sentence would be "satirical." The word "ebullient" (joyful) nor "somber" (mournful) nor "quizzical" (puzzling) nor "irate" (angry) fit.

17. **Choice A** is correct. The phrase "marketing virus" in this context is a positive one because this author learned by accident, along with the Grateful Dead, that free recording and distribution of videos of their concerts spread their fame and actually *boosted* sales of their albums. This spread like a "virus" but it clearly was a *positive* result unlike most viruses.

18. **Choice B** is correct. The author discusses VCR's and software as parallel examples whose sales have benefited from "unauthorized" copying of their material. He is using this information (along with statistics) to strengthen or "bolster" his primary argument.

19. **Choice C** is correct. The author of Passage 2 would come to the opposite conclusion of author 1. Whereas the first author thought he would not "make it", the second would contend that his fame would spread ("increased renown").

Section 10

1. **Choice B** is correct. The phrase "so that" is incorrect because it is synonymous with "therefore", indicating a cause and effect relationship which does not exist. Changing "so that" to "because" makes the sentence intelligible.

2. **Choice A** is correct. The original sentence is grammatically correct.

3. **Choice D** is correct. The original sentence is incorrect because it is incomplete. The verb "maintaining" must be changed to "maintain" to make any sense. This eliminates A, B and E. Choice C is incorrect because "and" is an inappropriate conjunction here. The word "by" is necessary to give the reason why sales of exports will increase.

4. **Choice D** is correct. The original sentence is far too roundabout and awkward. In addition, "actions" and "behaves" mean the same thing. A direct, concise way of communicating the idea is necessary and Choice D does this best.

5. **Choice D** is correct. The original sentence is incorrect because women cannot become "professions" but people in professions, commonly known as "professionals".

6. **Choice C** is correct. The original sentence is a run-on sentence. What follows the comma is a completely distinct idea and cannot be separated by a comma. Choice C makes a smooth transition which is grammatically correct.

7. **Choice B** is correct. The problem with the sentence as it stands is one of verb tense. The first part of the sentence is in the past, whereas, the verb "will spend" is in the future and incompatible. The verb "would spend" is in the past and agrees with "stimulated".

8. **Choice C** is correct. The original sentence is confusing. In addition, the word "as" is insufficient to join these two clauses. Choice C clarifies the idea and smoothly communicates it best.

9. **Choice D** is correct. The pronoun "you" incorrectly modifies "someone" It should be "he or she".

10. **Choice D** is correct. The original sentence is incorrect because "Brought to…education" modifies "his first book" which is not the idea to be communicated. "Lee" should, therefore, immediately follow the comma. This eliminates A and C. Choice D is the most concise.

11. **Choice C** is correct. The original sentence is confusing because we do not know to whom the "she" refers. Choice C correctly clarifies that it is her mother and not the daughter.

12. **Choice A** is correct. The original sentence is grammatically correct.

13. **Choice B** is correct. In the original sentence we have a shift in the subject from "we" to "impressions". Choice B keeps "we" as the subject performing the actions of reading and evaluating.

© 2009 Master Learning Strategies Inc.

14. **Choice D** is correct. The original sentence is incorrect because there is flawed comparison. As it stands, the sentence compares "songs" to "birds". The songs of the whales can only be compared to the songs of the birds. Choice D does this best.

Practice Test #7 - Math

Section 2
8 questions – first third - easy

1. **Choice A** is correct. "… are *also in* set Y?" Look at each member in set X and see if it is set Y. Count it only if the answer is yes. 30 – No; 31 – No; 32 – Yes; 33 – Yes. There are two in both sets.

2. **Choice C** is correct. Linda traveled twice as far so she traveled 20 miles. She took half the time so she took 1 hour. She traveled 20 miles in 1 hour.

3. **Choice C** is correct. Plug in our own numbers. Let $k = 3$. Then $x = 3(3-2) = 3$. We need to check their answers for the value $x + 1 = 4$

   A) $3^2 - 3 = 6$ WRONG   B) $3^2 - 3 * 3 = 0$ WRONG

   C) $3^2 - 2 * 3 + 1 = 4$ D) $3^2 + 6 + 1 = 16$ WRONG

   E) $3^2 - 1 = 8$ WRONG   Only C remains

Second third - medium

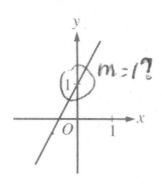

4. **Choice B** is correct. In $y = ax + b$, b is where the graph crosses the y-axis. In the graph that value is 1. In $y = 2ax + b$ the y-intercept is this same value. Cross off any graph that does NOT cross the y-axis at 1. A, D and E should be crossed off. The original graph has a slope that seems to be near 1. It might be a little bigger but it is close to 1. So a is 1 or a little bigger. $2a$ would be 2 or a little bigger. Which of the two remaining graphs have a slope that is at least 2? C looks flatter that the original graph so it has a slope closer to 0. Cross it off. Only B remains

5. **Choice A is correct.** To find the perimeter we need to find the length of the hypotenuse. Mr. Pythagoras can help. $c^2 = x^2 + x^2$ or $c = \sqrt{2x^2}$. So the perimeter is $2x + \sqrt{2x^2}$. Math types can simplify this but we don't have to do that. Let's also approximate the perimeter they gave us. $4 + 2\sqrt{2} \approx 6.83$. The answers given aren't in order so we might as well start with A.

   A) $2*2 + \sqrt{2*2^2} = 4 + \sqrt{8} \approx 6.83$ Got it.

6. **Choice C is correct.** With 17 students the median will be at position 9. That makes 8 smaller scores and 8 larger scores. When Sam takes the test we will need to change the number of students who got a 95 to 3. Let's start counting. 1 + 3 = 4 so 4 students got 95 or above. 4 + 4 = 8 so 8 students got 90 or above. Remember we need the 9th position. The next student down will be the median score. That 9th position is an 85.

Last third - hard

---

7. Choice D is correct. Put our own numbers in here. What shall we put in for x? 16 containers hold a total of x gallons. Perhaps $x = 32$ would be good since that makes each container hold 2 gallons. Now the other 8 containers also hold this same 32 gallons. That makes them 4 gallons each. These are the larger containers and they hold 4 gallons when $x = 32$

   A) $4*32 = 128 = 4$ WRONG   B) $2*32 = 64 = 4$ WRONG

   C) $32/2 = 16 = 4$ WRONG   D) $32/8 = 14$ Possible

   E) $32/16 = 2 = 4$ WRONG   Only D remains

8. **Choice D** is correct. This is supposed to work for *any* rectangle that is not parallel to the axes. We know that when we multiply the slopes of perpendicular lines we get −1. So let's make a rectangle with one of the sides having slope 1. Both of the adjoining sides have slope −1. And the fourth side is parallel to our original side so it has slope 1. Now we multiply these four numbers. $1*(-1)*(-1)*1 = 1$

---

10 questions – first third - easy

9. **Choice 2/3, .666 OR .667** is correct. One hour has 60 minutes. If 20 minutes were commercials then 40 minutes were NOT commercials. The fraction that was not commercials is $40/60 = 0.66666$

10. **Choice 10/3 OR 3.33** is correct. "Product" means to multiply. As an equation we have $0.3x = 1$ Divide both sides by 0.3. $x = 1/0.3 = 3.3333$

11. **Choice 875** is correct. This is an SAT function problem. Let's look at the positions of the numbers. The y is on the top of the triangle. In the expression it is both exponents. We need to remember to "put the top on the top." x is on the left of the triangle and the left of the expression. y is on the right in both. This makes the value $10^3 - 5^3$. Don't try to simplify. Put it into our calculator $10 \wedge 3 - 5 \wedge 3 = 875$

Second third - medium

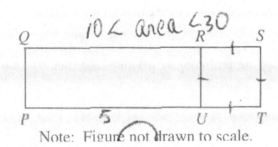

Note: Figure not drawn to scale.

12. **Choice 2 OR 3** is correct. Mark the info in the diagram. Put 5 by PU. UTSR is a square so this helps in finding the height. We need to find any one of the values possible for UT. UT is a positive integers so we shouldn't try any fractions.

$UT = 1$ means the height is 1 and the length is $5 + 1 = 6$. This makes the area $1*6 = 6$. Is this in the 10 to 30 range? WRONG.

$UT = 2$ means the height is 2 and the length is $5 + 2 = 7$. This makes the area $2*7 = 14$. Is this in the 10 to 30 range? Yes. Write it down and go to the next problem. For completeness here are the rest of the answers.

$UT = 3$ means the height is 3 and the length is $5 + 3 = 8$. This makes the area $3*8 = 24$. Is this in the 10 to 30 range? Yes

$UT = 4$ means the height is 4 and the length is $5 + 4 = 9$. This makes the area $4*9 = 36$. Is this in the 10 to 30 range? WRONG.

As UT increases the area increases. So any further increase will still be too large. No need to work any more.

13. **Choice 36** is correct. We could try to guess and check. Let's guess at the number of balloons and see if the fractions work out. One-third of the balloons are red. We have to make sure that the number of balloons is a multiple of 3. There are 18 blue balloons so we can start above that.

Let's start with 30 balloons.

$30 / 3 = 10$ red balloons. $10 / 2 = 5$ green balloons. 18 blue balloons. $10 + 5 + 18 = 33$ balloons. Not the 30 from the beginning. WRONG

Let's move up to 33 balloons

$33 / 3 = 11$ red balloons. $11 / 2 = 5.5$ green balloons. Error! Can't have half a balloon.

Continue moving up to 36 balloons.

$36 / 3 = 12$ red balloons. $12 / 2 = 6$ green balloons. 18 blue balloons. $12 + 6 + 18 = 36$ balloons. This matches so it is the answer.

Math Method: red + green + blue = total

$\frac{1}{3}b + \frac{1}{2}\left(\frac{1}{3}b\right) + 18 = b$ Multiply both sides by 6

$2b + b + 108 = 6b$ Subtract $6b$ from both sides

$108 = 3b$ Divide both sides by 3

$36 = b$

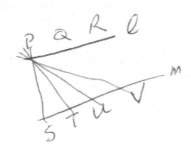

14. **Choice 12** is correct. Make a quick sketch. From P we can draw 4 lines. From Q we can draw another 4 and they are all different. And another 4 from R makes 12 lines in all.

15. **Choice 5 is correct.** We can use the guess and check method here. Find $2^7 = 2\wedge 7 = 128$

$x = 1$ gives us $2^1 = 2$ making the problem $2 + 2 + 2 + 2 = 8 = 128$ WRONG

$x = 2$ gives us $2^2 = 4$ making the problem $4 + 4 + 4 + 4 = 16 = 128$ WRONG

$x = 3$ gives us $2^3 = 8$ making the problem $8 + 8 + 8 + 8 = 32 = 128$ WRONG

$x = 4$ gives us $2^4 = 16$ making the problem $16 + 16 + 16 + 16 = 64 = 128$ WRONG

$x = 5$ gives us $2^5 = 32$ making the problem $32 + 32 + 32 + 32 = 128$ Right – Our answer

Math Method: $2^x + 2^x + 2^x + 2^x = 4 * 2^x$ So the original problem becomes $4 * 2^x = 128$ or $2^x = 32$ which

means $x = 5$

Last third - hard

16. **Choice 71 is correct.** If the average is 15 then the total of all the cards would be $5 * 15 = 75$. If four people

wrote low numbers it would allow that one person to write a high number. They have to write positive

integers. The smallest number they can write is 1. All four of them writing 1 means their total is 4. That

leaves $75 - 4 = 71$ for the high writer.

17. **Choice 10/7, 1.42 OR 1.43 is correct.** When Alice is starting to walk back, her first 10 steps get her back to

her starting spot. Now the last 7 cover the same distance as Corinne's 10 steps. Alice's steps are bigger than

Corinne's. Suppose Corinne is small and takes 1 foot steps. Then Alice takes 7 steps to cover 10 feet. That

makes her step $10 / 7 = 1.428$ The problem asks for "How many times the length of Corinne's step?" Making

Corinne take 1 foot steps makes the length of Alice's step that answer to the problem

18. **Choice 3 is correct.** Guess and check method will give us a place to start and a feel for what the problem is

asking.

$m = 1$, $f(2*1) = 2^2 + 18 = 22$, $2f(1) = 2(1^2 + 18) = 38$ Does $22 = 38$? WRONG.

$m = 2$, $f(2*2) = 4^2 + 18 = 34$, $2f(2) = 2(2^2 + 18) = 44$ Does $34 = 44$? WRONG but closer. Continue going up.

$m = 3$, $f(2*3) = 6^2 + 18 = 54$, $2f(3) = 2(3^2 + 18) = 54$ Does $54 = 54$? Success.

Math Method: $f(2m) = 2f(m)$ means

$(2m)^2 + 18 = 2(m^2 + 18)$ Simplify the expression

$4m^2 + 18 = 2m^2 + 36$ Combine like terms

$2m^2 = 18$ Divide by 2

$m^2 = 9$ gives $m = \pm 3$ but m has to be positive so $m = 3$

Section 5

20 questions – first third - easy

1. **Choice E** is correct. We are given four terms so we only have to find two more. Process is add 1 and then double.

   Fifth term: Add 1 to 30 and get 31. Double 31 and get 62.

   Sixth term: Add 1 to 62 and get 63. Double 63 and get 126.

2. **Choice E** is correct. $a(x + y) = ax + ay = 15 + ay$ 15 plus what we want is 45. We want 30.

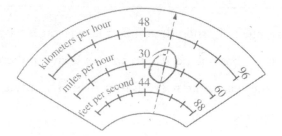

3. **Choice B** is correct. Looking at the Mile per hour mark we want to approximate the needle reading circled. By eye it looks a little less than 40. Let's find out how much each mark on the mph arc is worth. From 0 to 60 there are 8 equal sections. Each of the would be one-eighth of 60 or $60 / 8 = 7.5$. We want the reading that is one mark past 30. $30 + 7.5 = 37.5$ Success.

4. **Choice C** is correct. We can make two different numbers with a 4 in the front. (456 and 465). We can make 2 different numbers with 5 in the front and 2 more with 6 in the front. That makes 6 in all.

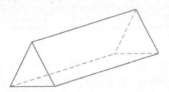

5. **Choice B** is correct. There are two triangles (the front and the back) and 3 rectangles (the bottom and the two tent sides). We can put in our own values for the areas and check their answers. $t = 7$ and $r = 5$. To find the total area we add each small piece together. So we add two triangles plus three rectangles. $2 * 7 + 3 * 5 = 29$

A) $2 * 5 + 7 = 17 = 29$ WRONG

B) $3 * 5 + 2 * 7 = 29$ Possible

C) $4 * 5 + 3 * 7 = 42 = 29$ WRONG

D) $6 * 5 * 7 = 210 = 29$ WRONG

E) $5^3 * 7^2 = 125 + 49 = 174 = 29$ WRONG

Only B remains

6. **Choice C** is correct. Plug in their answers starting with C

C) $\dfrac{3+1}{2^3} = \dfrac{4}{8} = \dfrac{1}{2}$ Success

7. **Choice E** is correct. Plug in our own numbers. $p = 2$. "The average of the weights of 14 books is 2 pounds." The total weight is then 28 ponds.

A) $14 + 2 = 16 = 28$ WRONG

B) $2 - 14 = -12 = 28$ WRONG

C) $2 / 14 = 0.14 = 28$ WRONG

D) $14 / 2 = 7 = 28$ WRONG

E) $14 * 2 = 28$ Possible

Only E remains

Second third - medium

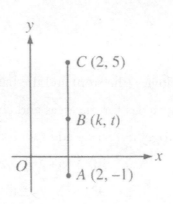

8. **Choice C** is correct. B is halfway from A to C. $AC = 6$ so halfway would be 3. 3 above −1 is 2

   Math Method: The midpoint formula for the y-coordinate is $\dfrac{y_1 + y_2}{2} = \dfrac{-1 + 5}{2} = \dfrac{4}{2} = 2$

9. **Choice B** is correct. We have a multiplication problem that is supposed to equal 0. That only happens when one of the multipliers is 0. We are given that $x > 1$. Let's look at each multiplier.

   $(2x + 3)$ If x is positive then so is $2x$. Then add 3 and it is still positive. $(2x + 3)$ is positive!

   $(x - 1)$ When $x > 1$ the $x - 1 > 0$ so $(x - 1)$ is also positive!

   k The other two factors are positive and one of the three has to be 0. this is the only one left that could be 0. So it has to be 0.

10. **Choice A** is correct. Let's look at each statement remembering that "Williams Men are all over 6 feet tall."

    A) Suppose John represents any man who is shorter than 6 feet. If John was a Williams Man then he makes the known fact false. That known fact has to stand so John can't be a Williams Man.

    B) Yao Ming is over 6 feet tall and he is not a Williams Man. Statement B is FALSE

    C) Yao Ming is not a Williams Man. He is also over 6 feet tall. Statement C is FALSE

    D) Susan Williams is 6 feet 4 inches. She is not a man. Statement D is FALSE

    E) If John Williams is 5 feet 7 inches then he violates the original know statement. Good thing he is really 6 feet 7 inches. Statement E is FALSE.

11. Choice B is correct. Test their answers starting with C. The formula for circumference is $2\pi r$

    C) $2\pi * 1 = 2\pi$ WRONG and too big.

    B) $2\pi * 0.5 = \pi$ Success

12. Choice D is correct. "...y is directly proportional to x^2" becomes the equation $y = kx^2$ Use the given values to find the value of k. $\frac{1}{8} = k\left(\frac{1}{2}\right)^2 = k\frac{1}{4}$. Multiply both sides by 4 and get $\frac{1}{2} = k$ which we put back into the equation to get $y = 0.5x^2$ Now substitute their answers to see which one works. Start with C looking for $y = 9/2 = 4.5$

C) $y = 0.5(9/4)^2 = 2.53 = 4.5$ WRONG and too small

D) $y = 0.5(3)^2 = 4.5$ Success

13. **Choice D** is correct. All the letters represent positive numbers so that makes this easier. Let's look at the first equation. $4x = 6u$. Which is bigger, x or u.? Let $x = 3$, then $4x = 12$. That makes $u = 2$ so $6u$ and equal 12. In this manor we can see that $u < x$. Look through all the answers they give us and cross off any that have x as the smaller. We get to cross off A, B and C.

Only D and E are left. Can we find a difference here? In D w is the smallest and in E u is the smallest. Let's try to see how they are related. We know that $6u = 7w$. What if they both multiplied to 42? That would mean $u = 7$ and $w = 6$. W is the smaller one. Cross off E. Only D remains

Last third - hard

14. **Choice B** is correct. A function problem! Plug in and solve. $h(t) = -60 = 2(t^3 - 3)$ divide by 2

$-30 = t^3 - 3$ Add 3

$-27 = t^3$ What is the value of t? It must be negative so test a few. $(-2)^3 = -8$. $(-3)^3 = -27$ so $t = -3$. Now plug into what they want us to find. $2 - 3t = 2 - 3(-3) = 11$

© 2009 Master Learning Strategies Inc.

15. **Choice D** is correct. Plug in our own numbers and test. Let's make it easy to start. If x is divisible by 3 let's let $x = 3$. Also if y is divisible by 5 the let $y = 5$.

I. Is $3*5 = 15$ divisible by 15? Possible

II. Is $3*3 + 5*5 = 34$ divisible by 15? WRONG

III. Is $5*3 + 3*5 = 30$ divisible by 15. Possible

Cross out C and E because they both include II which we know to be WRONG. It also looks like I and III will always work since we got so many 15s in the calculations. If time is a problem, guess D and move on. If you can afford to spend more time here is additional information.

To say that a number is divisible by 3 means that you can find some smaller integer times 3 to give you the original big number. In math speak $x = 3a$. Likewise we can consider divisible by 5 to give us $y = 5b$. Now let's look again at I and III.

I $xy = (3x)(5b) = 15ab$. We can see easily that 15 does divide this expression.

III $5x + 3y = 5(3a) + 3(5b) = 15a + 15b = 15(a+b)$ this is also divisible by 15. They do **both** work.

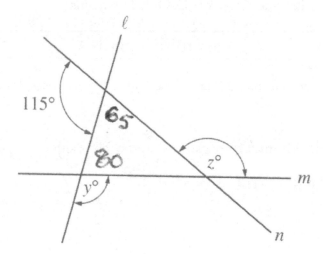

16. **Choice E** is correct. We can calculate the angle next to the 115°. Subtract from 180° and get 65°. Write it in the diagram. Can we figure anything else out? Doesn't seem like we can but the answers are all nice numbers. No variables. Let's plug in our own number for one of the angles in the triangle and see if it helps. That bottom left angle in the triangle looks a little smaller than a right angle. Write in 80 and see what we get. The third angle in the triangle would be 35 by subtraction. This makes $y = 100$ and $z = 145$.

$100 + 145 = 245$. That is one of their answers. It works for this special case so it probably works for all cases.

© 2009 Master Learning Strategies Inc.

17. **Choice D** is correct. Can we figure out what the actual number is? The three numbers add to 111 so they are all around $111/3 = 37$. 35, 37 and 39 would be the numbers. n represents the smallest of them so $n = 35$

   A) $3(35) = 105 = 111$ WRONG

   B) $3(35) + 2 = 107 = 111$ WRONG

   C) $3(35) + 4 = 109 = 111$ WRONG

   D) $3(35) + 6 = 111$ Possible

   E) $3(35) + 9 = 114 = 111$ WRONG

   Only D remains

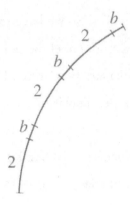

18. **Choice A** is correct. We need to find out what part of the circle a single b size arc is. There are 18 arcs of size 2 and 18 arcs of size b that total to 45. In math speak we would have $18*2 + 18b = 45$. Solving this we get $18b = 9$ or $b = 0.5$. This is $0.5/45 = 0.0111$ of the circumference. It is also that fractional part of the $360°$ around the circle. $0.0111*360 = 3.996$. This is so close to $4°$ that the difference must be round off error.

19. Choice C is correct. Next year Andrew will pay 10% more for his car. 10% of $300 is $30. So next year he will pay $330. We need to test their answers to see which one gives 330 in year 1. Start with C

   C) $300*(1.1^1) = 330$ Got it. Can it be this simple? Yes but let's look at year 2. Here Andrew pays 10% more than 330 or $33 more. That makes his bill 363. Test again for year 2. $300*(1.1^2) = 363$ Works again. It is the right answer.

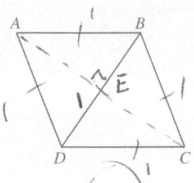

Note: Figure not drawn to scale.

20. **Choice B** is correct. Be Careful.. We want to find a ratio where the bottom number is BD. Let that be 1. All the five lengths are the same so make them all 1. So we have two equilateral triangles stuck together. We need to find AC which is not shown. Draw it in. Label the point where it hits BD as E. What does it look like AC does to BD? Does it look perpendicular? Be Careful. Does it look like it cuts it in half? Be Careful. Remember in Geometry how to make a perpendicular bisector of BD? Equal arcs from B and D cross on the top and on the bottom. Then you connect those points. If we look at the diagram we can imagine those arcs crossing at A and C. So AC is perpendicular to BD and it did cut BD in half. So $BE = 0.5$ $BE = 0.5$. Now we have the lengths two sides of a right triangle. $BE = 0.5$ and $AB = 1$. Mr. Pythagoras comes to our rescue again.

$0.5^2 + AE^2 = 1^2$ or $AE^2 = 1 - 0.5 \char`^2 = 0.75$ and $AE = 0.866$. That is also the length of EC by the same reasoning. So $AC = 1.732$ by adding both small lengths. The question asks for the ratio of $AC / BD = 1.732 / 1$ Let's check which answer gives us this ratio. The number are not in order so we can't shortcut and start with C. So we start with A.

A) $\sqrt{2} / 1 = 1.414$ WRONG

B) $\sqrt{3} / 1 = 1.732$ Success

Section 8

16 questions – first third - easy

.1 **Choice C** is correct. Divide the given equation by 100 on both sides. This gives us

$67 = 6k + 7$ subtract 7

$60 = 6k$ divide by 6

$10 = k$ which is answer C.

2. **Choice B** is correct. Plug in their numbers and see what works.

   A) 3 more than –5 is –2. It is negative. Good so far. 5 more than –5 is 0. It is not positive. WRONG

   B) 3 more than –4 is –1. It is negative. Good again. 5 more than –4 is 1. It is positive. This works. Success.

3. **Choice E** is correct. Be Careful. The dotted line bisects a 70° angle. Both of the smaller angles are half of 70. Write in 35 on each of them. We do the same thing for the 40° angle. Write in 20 for each. What is the value of x? Add the two pieces we found. $35 + 20 = 55$

4. **Choice C** is correct. Since the probability of picking an apple is 2/5, the result of multiplying the number of pieces of fruit by 2/5 has to come out as a whole number. No decimals allowed. $2/5 = 0.4$ so we could multiply each answer by 0.4 until we got a result that had a decimal part. Or we could notice that since 5 does not divide 2 it has to divide the number of pieces of fruit. Thus the number of pieces of fruit must be a multiple of 5. Either way 52 is the offending number of pieces of fruit.

5. **Choice C** is correct. The perimeter of the square is 12. The perimeter of the triangle is also 12. Each of the 3 sides must be 4 so the total is 12.

Second third - medium

6. **Choice D** is correct. It doesn't seem to matter much what the exact value of k is. It just needs to be positive. Let $k = 3$ and plug in to find the greatest value.

   A) $2(3)(-1) = -6$

   B $4(3)(-1)^2 = 12$

   C) $6(3)(-1)^3 = -18$

   D) $8(3)(-1)^4 = 24$

   E) $10(3)(-1)^5 = -30$

   24 is the largest. Perhaps we should have seen the powers of –1 and tossed out the odd powers that produced negative answers.

7. **Choice E is correct.** The order in terms of how fast she covers the distance is Slow – Fast – Medium. How steep the graph is shows the rate that she is covering the distance. Steeper graphs represent faster movement. Let's look at each graph and pick out the three speeds. Remember we want Slow – Fast – Medium as the answer.

A) Slow – Medium – Fast. WRONG

B) Medium – Fast – Slow. WRONG

C) Fast – Medium – Slow. WRONG

D) Fast – Slow – Medium. WRONG

E) Slow – Fast – Medium. Success

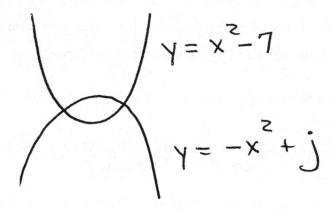

8. **Choice A is correct.** A point of intersection is a point whose coordinates work in both equations. Let's put it in and see what we get. $\left(\sqrt{6}\right)^2 - 7 = -1$ so the y-value is -1 on both graphs. Check out the other equation.

$-\left(\sqrt{6}\right)^2 + j = -1$ Simplify

$-6 + j = -1$ add 6

$j = 5$ and we have our value of .

9. **Choice A is correct.** Plug in their answers and see. Start with C

C) $|2-6| = |-4| = 4 < 3$ WRONG. Go smaller

B) $|2-5| = |-3| = 3 < 3$ WRONG but really close

A) $|2-4| = |-2| = 2 < 3$ Success

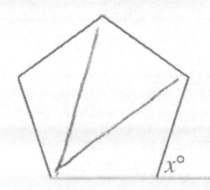

10. **Choice C is correct.** There is a short way to do this problem or a shorter way. It depends if you remember the formula for this type of problem.

   Don't Remember: Draw two diagonals from one vertex. All 5 of the original polygon angles add to the same as the 9 angles of the three triangles. The three triangles make $3*180 = 540$. So the 5 polygon angles also total 540. But all 5 are the same size so they are each $540/5 = 108$. By subtraction $x = 180 - 108 = 72$

   Do Remember: The angle shown is an exterior angle and the polygon is a "regular" polygon. That means all sides are congruent as are all angles. In this situation the size of one exterior angle is $360/n$ where n is the number of sides in the polygon. In this problem $n = 5$ so $360/5 = 72$

11. **Choice C is correct.** $3/8$ of something is 6. Plug in their answers to find the correct one. Start with C.

   C) $(3/8)*16 = 6$ Bingo! Go to the next problem

Last third - hard

12. **Choice E is correct.** The question asks what "x must be" Let's see if we can find examples to disprove the wrong answers from the SAT writers.

   A) a negative integer. Let $x = -2$, then $(-2+3)/2 = 2.5$. It doesn't work so A is WRONG

   B) a positive integer. Let $x = 2$, then $(2+3)/2 = 2.5$. It doesn't work so B is WRONG

   C) a multiple of 3. Let $x = 6$, then $(6+3)/2 = 4.5$. It doesn't work so C is WRONG

   D) an even integer. Let $x = 2$, then $(2+3)/2 = 2.5$. It doesn't work so D is WRONG

   E) an odd integer. All the others didn't work so this must be the answer. How do we check that. Look at the formula. The top starts out $(x+3)$. If x is odd then we have an odd plus an odd which gives even. Even over 2 is an integer. That's why it has to work when x is odd.

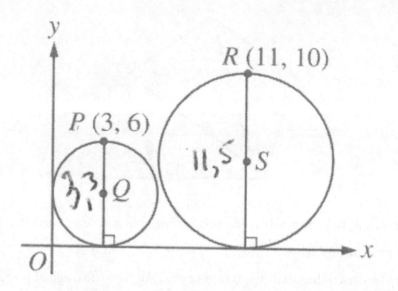

13. **Choice B** is correct. The "hard" part of this problem is figuring out what the coordinates of the points Q and S are. Look at Q. It is directly below point P. So it has the same *x*-coordinate. It goes half way down to the *x*-axis so the *y*-coordinate is half of 6. That makes the point $P(3,3)$. Similar reasoning makes the point $S(11,5)$. Slope is rise over run. The rise is $5 - 3 = 2$. The run is $11 - 3 = 8$. That makes the slope $2/8$.

14. **Choice B** is correct. We need to plug in our own numbers here. Plug in for *n* and see what *p* must be. And it must be one of the ones listed. We are told the *n* is bigger than 1.

Let's start with $n = 2$. $2 + 3 = 5$ and $2 + 10 = 12$. Does anything divide evenly both 5 and 12? No.

Next try $n = 3$. $3 + 3 = 6$ and $3 + 10 = 13$. Does anything divide evenly both 6 and 13? No.

Next try $n = 4$. $4 + 3 = 7$ and $4 + 10 = 14$. Does anything divide evenly both 7 and 14? Yes. 7. And that is one of the answers. Not as hard as they intended.

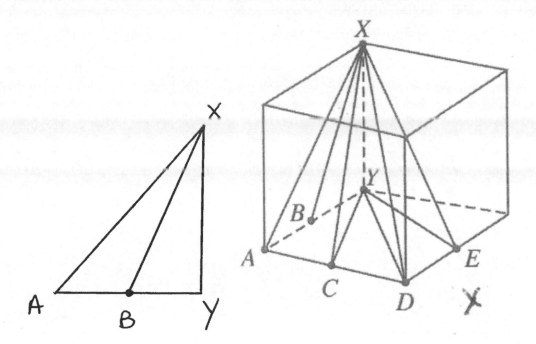

15. **Choice D** is correct. Let's first compare <XAY with <XBY. They are both on the back left side of the cube. Draw a little diagram of those angles. Which angle size is smaller? <XAY because it is in further away. We can see that the closer we get to the right angle at Y the bigger the angle becomes. Now we know that B is not the right answer. The SAT writers tried to make this problem hard by putting it in three dimensions. Then they made it easier by having all the angles be part of right triangles with one side XY. Take all those triangles and close them like the pages of a book so they are all on the back left side. All 5 triangles have the same height XY which we could think of as the spine of the book. They all have a right angle at Y. But all the third points are somewhere along the bottom edge of the book. We discovered before that the farther the angle was from Y the smaller the angle was. So we just have to find the point that is farthest from Y. We know A is further than B. How about C. Look at the original diagram. Which is farther, A or C. C it is. Now which is farther, C or D. One last point to check. Is D or E farther from Y? D again so <XDY is the smallest angle.

16. **Choice D** is correct. Sometimes problems like this become very easy if you first factor an expression that the SAT writers give you. $x^2 y - xy^2$ has two terms and they both have something in common. We can "take it out" and get a simpler expression.

$x^2 y - xy^2 = xy(x - y)$ Does that help? Yes because we know the $xy = 7$ and $x - y = 5$. Substitute them in and see what we get. $xy(x - y) = 7 * 5 = 35$ Who sweet it is when we find those hidden traps!

Practice Test #8 - Verbal

Section 3

1. **Choice C is correct.** The problem with the original sentence is two-fold. There is a lack of parallelism and awkward "ing" construction. The phrase "strongly opposed" would suggest "enthusiastically supported" to be parallel. Also, "being enthusiastic" is a construction that should be avoided.

2. **Choice D is correct.** The sentence as it stands is incomplete because it lacks a verb. Choices A, B and C can all be eliminated for the same reason. Both D and E have the verb but "and" in Choice E, without a comma, makes it a run-on sentence.

3. **Choice A is correct.** The sentence is correct. as it stands.

4. **Choice D is correct.** Choice A is incorrect because it is both wordy and confusing. To whom or what does "they" refer? Choice D is concise and straightforward.

5. **Choice E is correct.** Choice A is incorrect because "the house" is modified by "While driving" because it immediately follows the comma. Choices B and C do the same. D is incorrect because the "family's attention" is now driving.

6. **Choice D is correct.** The original sentence is incorrect because it is a comma splice, that is, the comma after "tree" is insufficient to separate two independent clauses. "Because" fixes the problem in Choice D by making it a cause and effect relationship.

7. **Choice B is correct.** The original sentence is incomplete because it lacks a verb. Choice B provides the verb "are" which clarifies the idea. It is smooth and grammatically correct.

8. **Choice C is correct.** The original sentence is technically grammatically correct. However, it is too wordy to be the best choice. Choice C is a better approach.

9. **Choice C is correct.** The original sentence is incorrect because there is a lack of parallelism. The construction is "no different_____than_____". If in the first blank we have "for children" then in the second we should have "for young adults".

10. **Choice B is correct.** The problem with the original sentence is the ambiguity of the word "it". The pronoun must be clarified because it could refer to reason, popularity, music, singers etc. Choice B indicates that it refers to their music and this, of course, makes sense.

© 2009 Master Learning Strategies Inc.

11. **Choice D** is correct. The original sentence is incorrect because the subject "I" should immediately follow its modifier. Choice D is the only sentence that does that and is, therefore, the only possible response.

12. **Choice B** contains the error. Choice B contains the error because the verb "is", being singular, does not agree with the plural object "plans". The verb "are" must be used in order to be correct.

13. **Choice B** contains the error. The word "keeping" is inappropriate here. The infinitive "to keep" should follow "have managed".

14. **Choice E** is correct. This sentence is grammatically correct as it stands.

15. **Choice D** contains the error. The proper word here is the adverb "calmly" which modifies the verb "examine".

16. **Choice A** contains the error. The singular verb "has" cannot agree with the plural subject "details". It must be changed to "have" in order to be correct.

17. **Choice D** contains the error. The problem here is one of tense. The action happened in the past ("were watching"), therefore, "are" should be replaced by "were".

18. **Choice D** contains the error. Appropriate construction should be "either…or" or "neither…nor", never, "neither…or".

19. **Choice C** contains the error. Again, the problem here is one of agreement in number. "Ethnographers" , being plural, must have committed their "lives" not "life" to studying.

20. **Choice A** contains the error. We have a lack of agreement in tense here. The verb "sprained" indicates that the action occurred in the past. Thus, the verb should be "spent" not "spends".

21. **Choice A** contains the error. The phrase "In a world that the rate…" is simply not idiomatically correct. A more appropriate way to express this would be "In a world in which the rate…"

22. **Choice A** contains the error. "I" is used as the subject of a sentence and precedes the verb. "Me" is the object of a sentence and follows the verb. An easy way to determine which to use is to drop "Juan". Therefore, the sentence becomes "Ms. Tanaka asked *me*…"

23. **Choice E** is correct. This sentence is grammatically correct as it is.

24. **Choice D** contains the error. Since "workers" is plural, it requires a the plural verb "own".

25. **Choice A** contains the error. One does not "listen *at*" something but "listens *to*" something.

26. **Choice C** contains the error. "She" is ambiguous here because we don't know if it refers to the office manager or Ms. Andrews. In order to be correct, either one would have to be specifically mentioned in place of "she".

27. **Choice E** is correct. This sentence contains no error.

28. **Choice A** contains the error. We have an error in number here. Since "they" is the subject, "as candidates" would be the appropriate change.

29. **Choice E** is correct. The original sentence is grammatically correct.

30. **Choice C** is correct. The pronoun "they" is ambiguous here and needs to be clarified. Choice C is the best way to do so.

31. **Choice D** is correct. The original construction is incorrect because the second sentence is a fragment. Choice A is incorrect because "by which" is an improper idiom. B is incorrect because the cause and effect relationship is not illustrated. C is incorrect because "plunges" is the wrong tense. Choice D is the best way to communicate the idea.

32. **Choice D** is correct. Choice A is poor because "this was that it was" is both confusing and awkward. Choice D is best because it is clear and flows smoothly.

33. **Choice B** is correct. The second paragraph enumerates the results of his safety device, namely, that buildings were built higher because people felt safer in elevators than they had before. Choice B is the best response because it is a topic sentence which introduces the reader to the "consequences" of the device, after which the effects are listed.

34. **Choice E** is correct. The original sentence as it stands is a comma splice because the comma is insufficient to separate two independent clauses. Either they must be separate sentences all together or they need to be separated by a semicolon. Choice E is the only answer that does so.

35. **Choice D** is correct. Sentence 10 deals with "birdcage" elevators but doesn't say anything about them which relates to the author's main idea. All of the other choices are pertinent to the discussion.

1. **Choice A** is correct. The second blank is easier to find. If the principal "apologized", then she would announce that the students suspected were *forgiven*. The only word which has that meaning would be "exonerated". Therefore, A is the only possible answer.

2. **Choice C** is correct. The word "although" immediately sets up a contrast. Marshall did not want his papers to be public knowledge so he would "stipulate" or "insist" exactly that. Choices A, B and D are immediately eliminated. The Library of Congress certainly did not "honor" his request but "disregarded" it.

3. **Choice A** is correct. The flow of the sentence would indicate that the second blank would mean the same as "mended". As we look at only the second word choices, "repair" is the only possibility. The word "disposal" clearly makes sense.

4. **Choice D** is correct. The phrase "terminal flourish" means that it occurs at the end. The best possible answer, then, would be "conclude". Nothing else fits.

5. **Choice C** is correct. The construction of the sentence indicates that the blank is synonymous with "swell". The word "distend" means to swell. But if we didn't know that, all the others can be eliminated because they mean the opposite.

6. **Choice E** is correct. The first blank means "selfless" and the second means "worthy of imitation". To be "altruistic" is to be selfless and, certainly, those worthy of imitation would be "examples" to others or "exemplars", same word.

7. **Choice A** is correct. The blank must be synonymous "fawning" (bowing or cringing in a servile manner). The word "obsequious" means subservient or like a servant. All of the other choices are self-explanatory.

8. **Choice D** is correct. The second blank is easier to find. Conservationists would promote a policy of *care* in the use of resources. A "husbandman" is a gardener or caretaker. "Husbandry", therefore, is the judicious use of resources. "Exploitation" is the wanton disregard of the consequences of one's actions. In other words, "to take advantage of ".

9. **Choice C** is correct. Clearly if she keeps checking her watch, she is concerned about the "schedule" and not the event itself.

10. **Choice D** is correct. Her presentation has to do with her mother who is well-known. If she is to shed " a *different* light" on her mother, her personal insights as a daughter would certainly be drawn upon.

11. **Choice A** is correct. The third sentence is particularly dramatic. The phrase "...immediately seizes the attention of the national media" certainly seems a bit exaggerated and highlights the drama.

12. **Choice E** is correct. If the media "touts" something and it causes the public to be "misled", then the author must be critical of the role of the media.

13. **Choice B** is correct. What makes a professional a professional in a certain field is the training he or she has had. It would not be surprising, therefore, that the "approach" of each would be different and that they would lead to different responses or conclusions.

14. **Choice E** is correct. If the engineer is suggesting that the stalls should be decreased, then obviously one could fit more cows in the barn without additional buildings.

15. **Choice D** is correct. Not surprisingly, the psychologist might think that the cow's "mental outlook" would have an effect on milk production. The terms "mellow" and "reduce boredom" indicate that the psychologist believes that "contented" cows will produce more milk.

16. **Choice C** is correct. The "old joke" has little to do, directly, with the main idea of the passage about physicists. It does, however, serve to "introduce the topic" in an interesting manner.

17. **Choice A** is correct. The analogy here is preceded by the idea that there are very few things "we know how to solve exactly". Thus, there is quite a bit of "mystery" in how we solve problems. Consequently, "if it works, exploit it". Or in modern terms, "if it ain't broke, don't fix it". This implies that producers don't always know "why a film succeeds."

18. **Choice B** is correct. The suggestion about "thinking simply" is followed by an explanation of what that means, namely, "getting rid of irrelevant details". In other words, simplifying a problem, or getting to its essence, is essential to solving it.

19. **Choice D** is correct. Attention Deficit Disorder is actually a misnomer. That is, people with ADD actually pay attention to _everything_ and that's why they can't focus on anything. Most of us do not have this difficulty precisely because we "filter out" non-essential details or we "prioritize". Most seem to have this ability from the time they are born.

20. **Choice C** is correct. The word "empirical" means as determined by observation or experimentation. The author suggests in these lines that "facts" determined by observation may not be "facts" at all because our observations may mislead us. It was only as Galileo got the "medium" (air) out of the way that he understood what others did not.

21. **Choice B** is correct. Removing "particular circumstances" , again, refers to the medium of air or the "object's environment".

22. **Choice D** is correct. See the previous two answers.

23. **Choice B** is correct. The phrase "the fault of another" is elaborated upon in the opening of the final paragraph. Galileo faults Aristotle for his approach as well as his conclusions.

24. **Choice A** is correct. Sometimes the "details" actually cloud the truth. The story of Galileo and motion illustrates how the "detail" of air was too much information and "got in the way" of the proper understanding of motion.

Section 6

1. **Choice C** is correct. Once again, what follows the comma defines the blank. "Expressive movements" are "gestures".

2. **Choice C** is correct. The first blank is easier to find and is described by the phrase "chief advice-giver". One with such a title would have "lots" of knowledge so either A, B or C would work. Louisa Vigil would be "considered" this if she has lots of knowledge, so, "regarded" would be the only choice.

3. **Choice C** is correct. If "only" enthusiastic responses have been generated, then the blank must be synonymous with "praise". The only possible answer is "plaudits" which has the same root as "applause". None of the other choices fit. The word "pathos" means empathy or emotion.

4. **Choice E** is correct. The word "pungent" (strong) is exclusively used with the sense of smell. Only A and E are possibilities. In order to make sense, the second blank can only be "identify" not "cultivate".

5. **Choice A** is correct. The blank refers to "The announcement". The only possible answer is the "disclosure" (revelation).

6. **Choice D** is correct. Passage 1 by using words like "crucial" and "critical" and phrases like "no other period of human life", implies that outside of the first three years the brain is not nearly as capable of adaptive change. The author of Passage 2 not only questions that assumption but gives the example of an amputee as evidence to the contrary.

7. **Choice D** is correct. Keeping the previous answer in mind, both author's would certainly agree that the first three years are important for the development of all human beings.

8. **Choice B** is correct. The author of Passage 2 would clearly be "skeptical" of such a claim. "Indignation" (anger) nor "humor" nor "ambivalence" (indifference) nor "approval" fit.

9. **Choice C** is correct. These lines clearly indicate the connection between what parents have always felt and thought concerning a newborn's basic needs, and scientific data which now confirms it.

10. **Choice D** is correct. This passage says little about the _content_ of Jacobs' writing. It does describe the "narrative choices" she had, that is, the way that she wrote, to whom she wrote, how she would present herself to them etc. These were all questions she was confronted with and needed to answer in order for her to be effective in reaching her audience and effecting change in their attitudes.

11. **Choice D** is correct. In lines 9-10 Douglass called upon their "deepest principles of individualism" which is synonymous with "revered concepts" and follows that with the example of slavery which takes that away.

12. **Choice D** is correct. Although "exercise" (not physical exercise) is close, "formulate" is a better choice. The word "formulate" means to put into a systematized statement or expression or devise a strategy. This is exactly what some Northern White women were doing with respect to the analogy between slavery and the oppression of women.

13. **Choice B** is correct. These lines indicate that those who sought to improve their lot did so by clinging to "true womanhood and domesticity" in support of that change. What is "true womanhood and domesticity"? It is certainly being a "better mother", but not just that. It is the liberty to use all her gifts, physical, mental and spiritual, as an _equal_ partner with her husband, in the _entire_ success of the family inside and outside the home.

14. **Choice A** is correct. Jacobs' decisions about her narrative, as in the case of the decisions of most prudent people, were based upon how *practical* or "pragmatic" they would be. For example, the passage indicates that she may have written in a completely different manner if her audience was an audience of slave women. However, since most slave women either could not read or did not have access to her narrative, it wasn't practical or "pragmatic" to do so. "Disingenuous" (giving a false impression, insincere) nor "scholarly" (studious, academically inclined) nor "presumptuous" (overstepping one's bounds) nor "melodramatic" (extravagantly theatrical) fit.

15. **Choice B** is correct. Since the passage details exactly what Jacobs felt and did given her circumstances, and supported what she did and how she did it, the tone of the passage can be described as "analytical and appreciative". The is no supporting evidence for "disappointment and criticism" nor "regret and anger" nor "irony and jocularity".

16. **Choice A** is correct. Choice A is clearly the best response. The passage is not only a recounting of "three encounters" with this vicious boy, but the shameful (ignominious) exit of the author from the town which resulted from these encounters.

17. **Choice B** is correct. The first paragraph describes how the townspeople reacted to his return. Though they clearly knew who he was, they did not greet him personally ("distanced") because he was a celebrity ("smug") to them.

18. **Choice C** is correct. His "progress" is preceded by the phrase "Casting my eyes along the street". It is clear, therefore, that the former refers to the latter and the remainder of the paragraph describes his first encounter with "Trabb's boy". He thinks of his stroll as a "procession".

19. **Choice C** is correct. The narrator's look on his face, one of "serene and unconscious contemplation" of him, indicates his desire to show no interest or "feigned indifference" of the boy.

20. **Choice E** is correct. If something is "visited" upon someone it is usually *thrust* upon them. This word is also typically used of something which is negative. The term "afflicted" carries with it the same connotation.

21. **Choice B** is correct. Clearly the narrator was not amused by the boy but the townspeople were. As well, the boy's actions and gestures must have been "derisive" toward the narrator or he would not have been shamed upon his exit from the town but he was.

22. **Choice B** is correct. The boy is imitating the narrator's aloofness and mocking him for acting that way.

23. **Choice E** is correct. This entire passage is simply that of a writer recounting an unpleasant personal experience. None of the other choices are supported by the text.

24. **Choice B** is correct. The comedy in the passage stems from the polar opposite attitudes of the narrator and the boy. The narrator is reserved and aloof while the boy is boisterous and bizarre.

Section 9

1. **Choice C** is correct. The key context clues here are the two authors in the compound subject and the phrase "mingling their individual styles". These clues indicate that their _combined_ efforts led to success. The word "collaborative" is synonymous with combined. "Stratified" (layered) nor "fitful" (restless) nor "vicarious" (living through another's experience) nor "corresponding" (parallel) fit.

2. **Choice E** is correct. The phrase "but unfortunately" indicates a contrast. If the audience members were "eager", then the topic must have been "interesting" or "stimulating", the only two possibilities. The second answer is "soporific" (inducing sleep or lethargy), but if we did not know that, "rousing" is not the opposite of "stimulating" so it cannot be the correct amswer.

3. **Choice E** is correct. The flow of the sentence indicates that the answer is synonymous with "touched". The word "tactile" means exactly that. "Odoriferous" (smelly, morally offensive) nor "archaic" (ancient) nor "aural" (having to do with hearing) nor "rustic" (pastoral, rural).

4. **Choice D** is correct. The context clues are "deft performance" and "hand is quicker". These clues indicate manual dexterity and skill. This is synonymous with "adroitness". "Discernment" (good judgment) nor "tenacity" (persistence) nor "hilarity" (humor) nor "insecurity" fit.

5. **Choice D** is correct. The word "Although" immediately indicates a contrast in the sentence. The second blank is easier to find since it must be a _negative_ attribute and there are only two on the list of second choices: "inadequacy" and "ineptitude" (lack of ability). The corresponding choice with the correct answer must then be _positive_. The word "prominence" (fame) is.

6. **Choice C** is correct. What follows the colon defines the blank. "A public declaration of motives" is "a manifesto", much like the Declaration of Independence was for the colonists.

7. **Choice A** is correct. The author of Passage 1 indicates in line 42 that Williamsburg is a destination for family vacations while the author of Passage 2 states that places like Colonial Williamsburg are "staggeringly profitable". Both suggest that Williamsburg has achieved "popular acceptance" in the U.S.

8. **Choice B** is correct. The phrase "Unless one knows a great deal…" precedes the mention of the Forum, Acropolis and National Gallery. This indicates the necessity of "expert knowledge".

9. **Choice D** is correct. The "ribbon" and "sign" in European museums is contrasted with Colonial Williamsburg in that at Williamsburg visitors can actively participate in the community and not be "kept away" from a link to their history.

10. **Choice C** is correct. The information which follows the phrase "most startling" is that the guides have "no set speeches" indicating a refreshing and unusual degree of "freedom" that the tour guides have.

11. **Choice A** is correct. The author of Passage 1 suggests that Americans "refuse to believe that education need be a chore" and, therefore, we have a number of creative ways to teach people of all ages. Colonial Williamsburg is one way, and a similar "solution" to this "chore" would be a "computer game that teaches geography."

12. **Choice D** is correct. The word "studious" of course means carefully investigated. This would indicate that the reproduction of Colonial Williamsburg was not haphazard but carefully "deliberate".

13. **Choice C** is correct. Obviously the word "plays" here means "acts as" God.

14. **Choice E** is correct. This "type of crime" is "ominous" (threatening) because it is not only popular, but as the following line indicates, "gives a license to destroy".

15. **Choice D** is correct. We can see from the reading that the author of Passage 2 is strongly opposed to the concept of Colonial Williamsburg because so much of what has been reproduced is one person's one-sided view of history, that is, much of the "real" history has been destroyed for a "sanitized" (cleansed) view of history.

16. **Choice E** is correct. Line 13 states that many historians view Williamsburg as "harmless" but the author of Passage 2 would strongly disagree and would say that "serious damage" has been done to actual historical buildings but also presenting a false view of history.

17. **Choice E** is correct. The "freedom" that the Williamsburg guides have in making their speeches is viewed as positive by the author of Passage 1, but the author of Passage 2 would be upset by the lack of authenticity by such speeches as examples of the "tendency to take liberties" with historical facts.

© 2009 Master Learning Strategies Inc.

18. **Choice C** is correct. Clearly we can see that the author of Passage 1 approved of Colonial Williamsburg, whereas the author of Passage 2 strongly opposed it. We would, therefore, look for a positive attribute from the first author and a negative one from the second. "Admirable" would certainly fit the former and "lamentable" (unfortunate) would fit the latter. No other pair of choices is supported by the text.

19. **Choice C** is correct. Both authors would say that it is challenging to represent history in a realistic ("authentic") way, but also, to do so in a fashion that would allow the visitor to "participate" in the history, that is, make it "accessible".

Section 10

1. **Choice B** is correct. The original sentence is very awkward and wordy. Choices A, D and E all use the pronoun "it" after it is already introduced in the sentence. This makes each redundant and awkward. Choice B is the smoothest and most concise.

2. **Choice A** is correct. The original sentence is correct. as it stands.

3. **Choice B** is correct. The sentence as it stands is a comma splice since the comma separates two independent clauses without a coordinating conjunction. B is the only choice that has the appropriate construction. Both C and D have semicolons which can separate independent clauses. However, in the second parts of each sentence, the subject is "biography" not "biographer" as it should be.

4. **Choice A** is correct. The original sentence is correct. as it stands.

5. **Choice E** is correct. The phrase "because of having" is an awkward, roundabout way of communicating the idea which is succinctly communicated in Choice E.

6. **Choice E** is correct. The sentence is incorrect as is because of a modifier error. As it stands, "the task" is "laughing". Since laughing modifies "tourists", "tourists", must immediately follow the comma. C is incorrect because "facing" should be "faced". D is incorrect because there is no need for the word "nevertheless".

7. **Choice D** is correct. We have an error here in agreement. "One" is a singular subject which requires the singular verb "was" not "were".

8. **Choice A** is correct. The current sentence is grammatically correct.

9. **Choice C** is correct. As it stands the pronoun "it" refers to "damage" not "strip-mining" as it should. Choice C puts these terms in their proper positions.

10. **Choice A** is correct. The sentence is grammatically correct as it is.

11. **Choice E** is correct. The phrase "Insofar as" means "to the degree that" and does not fit the context. We need a word that illustrates the cause and effect relationship indicated. "Since" or "Because" would do the trick. Choice E is the best choice.

12. **Choice D** is correct. The original sentence is redundant. The construction "as____as" means "equally". Choice D is the proper way to communicate the idea.

13. **Choice E** is correct. The proper construction should be "refuse to_____or to_____". If an infinitive is used in the first part of the comparison, it should be used in the second.

14. **Choice A** is correct. The original sentence is grammatically correct.

Practice Test #8 - Math

Section 2
8 questions – first third - easy

1. **Choice E is correct.** The old rate is $4.50/3 = 1.50$. Increase that by 0.50 and the new rate is $2. 5 pencils at $2 each is $10.

2. **Choice E** is correct. As x goes from 1 to 2 the y-value goes from 3 to 7. So this line goes up 4 over 1. The slope is 4. Cross out A, B, and C.

   We check D by putting in a pair of x and y-values. Does $3 = 4*1$. WRONG.

   Only E remains but lets test quickly.

   Does $3 = 4*1-1$ Yes

   Does $7 = 4*2-1$ Yes so it will work for the rest of the line.

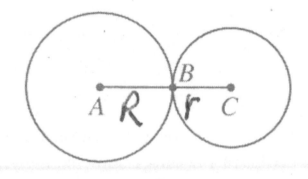

Note: Figure not drawn to scale.

3. **Choice B** is correct. The ratio of the circumferences of two circles is equal to the ratio of their radii. In this problem the big circle circumference is twice the little circle's circumference. So the radius of the big circle is twice the little circle's radius. Now test their answers starting with C.

   C) $r = 3$ so $R = 6$. Does that add to 6? WRONG. We need to get smaller.

   A)) $r = 1$ so $R = 2$. Does that add to 6? WRONG. Too small.

   B)) $r = 2$ so $R = 4$. Does that add to 6? Success

© 2009 Master Learning Strategies Inc.

Second third - medium

4. **Choice B** is correct. Test each point to see what works. We need to test in $|x| - |y| = 3$

   A) $(-3,-6)$ Does $3 - 6 = 3$ WRONG

   B) $(-4,-1)$ Does $4 - 1 = 3$ Success.

SURVEY RESULTS

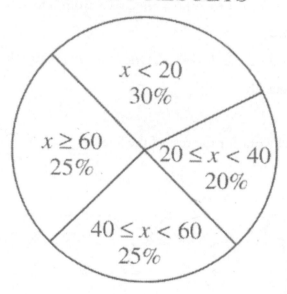

$x < 20$
30%

$x \geq 60$
25%

$20 \leq x < 40$
20%

$40 \leq x < 60$
25%

5. **Choice D** is correct. From the pie chart we can see that 20% of the people said their age was between 20 and 40. 30% said their age was less than 20. That makes a total of 50% below age 40. 50% is half. Half of 1,000 people is 500 people.

6. **Choice D** is correct. When we divide by a number the remainder is always less than the number by which we are dividing. That means when we divide by 3, all the remainders are less than 3. Cross off any list that contains a number that is 3 or larger. This lets us cross off A, B, C and E since they all have a 3. Only D remains.

Last third - hard

7. **Choice C** is correct. The sentence "y is inversely proportional to x" yields the formula $y = k / x$. Put in the two known values to calculate the value of k. $15 = k / 5$. Multiply by 5 and we get $k = 75$. That makes the formula $y = 75 / x$. What is the value of y when $x = 25$? Substitute. $y = 75 / 25 = 3$. Success.

8. **Choice A is correct.** This is a hard problem. Answer E is too attractive to poor students to be the correct

answer. Let's look for a solution. Plug in their answers and see what works. Start with C

C) $2x + z = 2*10$ and $2x + 2*10 + z = 20$ Subtracting 20 from the second equation gives $2x + z = 0$ Can

$2x + z$ be 20 and 0 at the same time? WRONG. Try lower

B) $2x + z = 2*8$ and $2x + 2*8 + z = 20$ Subtracting 16 from the second equation gives $2x + z = 4$ Can $2x + z$

be 16 and 4 at the same time? WRONG. Try lower

A) $2x + z = 2*5$ and $2x + 2*5 + z = 20$ Subtracting 10 from the second equation gives $2x + z = 10$ Can $2x + z$

be 10 and 10 at the same time? Success

Math Method: In $2x + 2y + z = 20$ we can replace the $2x + z$ with the $2y$ that the first equation says is equal

to it. Here is the work

$2x + 2y + z = 20$ Substitute

$2y + 2y = 20$ Combine like terms

$4y = 20$ Divide by 4 and get $y = 5$

---

10 questions – first third - easy

---

9. **Choice 13/2 OR 6.5 is correct.** $2(x - 3) = 2x - 6 = 7$. Add 6 and get $2x = 13$ or $x = 13/2 = 6.5$

10. **Choice 10 is correct.** Put in 4 for x and evaluate. $y - 4 = 3(4 - 2)$ so $y - 4 = 6$ or $y = 10$

11. **Choice 45 is correct.** How much gas did car A use for the 60 miles. Every 20 miles car A used 1 gallon. The

full trip used 3 gallons of gas. How far would car B go on 3 gallons? $3*15 = 45$

Second third - medium

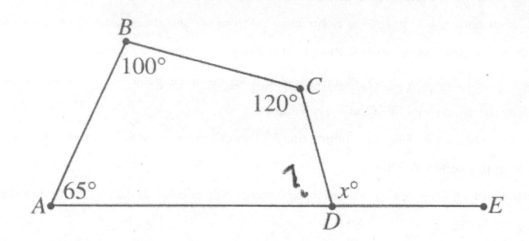

12. **Choice 105** is correct. The four angles inside the polygon add up to 2 triangles worth or 360°. By subtraction we get 75°. The rest of 180 will be x. $180 - 75 = 105$

13. **Choice 12.5 OR 25/2** is correct. 20 and 8 have an average of $(20 + 8) / 2 = 14$ so 14 is the third term. The fourth term is $(8 + 14) / 2 = 11$. Then comes $(14 + 11) / 2 = 12.5$ and we have arrived at the first term that is <u>not</u> and integer.

14. **Choice 3/50 OR .06** is correct. Plug in our own numbers and calculate. $z = 100$ is a nice place to start. $y = (3 / 10) * 100 = 30$ gives y. Now find x. $x = (1 / 5) * 30 = 6$. The question is "x is what fraction of z?" $6 / 100 = 0.06$

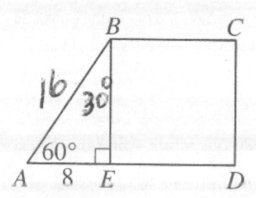

15. **Choice 192** is correct. In a 30–60–90 triangle the side opposite the 30° angle is half the hypotenuse. This is a favorite SAT triangle and it is well worth memorizing this fact. So the hypotenuse is 16. Mr. Pythagoras will calculate the third side as $\sqrt{256-64} = \sqrt{192}$. That is one side of a square. The other sides are the same. The area of the square is just $\left(\sqrt{192}\right)^2 = 192$

Last third - hard

---

16. **Choice 8/7 OR 1.14** is correct. Think of 7 pounds of this mixture. There will be 5 pounds of peanuts and 2 pounds of cashews in the 7 total pounds. What is the ratio of cashews to total? $2/7$ is the answer. If we have 4 pounds total then $(2/7)*4 = 1.1428$ is the weight of the cashews.

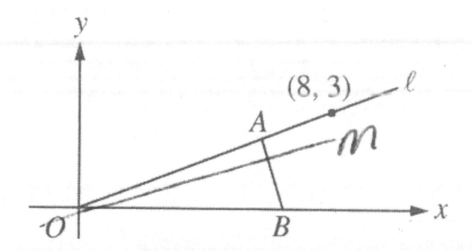

17. **Choice 0 < x < .375** is correct. The slope has to be positive. It also has to be less than the slope of OA. For $\overrightarrow{OA}$ the rise is 3 and the run is 8 so the slope is $3/8 = 0.375$. Pick any positive number less than this. 0.3 would be fine. So would 0.1.

18. **Choice 1350** is correct. In 1996 the school had the median enrollment of the 5 years. That means there were 2 years with a larger enrollment and two years with a smaller one. 1995 and 1993 were both higher. That forces 1992 to be lower than the median. 1350 is the largest number that is smaller than 1351.

Section 5
20 questions – first third - easy

1. **Choice B** is correct. This is quite easy and we should notice that both fractions have the bottom number two less than the top number. But if we didn't notice this we should start by plugging in their numbers and see which one works. Start with C. $39/37 = 1.054$

   C) $41/39 = 1.051$ CLOSE! Others any better?

   B) $39/37 = 1.054$ Yes. This one matches. Success

	Juniors	Seniors	Total
Boys	k 1	n 2	m
Girls	r 4	s 3	t
Total	w	x	z

2. **Choice E** is correct. Plug our own numbers in and calculate the totals. $m = 1+2 = 3$; $t = 4+3 = 7$; $w = 1+4 = 5$ and $x = 2+3 = 5$. That makes $z = 3+7 = 10$ or $z = 5+5 = 10$. Checks both ways. Now check their answers.

   A) $1+3 = 10$ WRONG

   B) $3+5 = 10$ WRONG

   C) $4+3 = 10$ WRONG

   D) $4+3+7 = 10$ WRONG

   E) $1+2+4+3 = 10$ Possible

   Only E remains

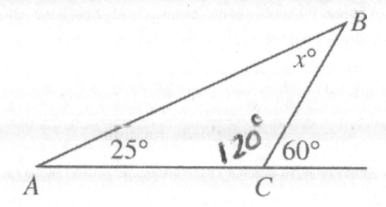

3. **Choice C** is correct. Subtraction gives us 120° for the measure of the angle inside the triangle at C. Now what do we add to 154 to get 180. Subtraction again gives us 35°

4. **Choice D** is correct. The Martins have to save $600 at $15 per month. 15 times what will give us 600? Division gives us $600 / 15 = 40$

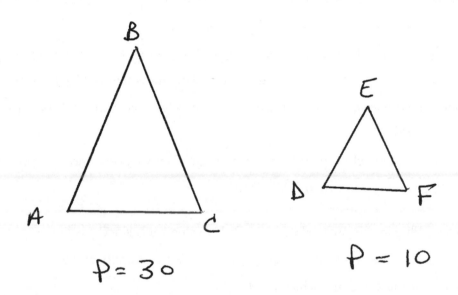

5. **Choice B** is correct. The perimeter of the big triangle is 3 times the perimeter of the small triangle. So the big perimeter is 3 time 10 or 30. $\triangle ABC$ is equilateral so all three sides have the same length. $30 / 3 = 10$

6. **Choice A** is correct. If we want to find the number of days it takes to mint coins, we need to find out how many coins they mint in a day. At one a second the number of coins will equal the number of seconds. So how many seconds are there in a 10-hour work day? 60 seconds in a minute times 60 minutes in an hour times 10 hours in a work day gives $60 * 60 * 10 = 36,000$. Now how many days will it take to mint those 360,000 coins? $360,000 / 36,000 = 10$

7. **Choice C** is correct. We know the average of two numbers is 12. What is the sum of those two numbers?

$2*12 = 24$. So the sum of x and $3x$ is 24.

$x + 3x = 24$ Combine like terms

$4x = 24$ and $x = 6$ by division.

Second third - medium

8. **Choice C** is correct. We are trying to find the TRUE statement. If we examine each statement and try to find an example that disproves it, we will eliminate all but the correct answer. Let's look at each one now.

   A) Joan is a member of the chess club. Is she a swim team member? She might be and she might not be. If she is not a swimmer then we don't know anything about her grade. Her being a tenth grader does not violate anything we know. This statement is WRONG

   B) There are two kinds of chess club members. Swim team members and those who aren't on the swim team. We know that those on the swim team are not tenth graders. What do we know about those chess club members of the swim team? Nothing! They may or may not be tenth graders. We don't know and can't say for sure that there is or isn't a tenth grader there. This statement is WRONG

   C) We know that some of the chess club members are on the swim team. If Ed was one of those people then we know Ed is a swimmer and is not a tenth grader. This statement is TRUE. Success

   D) There are no tenth graders on the swim team. 0 can not be greater than a number that is 0 or positive. WRONG

   E) If there are any tenth grade chess players then this is true. But we don't know if there are any so the number might be 0. 0 is not greater than 0. WRONG

9. **Choice D** is correct. Plug in our own values here. Pick a value for x since it is in two places. Makes the solution easier. $x = 5$ and plug it into the equation. $3*5 + n = 5 + 1$ Simplify and get $n = 6 - 15 = -9$. Now test the answers looking for the value of n which is –9.

   A) $4*5 + 1 = 21 = -9$ WRONG

   B) $2*5 + 1 = 11 = -9$ WRONG

   C) $2 - 5 = -3 = -9$ WRONG

   D) $1 - 2*5 = -9$ Possible

   E) $1 - 4*5 = -19 = -9$ WRONG

   Only D remains

© 2009 Master Learning Strategies Inc.

10. **Choice E is correct.** Let's understand what this function problem means by that funny symbol. $\boxed{2}$ means multiples of 2 The set would be 2, 4, 6, 8 10 and so on. $\boxed{3}$ gives multiples of 3 which are 3, 6, 9, 12, 15 …. Finally $\boxed{5}$ gives 5, 10, 15, 20, 25 … We have to check each proposed set to see if *all* its members are contained in *all* three sets that we listed above. Let's look at each answer.

A) $\boxed{5}$ is the set listed above. The first number is 5. Is that in *all* three sets? It is not in $\boxed{2}$ since they are even numbers and 5 is odd. WRONG

B) $\boxed{6}$ is multiples of 6. Is 6 in $\boxed{2}$? Yes. Is 6 in $\boxed{3}$? Yes. Is 6 in $\boxed{5}$? No. WRONG

C) $\boxed{10}$ is multiples of 10. Is 10 in $\boxed{2}$? Yes. Is 10 in $\boxed{3}$? No. WRONG

D) $\boxed{21}$ is multiples of 21. Is 21 in $\boxed{2}$? No. WRONG

E) $\boxed{60}$ is multiples of 60. Is 60 in $\boxed{2}$? Yes. Is 60 in $\boxed{3}$? Yes. Is 60 in $\boxed{5}$? Yes. If this were a Math class we might have to look further at this set. But this is the SAT and one of the answers they give is the one they give credit as the correct answer. A, B, C, and D were shown not to be the correct answer. Put down E.

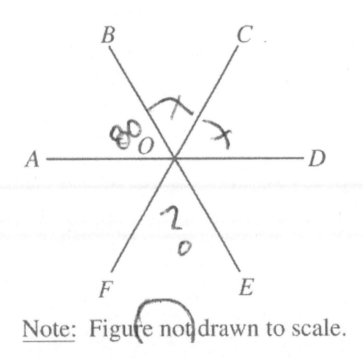

Note: Figure not drawn to scale.

11. **Choice B is correct.** In the diagram we should enter what is written for us. Put in 80° and the two equal size angles where they belong. This makes an 80° angle and two equal size angles that add to 180°. By subtraction we know that the two equal size angles add to 100° which makes them 50° each. Write that in the diagram. What angle do we want to find? <EOF is a vertical angle to <BOC that we calculated as 50°. Success.

12. **Choice C** is correct. We want to find the *least* value so we should start with the smallest one they give us and keep going up until we get to one that works. "Works" means that it produces an integer. That will be their answer. We should be surprised if the smallest number they give us actually does work.

A) $\sqrt{\dfrac{5*3}{3}} = \sqrt{5} = 2.236$ NO

B) $\sqrt{\dfrac{5*5}{3}} = \sqrt{8.333} = 2.887$ WRONG

C) $\sqrt{\dfrac{5*15}{3}} = \sqrt{25} = 5$ Success

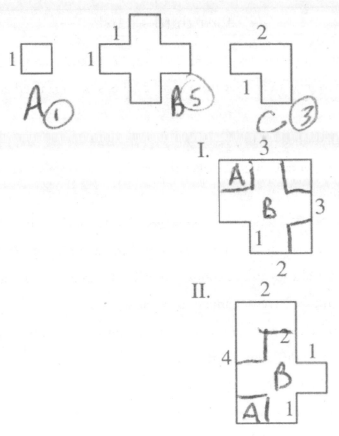

13. **Choice C** is correct. We need to test each and see if we can put the puzzle pieces into the shape. Shape A has 1 square, shape B has 5 squares and shape C has 3 squares as the area. That is a total of 9 squares.

I. We should put in the biggest shape, B, first. Since it is three high and 3 wide it is forced to go right in the middle. This is a nice fit on the lower left. There are three little square spots left. We can put A into one of them. Now we need to fit in C. It is too big to go in any of the left over places. We have no room for movement of shape B so we are stuck. I is not possible. Cross off B and E as answers since they include I..

II. Again we should put in the shape B first. Since it is 3 wide we are forced to put it right where the shape 2 juts out on the right. There is no room to move it so any solution has to have this shape right here. There is a little spot for shape A down in the lower left. What is left? A little L shaped piece is left. Rotate shape C 90° to the left and it just fits the spot we have left.. So we can do II. Cross off anything that doesn't include II. Cross off A and D. Only C remains. That is their answer and we didn't have to try III.

© 2009 Master Learning Strategies Inc.

14. **Choice D** is correct. Prime numbers are 2, 3, 5, 7, 11, 13, 17, 19 and so on. Pick out numbers from this list, 2 at a time, that multiply to give an answer from 21 to 29. Let's be organized and start with 2 as the first number.

$2 * 11 = 22$ so that is the first one.

$2 * 13 = 26$ and we have a second. Using 17 makes the product too large so we have all the ones that use 2. Now we go to 3 and look.

$3 * 7 = 21$ works. Pair number 3. 3 times 11 is too large so we are done with 3. The next number is 5.

$5 * 5 = 25$ works *but* we were told the two numbers we picked had to be *different*. 7 is too big so we are done with 5. Go to 7. 7 times 3 is already in our count. Go to 11. 11 times 2 is in our count also. Looks like we are at the end of the list and we have our answer as 3 pairs.

Another Look: Instead of taking pairs of primes and multiplying we could look at all the potential answers and see if they factor into two different primes.

$21 = 3 * 7$ Count it as number 1.

$22 = 2 * 11$ Count it as number 2.

23 is prime so it can't be factored.

$24 = 2 * 12 = 3 * 8$ These are the only pairs with a prime. None of them is a pair of primes. Don't count this one.

$25 = 5 * 5$ This works as two primes but the aren't *different*.

$26 = 2 * 13$ Count this as number 3.

$27 = 3 * 9$ No pair of primes here.

$28 = 2 * 14 = 7 * 4$ Same as 24. Don't count this.

29 is prime so can't be factored.

Just as in the other method we got 3 results.

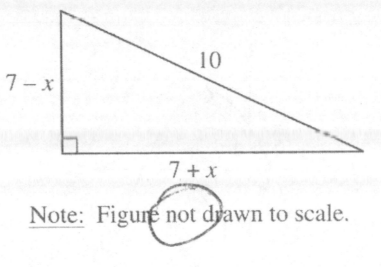

Note: Figure not drawn to scale.

15. **Choice A** is correct. This is a right triangle problem. $49 + x^2$ looks like they are asking for us to use the Pythagorean Theorem. Let's at least start it as it gives us a way to begin.

$(7 - x)^2 + (7 + x)^2 = 10^2$ Looks like we have to use FOIL

$(49 - 7x - 7x + x^2) + (49 + 7x + 7x + x^2) = 100$ Combine

$98 + 2x^2 = 100$ How does this compare with $49 + x^2$ which is what they want. Dividing by 2 will make the left side the same as what they want.

$49 + x^2 = 50$ and now we have their answer.

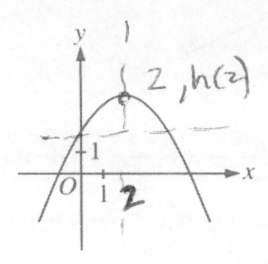

16. **Choice A** is correct. They tell us that $h(2)$ is the maximum value. That means that the x value is 2. They ask

us to find a when $h(a) = 0$. Where is the y-value zero? On the x-axis of course! Where does the graph cross

the x-axis? Once to the left of 0 and once further out on the right. Let's look at their answers.

A) –1. Possibility

B) 0 WRONG. It is up above 1 when $x = 0$

C) 2 WRONG. This is the max point.

D) 3 Doesn't look right and the graph is drawn to scale

E) 4 Possibility.

We have two answers that might be right. Let's use the edge of the test paper to measure. 0 to 1 gives us a

unit. Mark off more units and see what we get. The left side seems to cross at –1 and the right side looks

more like 5 than 4. A is our measurement choice. Mark it down and move on the next problem. If you are

interested in a math type reason here it is. This graph is symmetric. That means it looks the same on both

sides. 2 is the x–value for the max point. One unit to the right and the left of 2, that is 3 and 1, will give the

same y-value on the graph. 2 units to the left and right of 2, that is 0 and 4, will also give the same y-values.

We know that at 0 the graph is above 1 so at 4 it will also be above 1. That makes 4 not a place where it

crosses the x-axis.

17. **Choice D** is correct. We are in the hard section. E will not be the answer. When two things are equivalent that means we can set them equal to each other. Let's do it.

$x^2 + kx + 7 = (x+1)(x+h)$ Looks like FOIL again.

$x^2 + kx + 7 = x^2 + x + hx + h$ The x^2s match. Great! What about the x terms and the ones without an x? They will have to match in order for the expressions to be equivalent. We want to find k which is part of the x terms. But there is also an h in the x terms. Look at the terms without an x. To be *equivalent* the left side and the right side will have to match. So $7 = h$. Great. Now look at the x terms again only this time put the 7 in for the h. $kx = x + 7x = 8x$. Bingo. $k = 8$

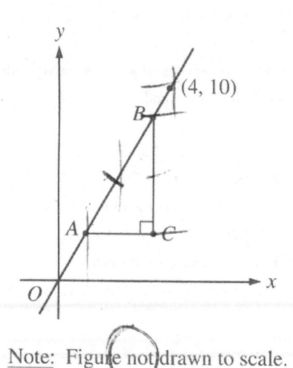

Note: Figure not drawn to scale.

18. **Choice A** is correct. AC is not 4 units long because C is to the left of $(4, 10)$. So we can cross off E whose short leg is 4. Does AC look closer to 2 units or 3 units? It looks much closer to 2 units according to the edge of the test measuring. There are two answers with 2 as the short leg. Let's try the Pythagorean Theorem on them.

A) $4 + 25 = 29$ Possible

B) $4 + 25 = 49$ WRONG

Choose A.

19. **Choice E** is correct. Plug in their values to see which one works.

    A) $\sqrt{\dfrac{3}{\sqrt{2}}} \approx 1.45$; $\frac{1}{2}(2*1.45-1)=0.95=4$ WRONG

    B) $\sqrt{\dfrac{7}{2}}=1.87$; $\frac{1}{2}(2*1.87-1)=1.37=4$ WRONG

    C) $\sqrt{\dfrac{9}{2}}=2.12$; $\frac{1}{2}(2*2.12-1)=1.62=4$ WRONG

    D) $\sqrt{\dfrac{49}{4}}=3.5$; $\frac{1}{2}(2*3.5-1)=3=4$ WRONG

    E) $\sqrt{\dfrac{81}{4}}=4.5$; $\frac{1}{2}(2*4.5-1)=4$ Success at last.

20. **Choice E** is correct. We need to plug in our own values and see what works. "Works" means that the number we get is even and when divided by 2 is odd.

    Pick $k=1$

    A) $2*1=2$; Is 2 even? Yes; Is $2/2=1$ odd. Yes – Possible

    B) $2*1+3=5$; Is 5 even? No! WRONG

    C) $2*1+4=6$; Is 6 even? Yes; Is $6/2=3$ odd. Yes – Possible

    D) $4*1+1=5$; Is 5 even? No! WRONG

    E) $4*1+2=6$; Is 6 even? Yes; Is $6/2=3$ odd. Yes – Possible

    So we have A, C and E left. Pick another value of k and plug in to those three again to find more wrong answers.

    Pick $k=2$

    A) $2*2=4$; Is 4 even? Yes; Is $4/2=2$ odd. No! WRONG

    C) $2*2+4=8$; Is 8 even? Yes; Is $8/2=4$ odd. No! WRONG

    E) $4*2+2=10$; Is 10 even? Yes; Is $10/2=5$ odd. Yes – Possible

    Only E remains

    Math Method: How do we force a number to be odd when we don't know what kind of an integer it is? Multiplying it by 2 makes it even and then adding 1 makes it odd. For k that means it looks like $2k+1$. Now we know we have an odd number. Multiply that by 2 and we get an even number. Then $2(2k+1)=4k+2$ which is answer E.

Section 8

16 questions – first third - easy

.1 **Choice A** is correct. With each of the 8 dinners we have 3 desserts so $8 * 3 = 24$

2. **Choice E** is correct. "The sum of $3x$ and 5" means $3x + 5$. Cross out answers where the left is not this. Cross out A, B and C. The right side calls for the "product" which is multiplying. D is division. Cross it off. E is multiplying. That's our answer.

3. **Choice C** is correct. The probability is the blue number over the total number. $15 / 90 = 0.166$. Either learn to reduce fractions or convert their answers with a calculator to get the answer they want. In case you missed it $1 / 6 = 0.166$

4. **Choice E** is correct. Cross multiply and get $2x = y$. How many integer pairs make this true? $(1,2)$ works. So does $(2,4)$ and $(3,6)$ and $(4,8)$ and … Is the point made? Let's just test $(4,8)$ in the original problem just to make sure.

$$\frac{x}{y} = \frac{4}{8} = \frac{1}{2}$$ Works!

ELLEN'S BOOKSTORE SALES

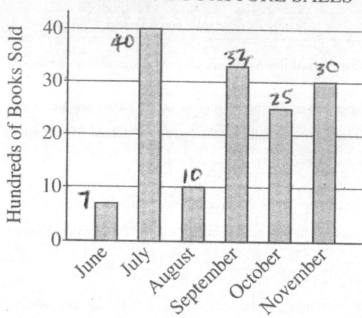

5. **Choice C** is correct. Look at the graph and calculate each pair. To help it may be good to write in what we think each bar represents.

   A) $700 + 4000 = 4700$

   B) $4000 + 1000 = 5000$

   C) $1000 + 3300 = 4300$

   D) $3300 + 2500 = 5800$

   E) $2500 + 3000 = 5500$

   4300 is the least number of books.

Second third - medium

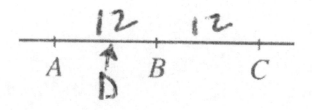

6. **Choice D** is correct. Write on the diagram the values we know. $AC = 24$ and B cuts it in half. That makes each piece 12. We are also told that D cuts AB in half. So what is DC? $6 + 12 = 18$

7. **Choice B** is correct. Plug in our own value for n here. Let $n = 3$. On my calculator $6*10^\wedge(-3) = 0.006$ and

$1*10^\wedge(-3) = 0.001$. $0.006 + 0.001 = 0.007$. Now see which of their answers gives this value.

A) $7/10 = 0.7$ WRONG

B) $7/(10^\wedge 3) = 0.007$ Possible

C) $7/(10^\wedge(2*3)) = 0.000007$ WRONG

D) and E won't make the 7 appear. They are both WRONG

Only B remains

8. **Choice B** is correct. One-fourth of a circle is $\frac{1}{4}*360 = 90°$ and $\frac{1}{5}*360 = 72°$ Subtraction tells us that there are

$90° - 72° = 18°$

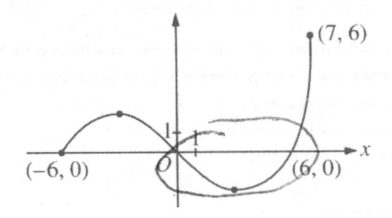

9. **Choice B** is correct. $f(x)$ means the y-values on the graph. Where are the y-values negative? What are the

x-values here? The y-value is negative when the x-value is from 0 to 6.

© 2009 Master Learning Strategies Inc.

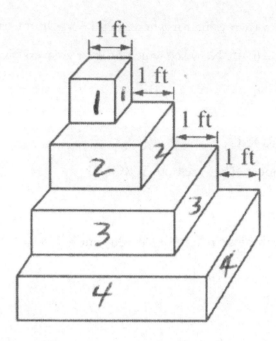

10. Choice C is correct. In each layer we multiply the length times the width times the height to find the volume of that layer. Then we add up all four layers. Now that we know how to do it. Let's do it!

Top Layer - $1*1*1 = 1$ cubic foot of marble.

Second Layer - $2*2*1 = 4$ cubic feet of marble.

Third Layer - $3*3*1 = 9$ cubic feet of marble.

Bottom Layer - $4*4*1 = 16$ cubic feet of marble

Total marble is $1 + 4 + 9 + 16 = 30$

11. **Choice A** is correct. Plug in our own numbers here and then test. Let $x = 3$. Then $4(2^3) = 4*8 = 32$. We need to find y so that $2^y = 32$. If we have trouble finding it use the calculator. $2\wedge 4 = 16$ and $2\wedge 5 = 32$ so we know $y = 5$. Now we test their answers looking for x which we know is 3.

A) $5 - 2 = 3$ Possible

B) $5 - 1 = 3$ WRONG

C) $5 = 3$ WRONG

D) $5 + 1 = 3$ WRONG

E) $5 + 2 = 3$ WRONG

Only A remains

Math Method: Follow the rules of exponents

$4(2^x) = 2^y$ Change 4 into a power of 2

$2^2(2^x) = 2^y$ Multiplying bases means adding exponents

$2^{x+2} = 2^y$ If the bases are $=$ then the exponents are $=$.

$x + 2 = y$ and we subtract 2 to solve for x

$x = y - 2$

Last third - hard

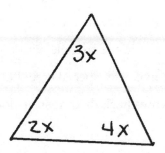

12. **Choice C** is correct. Add up the angles and we get 180° so

$2x + 3x + 4x = 180$ Combine like terms

$9x = 180$ divide by 9 to get $x = 20$

The angles are $2x = 40$, $3x = 60$ and $4x = 80$. Big angle minus small angle is $80 - 40 = 40$

13. **Choice D** is correct. Plug in our own numbers here. Let's make an 11 minute call. The first minute casts $0.50. The next 10 minutes cost $0.30 each so the cost for those 10 minutes is $10 * \$0.30 = \$3$. So the call costs $3.50. Now we test their answers for the one or ones that give $3.50

A) $0.8 * 11 = 8.8 = 3.50$ WRONG

B) $0.50 + 0.30 * 11 = 3.8 = 3.50$ WRONG

C) $0.50 + 0.30 * (11 + 1) = 4.1 = 3.50$ WRONG

D) $0.50 + 0.30 * (11 - 1) = 3.50$ Possible

E) $0.50 * 11 + 0.30 * (11 - 1) = 8.5 = 3.50$ WRONG

Only D remains

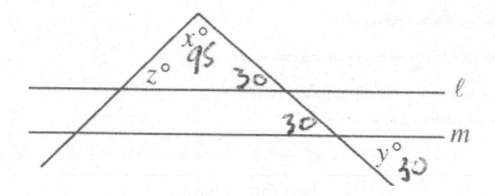

14. **Choice E** is correct. Plug in our own numbers here. Let $y = 30°$ Always remember "When parallel lines are cut by a third line, all the little angles have the same measure." That means that all four of those little angles are 30°. We are most interested in the one in the triangle with the x and the z. Now we need a value for x. Looks like a right angle but that might make it a special case. Let's let $x = 95°$. So what does that make z? By subtraction we get $180 - 95 - 30 = 55$. Now check their answers looking for 55°.

A) $95 + 30 = 55$ WRONG

B) $95 - 30 = 55$ WRONG

C) $180 - 95 = 55$ WRONG

D) $180 - 95 + 30 = 115 = 55$ WRONG

E) $180 - 95 - 30 = 55$ Possible

Only E remains

15. **Choice C** is correct. Looks very complicated. Let's plug in our own number and get a feel for the problem.

Let $n = 3$ That makes the left side $\frac{3}{2} * \frac{1}{3} * \frac{3}{4} = \frac{3*3}{2*3*4}$ Oh, look. The 3 cancels. When the 3 is cancelled we get

$\frac{3}{2*4} = \frac{3}{8}$ which is supposed to equal $\frac{5}{k}$ If we cross multiply $\frac{3}{8} = \frac{5}{k}$ we get $3k = 40$ or $k = 40/3 = 13.33$ That

isn't an integer. But when we started with 3 the top number of the left fraction was that same 3. Maybe we

should start with $n = 5$ Plugging 5 in for n gives $\frac{5}{4} * \frac{1}{5} * \frac{5}{6} = \frac{5*5}{4*5*6} = \frac{5}{4*6} = \frac{5}{24} = \frac{5}{k}$ which means $k = 24$.

That's one of our answers. Mark it down and get on to the last problem in the test.

16. **Choice E** is correct. Plug in our own numbers here. How many coworkers do we have? $m = 7$ is a nice size office. Suppose they all had to put in $50? That means the cost of the lunch is $7 * 50 = 350 = y$. If $p = 2$ coworkers failed to pay, then the other 5 had to pay the whole bill. $350 / 5 = 70$. The additional amount each had to pay is $70 - 50 = 20$. Let's plug in $m = 7$, $y = 350$ and $p = 2$ to see which answer gets 20.

A) $350 / 7 = 50 = 20$ WRONG

B) $350 / (7 - 2) = 70 = 20$ WRONG

C) $(2 * 350) / (7 - 2) = 140 = 20$ WRONG

D) $350 * (7 - 2) / 7 = 250 = 20$ WRONG

E) $2 * 350 / (7 * (7 - 2)) = 20$ Possible

Only E remains

© 2009 Master Learning Strategies Inc.

The Essay - Instructions

Expressing oneself with precise language is foundational to achieving success in college and beyond. It reveals not only the depth of a person's knowledge in a specific arena, but it is also a barometer of his or her ability to communicate. In this day and age, it is absolutely essential to be able to communicate well. We've all had teachers who have had more degrees than a thermometer but couldn't communicate to save their lives. If we have a strong command of the English language and can express ourselves with fluidity and confidence, orally and in writing, we will be much more apt to make a positive impact in our spheres of influence. Isn't that what it's all about?

The greatest change to the SAT is the addition of a writing section. Students will spend 25 minutes on an essay and 25 minutes on multiple choice grammar questions. Many students are dreading the essay. There is no reason to fear, however. The College Board, the test administrator, and Educational Testing Service, the test maker, both understand that it is very difficult to ask anyone to write well in just 25 minutes. Therefore, there will be some specific things that the graders will be looking for when they read your essay. We will arm you with the strategies necessary to write well on any topic, and give you our approach to some of the specific essays found on the Practice Tests of the College Board's Official SAT Study Guide for the New SAT.

1. **Read the <u>Prompt</u> and <u>Assignment</u> Carefully, at least Twice:** Although this may seem painfully obvious and elementary, it is extremely important. You may write the best essay since Thomas Jefferson but if it is off-topic you will receive a score of 0. The <u>Prompt</u> is usually an excerpt boxed-in and gives the point of view of a particular author. The <u>Assignment</u> is the question put to you and is related to the Prompt. Although you don't have to refer to the prompt, it is usually an excellent place from which to jump off.

2. **Write an Outline:** Take the first 5-7 minutes to organize your thoughts. Although you will not be required to write a "perfect" essay, you will not receive a good score (5-6) if it is not persuasive. It is almost impossible to be persuasive and logical if you're not well organized. It may seem like a "waste" of time to write an outline with so little time to begin with but this is not the case. A good outline will not only help you determine which position to take on a particular issue, it will also keep you focused on that position and more likely to write in a logical and cogent fashion. A T-chart, that is, a two-columned chart where pros and cons can be written, is an excellent tool to help organize your thoughts.

© 2009 Master Learning Strategies Inc.

3. **Organization.** The format of the essay should be the classic introduction body conclusion style. The introductory paragraph should be interesting and include a <u>Thesis Statement</u> which clearly indicates to the grader what your point of view is. The body should be comprised of at least two paragraphs which "flesh out" your Thesis. You should have two solid examples to illustrate your position. Although, in certain essays, you may be able to support both sides of an issue, it is probably better to take a firm stand on one side or the other. As a result, you will probably be more passionate and more persuasive. Finally, in the conclusion, drive home your point of view by restating your Thesis.

4. **Variety:** Variety in sentence structure (simple, compound and complex) and vocabulary is important. The College Board wants to make sure you know some polysyllabic words and how to use them in a sentence. Avoid being too casual in the way you write; you're not speaking on the phone with a friend. Avoid using the second person when writing an essay.

5. **Finish with a Flourish:** Just as you want to begin in an interesting way--"you only get one chance to make a first impression"-- in order to catch the grader's attention, (most graders will be reading 100-200 essays in one sitting—so light a spark!) you also want to finish in a memorable way—it's the last impression they'll have of you before they put a grade on you essay!

6. **Proofread!!!!** Leave 1 or 2 minutes at the end to find any obvious errors. You can receive a perfect score of 6 with some slight grammatical errors. Serious errors, to the point of obscuring the meaning of the sentence, will definitely reduce your score significantly.

Essay for Practice Test #1

What compels a person to change?

1. Inner compulsion:
    a. Conscience
    b. Excellence
    c. Success
2. Outer compulsion:
    a. Parents
    b. School
    c. Law
    d. Punishment

3. Examples:
    a. Prodigal Son
    b. Martin Luther
    c. Richard Nixon
    d. Michael Jackson

Pick the point of view for which you can make the strongest case. Include the strongest examples which will make your position more persuasive.

Thesis Statement: It is sometimes only from the darkest chasm of depravity that one finally perceives the light and is compelled to climb into its radiance.

Essay for Practice Test #2

Do changes that make our lives more convenient make them better?

<u>Pro</u>	<u>Con</u>
1. Medical Breakthroughs	1 Quality of Life
2. Computers	2. Identity Theft: Big Brother
3. Appliances	3. Nuclear War
4. Communication	4. Urbanization, Overpopulation
5. Transportation	
6. Agriculture	

Pick the point of view for which you can make the strongest case. Include examples from history, literature or personal experience.

Thesis Statement: History is replete with examples of man's inhumanity to man. Regardless of our advances in technology, however, the basic nature of man has remained unchanged since the Garden of Eden.

Essay for Practice Test #3

Does conscience have a greater influence on people than power, money or fame?

<u>Pro</u>	<u>Con</u>

1. American Revolutionaries
   a. Patrick Henry
   b. John Hancock
   c. Thomas Payne
	1. Professional Athletes; Movie Stars

2. Civil War a. Abraham Lincoln (Emancipation)	2. Hitler

3. Civil Rights
   a. Rosa Parks
   b. Dr. Martin Luther King Jr.
   c. Nelson Mandela
	3. John D. Rockefeller

Thesis Statement: Whether conscience has a greater influence on a person than power or money or fame is entirely dependent upon that person. One can think of strong examples throughout history on either side of the issue.